Maurice Gee

A LITERARY COMPANION

The Fiction for Young Readers

Maurice Gee's fiction for young readers

Under the Mountain (1979)
The World Around the Corner (1980)
The Fire-Raiser (1986)
The Champion (1989)

THE *O* TRILOGY
The Halfmen of O (1982)
The Priests of Ferris (1984)
Motherstone (1985)

The Fat Man (1994)
Orchard Street (1998)
Hostel Girl (1999)

THE SALT TRILOGY
Salt (2007)
Gool (2008)
The Limping Man (2010)

Maurice Gee

A LITERARY COMPANION
The Fiction for Young Readers

edited by
Elizabeth Hale

First published 2014
Copyright © Individual authors as listed in the Contents

The moral rights of the authors have been asserted.
ISBN 978-1-877578-84-7

A catalogue record for this book is available from the National Library of New Zealand. This book is copyright. Except for the purpose of fair review, no part may be stored or transmitted in any form or by any means, electronic or mechanical, including recording or storage in any information retrieval system, without permission in writing from the publishers. No reproduction may be made, whether by photocopying or by any other means, unless a licence has been obtained from the publisher.

Publisher: Rachel Scott
Editor: Gillian Tewsley

Printed in New Zealand by Printstop Ltd, Wellington

Front cover: 'Nelson, the centre of New Zealand' from a drawing by Gary Hebley for *The World Around the Corner* (1980)

CONTENTS

	Editors' note to the series Lawrence Jones and Elizabeth Hale	7
	Acknowledgements	9
	Introduction: Gee's novels for young readers Elizabeth Hale	11
1	**The early fantasy novels:** 'a kind of perturbation, held within the pages' Claudia Marquis	25
2	**The good, the bad – and ironic reversals:** Moralscape in Gee's realist historical quintet for young readers Diane Hebley	55
3	**Mining Gee:** *Salt, Gool* and *The Limping Man* Elizabeth Hale	83
4	**'What I must steer clear of':** The influence of his mother's stories on Maurice Gee Kathryn Walls	101
5	**Writing horizontally and vertically** in *The World Around the Corner* and *Hostel Girl* Louise Clark	123
6	**Patterns of exchange:** Setting, hero, villain and child in *The Champion* and *The Fat Man* Vivien van Rij	147
7	**Representation and responsibility** in *Under the Mountain* and *The Fat Man* Elizabeth Hale	163
	Notes	181
	Contributors	195
	Bibliography	197
	Index	202

EDITORS' NOTE

Maurice Gee's first published story, 'The Widow', appeared in *Landfall* in September 1955; his final novel for adult readers, *Access Road*, appeared in 2009 and in his final novel for young readers, *The Limping Man*, in 2010. In those years Gee has gained almost every honour that New Zealand society can bestow on a writer of fiction for adults: the Robert Burns Fellowship, the Literary Fund Scholarship in Letters (twice), the Literary Fund Award for Achievement (twice), the New Zealand Book Award for Fiction (four times), the Goodman Fielder Wattie Book Award (twice), the Montana New Zealand Book Award for Fiction and the Deutz Medal (twice), the Victoria University Writing Fellowship, the Katherine Mansfield Memorial Fellowship, an inaugural New Zealand Icon Award from the Arts Foundation of New Zealand, the Prime Minister's Award for Fiction, an honorary doctorate from the University of Auckland, and the inaugural Honoured New Zealand Writer at the 2012 Auckland Writers and Readers Festival.

Trevor James, who has written some of the most interesting and enlightening criticism of Maurice Gee's adult fiction, remarked in 1998 on the 'huge gap' where one would expect to find a body of critical discussion of Gee's work, and speculated concerning the cause:

> The relative lack of attention Gee has received from literary critics in New Zealand marks a huge gap in New Zealand literary criticism; certainly he has received far less than his stature as a writer deserves, and I suspect that this reflects the influence of literary fashion. Though Gee has been consistently praised by reviewers, the realistic 'surface' of his fiction appears the most likely deterrent to more sustained and rigorous critical attention.[1]

This book is the first in a two-volume series discussing the fiction of Maurice Gee. Over a career that spans 55 years so far, Gee has published 17 novels and more than 20 short stories for adult readers, and 13 novels for younger readers. These fictions create a variety of worlds. Denis Welch, in reviewing Gee's sixteenth novel for adults, *Blindsight*, in 2005, made a case for looking at all of Gee's fiction written for adults as creating a single, evolving fictional world, 'Geeland': 'a country of the mind that novel by novel has taken shape in our literary consciousness, to the point where – like the lifesize map in the Borges story that eventually covers and fits the actual land – it's almost indistinguishable from New Zealand'.[2]

The fiction for younger readers, however, ranges much more widely. The five realist historical novels, published at irregular intervals between 1986 and 1999, take place in a somewhat simplified but recognisable version of 'Geeland'. The eight other novels for younger readers, however, have at least elements of alternative worlds. The first, *Under the Mountain* (1979), takes place in the Auckland of Geeland, but aliens from two different planets infiltrate and influence it. In the second novel, *The World Around the Corner* (1980), Nelson (Saxton or Jessop in Geeland) has within it a gateway to the alternative world of the title. The novels of the *O* trilogy (1982–85) are likewise gateway books in which the movement is from the fictionalised Golden Bay to the alternative world of O and back. Finally, the *Salt* trilogy (2007–10) takes place entirely within a self-contained alternative world.

These two quite different but related bodies of fiction – Gee's writing for adults and his writing for young readers – are subject to different critical approaches in this two-volume series. Lawrence Jones, who has been writing and publishing on Gee's work for almost 40 years, constructs his text as a chronological narrative tracing, through close and contextual readings of all the works written for adults, the development of Gee's vision of a changing New Zealand and his narrative means for presenting it. In the present volume, Elizabeth Hale, who has previously co-edited a collection of essays on the fiction of Margaret Mahy,[3] decided on an approach that blends the chronological with a consideration of genre and topic.

The two volumes in this series discuss all of Gee's published fictions, from 'The Widow' in 1955 to *The Limping Man* in 2010. They present all of Gee's fictional worlds, from twentieth-century and early twenty-first-century New Zealand to the post-apocalyptic world of the *Salt* trilogy. Our hope is that these two volumes will be a useful companion in the reader's exploration of the worlds created by one of New Zealand's finest writers.

Lawrence Jones
and Elizabeth Hale

ACKNOWLEDGEMENTS

In late 2005, at a morning tea in the English Department at the University of Otago, Lawrence Jones told me he was working on a book on Maurice Gee. 'Oh,' I said, 'well, if you want anything on the children's literature, let me know.' The next day he wrote to me suggesting I take over the section on the children's literature, and I happily agreed. It has been a somewhat longer journey to publication than we anticipated; what was conceived of as a single book has become two: this current volume, and Lawrence's volume on Gee's fiction for adult readers to follow. My main acknowledgement is therefore to Lawrence, whose scholarly dedication to the literature of New Zealand is second to none. It is a privilege to be associated with him, and to be part of a project devoted to the remarkable writings of Maurice Gee. It has also been a privilege to work with the contributors to this volume – Claudia Marquis, Diane Hebley, Kathryn Walls, Louise Clark and Vivien van Rij – whose knowledge and expertise has greatly added to the richness of the project. My colleagues at the University of New England – Jennifer McDonell, David Roberts, Fiona Utley, Sascha Morrell, Susan Potter, Richard Scully, Natalia Tobin, Yvonne Griggs, Adrian Kiernander and Alan Davison – have been endlessly encouraging in research discussions, and I thank them for their support. I am especially grateful to the School of Arts at the University of New England, which supported me in the research and writing of this book through research leave, travel grants and funding to support the final stages of the project. Sarah Winters of Nipissing University read earlier drafts of my chapters and I am exceedingly grateful for her sound advice. My family, particularly my father John and mother Beatrice, offered insights, wisdom, advice and support at crucial moments. Otago University Press, under the guidance of Rachel Scott and the editing of Gillian Tewsley, has been wonderful to work with. I would also like to thank Gary Hebley for permission to use his beautiful illustration from *The World Around the Corner* for our cover image. Last, I'd like to take the opportunity to thank Maurice Gee himself for writing novels that struck me with the force of truth at a young age. Writers who write for young readers hold a special place in their imaginations; and my literary make-up (and that of hosts of other New Zealanders) is the richer for my youthful encounters with his works.

Elizabeth Hale

INTRODUCTION
Gee's novels for young readers
Elizabeth Hale

Maurice Gee is, unusually, an adult novelist who has written serious and compelling fiction for young readers, and his reputation is equal in both areas. The body of work Gee has produced for young readers is distinctive and valuable, and offers young readers, especially from New Zealand, unparalleled access to the creations of an extremely thoughtful writer.[1] He has made a major contribution to the quality and range of literature available for teenagers and children, creating a set of novels that engage in serious issues as the same time as they tell exciting and interesting stories.

This first volume of a two-volume series on the novels of Maurice Gee offers a critical guide to ways of seeing the literary worlds represented in his works for young readers. In some ways, the children's novels offer a view in miniature of Gee's entire oeuvre, especially in his employment of a deceptively simple and realistic style, and his preoccupying concern to engage fully in a social representation and critique of New Zealand. This is not to say that Gee's children's novels are simplistic or childish, though they are considerably shorter, use simpler language, work with more easily identifiable themes and engage in more obviously generic approaches to story. Gee himself indicated that he wrote his first children's novels as a break from the difficult work of his *Plumb* trilogy, employing a simpler mode of storytelling that got him away from the intense work of writing psychological realist fiction for adults. In suggesting that he wrote children's literature for 'fun', he may have been being dismissive of the genre, or simply modest. However, the verve and depth of the novels he produced belie any idea of 'childishness' in their creative power.

In 1979 Maurice Gee published his first children's novel, *Under the Mountain*. Since then the book has remained constantly in print, and it has been joined by 12 more novels for children and adolescents. They are distinctive for their suspenseful and exciting plots, moral rigour, and affectionate but critical representation of New Zealand. They are distinctive, too, because they are written with the interests of young New Zealand readers in mind (though they have sold widely overseas and have been translated into many other languages). They form a body of work that introduces readers to a range of genres: most obviously to the different modes of fantasy and realism, but also to adventure stories and mysteries, deeply felt psychological thrillers, and gangster stories. In addition, they educate readers in the social history of New Zealand: a place with an exciting history, a place profoundly literary – a place made of stories, where fantasy and adventure lurk around the corner.

They are also sometimes disturbing: Gee does not shy away from what he perceives to be necessary truths. Young readers are asked not merely to enjoy exciting chase scenes and fights against monsters or villains, but to think about what makes someone become wicked, and to consider the social responsibility for dealing with damaged or frightening people. They are asked to think about what it means to grow up; not merely to read unreflectingly about how protagonists find their place in the world but to think about what sort of world awaits them, the reader, as they grow up. They are asked implicitly to reflect on their own families and social circles, and to observe as young characters notice the strengths and weaknesses of people they admire and love.

Gee's novels for young readers are therefore generally not comedies, though there are comic moments. Indeed, if we might consider Margaret Mahy the great comedian of New Zealand children's literature, with Gee we are in darker territory: not precisely tragic, but sober, occasionally satirical, and philosophical.

The novels

Gee's first novel for young readers, *Under the Mountain* (1979), brings together elements of fantasy and science fiction with a realistic New Zealand setting. In this story, the Wilberforces, marauding aliens from another planet, have come to Earth and lurk beneath the volcanoes of Auckland. They plan to destroy the city and turn it to a sea of cold mud, their preferred habitat, before taking over the world. They are stopped by 11-year-old twins who, allied with a good alien from another planet, use their natural telepathic powers to destroy the Wilberforces before they destroy the city. *Under the Mountain*, which is aimed at readers aged from nine to 11, sets exciting action in a deliberately mundane suburban Auckland background, but enlivened by the volcanic geography of the city. In talking about this book, Gee says that he wanted to write a story that made New Zealand the most important place in the world. In 1981 *Under the Mountain* was adapted into a popular television series, screened in New Zealand and around the world; in 2008 production began on a feature film adaptation of the novel. As further testimony to the popularity of this book, it received the 2004 Gaelyn Gordon Award for a Much-loved Book.[2]

The second fantasy novel, *The World Around the Corner* (1980), is aimed at a slightly younger audience than that of *Under the Mountain* and the rest of his books, which target older children and young adolescents. In this novel, set in Nelson (where Gee and his young family were living at the time), eight-year-old Caroline finds a pair of magic eyeglasses that transform the world when she looks through them. The glasses are a magic talisman from another world, the 'world around the corner', a peaceful world that is under threat from a set of villains known as the 'Grimbles'. The glasses have been brought to our world by inhabitants of the other world (disguised as an elderly couple), to be recharged by the warmth of the sun. Caroline has to keep the glasses safe from the Grimbles, who have travelled to Earth to claim them; and restore them to their rightful owner, Moon-girl, who must wear them in order to defeat the Grimbles. Travel to and from the 'world around the corner' occurs at a gateway at the top of Nelson's Botanical Hill, the geographical centre of New Zealand. As in *Under the Mountain*, New Zealand's geography plays an important part in linking everyday reality with exciting fantasy adventure for young readers.

Gee's next three novels were also fantasy novels in which everyday New Zealand children are drawn into exciting, even epic adventures in an alternative world. In the *O* trilogy – *The Halfmen of O* (1982), *The Priests of Ferris* (1984) and *Motherstone* (1985) – the main action takes place in a secondary world, known as 'O', which is reached from New Zealand through a mineshaft in the hinterland of Golden Bay near Nelson. In each of the novels, two New Zealand cousins, Susan and

Nick, travel through the mineshaft to O. Each time, O has fallen out of balance and Susan and Nick help restore it to its natural order. In *The Halfmen of O* they help the good Mixies fight Otis Claw, a tyrant who has built an empire based on cruelty and pollution. Susan is the 'chosen one' who is able to restore free choice to the Halfmen, who are either pure good or pure evil and are thus imbalanced. In *The Priests of Ferris*, Susan and Nick return to O to find that hundreds of years have passed, and that a religious cult set up in memory of Susan has become a repressive regime and is spreading through fear and sacrifice. Appalled that the priests of Ferris are misusing her name, Susan works to restore the balance of power and dissolve the priesthood. In the final story in the trilogy, *Motherstone*, Susan and Nick return to O immediately after the events of *The Priests of Ferris*. Though the priesthood has been dissolved, some factions remain and are grasping for power by building nuclear bomb-like machines. Indeed, both good and evil sides are determined to use these machines; and Susan and Nick must again find a way to bring O into balance without destroying the world.

The *O* trilogy is epic in scope. It uses traditional fantasy tropes to explore the battle between good and evil, not only through the use of archetypes but by exploring different ways in which good and evil are socialised. For example, *The Halfmen of O* shows the corporate and imperial face of evil; *The Priests of Ferris* shows the destructive potential of corrupt religiosity; and *Motherstone* shows the destructive will to totalitarian power of both good and evil. That Susan and Nick have to put O to rights on three occasions in these novels suggests a pessimistic view of humanity on Gee's part. It suggests, too, a cyclical vision of human endeavour: O, like our own world (and our own country) will continually be in danger of falling into darkness and will continually require the efforts of rational people. With its combination of exciting action, vivid creation of a fantasy world accessed from New Zealand, and its moral and philosophical rigour, the *O* trilogy was very popular with readers and received critical acclaim: *The Halfmen of O* was a bestseller and was awarded the Children's Book of the Year in 1982; and in 1986 the New Zealand Library Association awarded Gee the Esther Glen Medal for *Motherstone*.

After this quintet of fantasy novels, Gee changed tack and wrote five historical novels set in different periods in New Zealand's history. The first of these is *The Fire-Raiser* (1986), a realistically told mystery story about an arsonist terrorising Jessop, a small town in the South Island (a fictionalised Nelson). Set during World War I, it explores the influence of the British Empire on New Zealand, and questions of patriotism and national and community identity. This book marks the beginning in Gee's work for children of a strong emphasis on the relationship between the individual and the community. Themes of insider and outsider status are explored through the xenophobia expressed by the community towards the German music teacher Frau Stauffel, and the outsider status of the arsonist Edgar Marwick, a disturbed loner who lives under the thumb of his rich and unpleasant mother. As in the fantasy novels, it is the children who take action where their adult parents are unable or unwilling to do so, and bring the arsonist to justice. The children demonstrate an openness of mind that Gee advocates, and 'Clippy' Hedges, a gifted teacher, symbolises the importance of humanist and scientific inquiry. *The Fire-Raiser* was well received in New Zealand and was adapted for television, using the script that Gee wrote, in the same year of its publication.[3]

On the heels of *The Fire-Raiser*'s success as a book and television series, Gee was asked to contribute another 'kidult' television series. He wrote *The Champion*, which screened in 1989, and published the book in the same year.[4] *The Champion* reveals a small-town New Zealand riddled with corruption, snobbery and racism. It is set during World War II in 'Kettle Creek', a version of Henderson where Gee grew up (then, it was a village; it has since been swallowed by Auckland's urban sprawl). Unlike the previous books, which have limited omniscient third-person narration, *The Champion* is narrated by 12-year-old Rex. The story concerns a black American soldier, Jackson ('Jack') Coop, who is on leave and is billeted with Rex's family. Rex, whose idea of soldiers and heroism is formed by the *Champion*, a magazine for boys, resents Jack, who is gentle and musical, but he notices how Jack's arrival brings into the open the hitherto unacknowledged racism of many of the people of Jessop. Like *The Fire-Raiser* before it and *The Fat Man* after, *The Champion* weaves together themes of war and peace, community ethics and outsiders, and racism.

The Fat Man (1994) again examines how outsiders are created by community, this time in Depression-era Loomis (a fictionalised Henderson). Jack is an outsider in *The Champion* because of his race and nationality, and his arrival in town exposes other unsavoury aspects of the town. In *The Fat Man*, Herbert Muskie, who was bullied as a child, has left the small town of Loomis for the United States, where he becomes a vicious criminal making money from bootlegging and possibly worse. He returns to Loomis and exacts revenge on his former classmates, Laurie and Maisie, now married with a child, Colin, through whose eyes the story is told. Colin watches as his parents and grandparents come under the spell of Muskie, a repellent but fascinating individual whose fatness indicates both his power and his victimhood. The novel ends with the death of Muskie who, pursued by the police, falls into a ravine from a broken flying fox that he has forced Colin to help him into. His death suggests that villains can be overcome. But the book is among other things a meditation on the origins of the wicked outsider; it asks whether evil is innate or created, and to what extent the community is culpable. The adults of Loomis, like the adults of Jessop, do not come out of the action well: Laurie and Maisie are inevitably diminished in their own eyes, and in Colin's – suggesting that for children, coming of age involves the diminishment of their parents. *The Fat Man* was awarded the 1995 AIM Supreme Award and Junior Fiction Award. (This caused some controversy as Gee bumped up against some of the strictures and sensitivities associated with writing for young readers (as Elizabeth Hale discusses in chapter 7).)

Orchard Street (1998) returns to Loomis at a different period: it is set during the 1951 waterfront dispute, the largest-ever industrial confrontation in New Zealand. Again, Gee draws on Henderson for details of setting and characterisation, exploring the effects of the dispute on the lives of several characters in Orchard Street. The story is told through the main character, Ossie, whose father is running an illicit printing press in support of the striking waterfront workers. Through Ossie's observations of his family and neighbours, *Orchard Street* shows how different people give in to, or resist, the stultification of conventional suburban life. *Orchard Street* thus also looks at the nature of community. It marks a departure from Gee's previous books, though, as the first of his novels for young readers that deals in any serious way with love and sex: Ossie's relationship with Teresa; his older brother Les's relationship with Eileen; and the outsider Bike Pike's jealousy of Eileen and Les.

The last of the realist novels, *Hostel Girl* (1999), set in the Hutt Valley in the 1950s, further develops ideas about teenage sexuality. This time, the historical moment that provides an anchor for the novel is the Mazengarb Report of 1954.[5] Overseen by Queen's Counsel Oswald Mazengarb, the *Report of the Special Committee on Moral Delinquency in Children and Adolescents* was initiated as an official response to the 'Petone incident', in which a teenager sex group in Petone came to the attention of authority. Gee uses the interest in controlling teenage sexuality as a key theme in his book. *Hostel Girl* is in part the story of the heroine Ailsa's coming of age and developing sexuality. Her mother is warden of a girls' hostel, and the other part of the story is about Gloria, an older and more sexually sophisticated girl who lives in the hostel and is being stalked by the creepy Errol Parkes. Parkes is a loner whose character seems to be strongly influenced by Hitchcock villains such as Norman Bates in *Psycho*, and the novel takes on the overtones of a psychosexual thriller. Ailsa and Calum, her love interest, discover Parkes' obsession with Gloria, and pursue (almost persecute) him. In a final chase scene, near the railway tracks that run through the Hutt Valley, he is killed by an oncoming train. Gee reworked *Hostel Girl* into an adult novel, *Ellie and the Shadow Man* (2002), indicating that he had found the ideas in the book worthy of further development.

Between 1999 and 2007 there is a break in Gee's output for young readers, though he remained in sight as a major force in New Zealand children's literature. In 2002 he was awarded the Margaret Mahy Medal by Storylines New Zealand, 'presented to a person who has made an especially significant contribution to children's literature, publishing or literacy, and [which] honours New Zealand's leading author for children'. Gee's lecture at the Margaret Mahy Award ceremony, 'Creeks and kitchens', gives insight into his thoughts about writing for children and is a useful resource for students and scholars.

With *Salt* (2007), the first in a trilogy of fantasy novels, Gee returned to writing for young readers. The *Salt* trilogy, which included

Gool (2008) and *The Limping Man* (2010), differed from the earlier fantasy novels in one key respect: instead of being set in another world, accessed from New Zealand by some kind of portal, the world portrayed is a fully realised other world. The main action of all three novels centres on the decaying, post-apocalyptic city of Belong. In each, the people of Belong are enslaved by power-hungry and corrupt men who use different forms of institutional power to achieve their ends. Pairs of young protagonists, girls and boys from different backgrounds, come together to fight these villains. In *Salt*, Pearl, a rich girl from Company class, teams up with Hari, a poor boy from the Burrows, to overthrow two men who manipulate the corporate structure of Company. These men, Ottmar and his son Kyle Ott, are exploiting the poor and the land by using poor people, press-ganged from the Burrows, to mine the radioactive 'salt' that they put in their weapons. Hari and Pearl, with the help of telepathic Dwellers who live out of the reach of the city, take on Ottmar and Kyle Ott – and win. They then retreat to the country, where they start a family.

However, though they have overthrown Ottmar they have not achieved peace, as becomes very clear in the next book, *Gool*, set 16 years later. When Hari is attacked by a 'gool', an alien creature from outside nature that symbolises pure evil, his daughter and son, Xantee and Lo, go to find the source of its power, the mother gool, who lurks beneath the city of Belong. The city is now caught between warring factions headed by Clerk, the executive of the decaying Company, and Keech, the leader of the poor folk from the Burrows. The gool feeds on evil, and feeds evil in its turn; it is overcome by Xantee.

The third book of the trilogy, *The Limping Man*, is set another 16 or so years later. Belong has now fallen into the control of a religious organisation, headed by Vosper, or the Limping Man. Vosper has the power of mind control and manipulates the people to do his bidding, all in the light of religious observance. The young protagonists Hana and Ben work with the Dwellers, Hari, Pearl, Xantee and Lo to overthrow Vosper. Hana discovers that Vosper's power comes from a hallucinogenic toad secreted in his headdress, and this knowledge enables them to overthrow Vosper. This time, the Dwellers, who have hitherto avoided Belong, use their own natural psychic powers to urge the citizens of

Belong to leave the city, form small communities and live in harmony with nature. The novel – and the trilogy – ends with some (limited) hope for the future.

The plots and thematic resonances of the *Salt* trilogy are extremely dense and multilayered; they provide stringent critiques of greed, capitalism, corporations, unions, religions, industrialisation, mass culture and pollution. All three novels promote a simple life lived in harmony with nature, and reward their protagonists with this life at the end of the novel. Interestingly, *Salt* is the first of Gee's novels in which the protagonists have sex and produce a child, revealing that he has found a way to write about such things for young adult readers.

It is unclear whether Gee plans to write any more fiction, for children or for adults. The *Salt* trilogy rounds off his output for young readers very nicely, drawing together the themes and approaches of his other novels, and doing so in a fully realised other world that possesses aspects of fantasy literature, but is written in a way that shows Gee's credentials as a serious writer of realist fiction, engaging in deep philosophical, psychological and social questions.

Gee's children's books remain popular and in print. Several of his books are studied in the national secondary-school curriculum, largely because of the ways they investigate different aspects of New Zealand's social history. Gee himself has remarked on the longevity of his books for children, noting that the children who read *Under the Mountain* in the 1980s are still fond of it and have passed it on to their children. What may have appeared to Gee to be a sideline when he embarked on writing children's novels has added greatly to his profile as a New Zealand writer.

The essays in this collection

Given the scope, range, depth, quality and overall value of Gee's contribution to New Zealand literature and children's literature, a volume that pays scholarly tribute to his work is appropriate. This volume contains seven chapters on Gee's 13 books for children. The first three chapters give an overview of his work; and the remaining four chapters look at different aspects of the books. Gee's work warrants careful reading and analysis. The contributors to this volume examine his novels from many angles, including genre, representation, character, plot, theme and context. Literature for young readers operates by its own set of rules, and these rules are given consideration. The result is a set of essays that show the consistencies and the variations in Gee's fantasy and historical novels for young readers.

Claudia Marquis, in chapter 1, gives a survey of the first five fantasy novels and explores the 'unexpected power' that readers find in them. She notes the schematic nature of the fantasy genre, and argues that it works with polarities in organising the conflict between its central characters, allowing Gee to project a sense of the threat of evil with great force and clarity. She examines the cost of the battle between good and evil in these novels. For Marquis, Gee's 'intensely suspicious relation to modern society' and 'ideological' bent can be seen in his fantasy novels, which advocate an environmentalism and a suspicion of power. Rather than being read as purely an allegory of our world, the *O* trilogy is far 'more fully a work of fantasy in so far as action is switched to an alternate world'.

Diane Hebley argues in chapter 2 that Gee's five realist historical novels may be seen as a quintet that provides a 'moralscape' for young New Zealand readers. She explains the historical texts and periods, New Zealand settings and other influences that shape these books. Each novel is set in a place where Gee has lived (i.e. fictional versions of Henderson, Wellington and Nelson), and all give evidence of his close observation of reality. Hebley shows how Gee's use of real events and real surroundings inflect his realist novels, lending a sense of 'moralscape' to their explorations of a range of moral problems, conundrums and situations. She shows how the novels explore the dynamics of family and community, but always in the explicitly New Zealand setting. Gee's five historical novels invest the New Zealand of their setting with a sense of important moral drama by portraying a wide array of moral, immoral or flawed behaviour in the adult characters. Young protagonists observe and learn from these behaviours, which contribute to the 'moralscape' that forms their own actions and outlooks.

In chapter 3, Elizabeth Hale looks at how Gee has used the image of mining to express the difference between what he believes he achieves in his adult novels and what he aims to do in his children's novels, making a distinction between open-cast and deep-shaft mining. In his character-driven adult novels, she suggests, Gee is mining deep, delving into the psyches of his characters, and turning over what he digs up. The children's novels, which are necessarily action-driven, he characterises as open-cast or horizontal in nature. Hale suggests that as well as using productive imagery of surface and depth in his work, Gee mines his own output deeply in the *Salt* trilogy, his final three fantasy novels; he returns to themes, images, character types and structural patterns from his other novels for young readers and pulls them together in a resonant and profound exploration of the possibilities of fantasy literature.

In chapter 4, Kathryn Walls looks at the writing of Gee's mother, Harriet Lyndahl Chapple Gee. Using the penname Lyndahl Gee, she wrote two stories: *Mihi and the Last of the Moas*, a verse adventure story for children in which Mihi, a young Maori boy, travels to the underworld to help save its ecology; and 'Double Unit', a psychological short story for adult readers. In both, Walls argues, we can see common concerns with Gee's work. She traces the influence of *Mihi* in the *O* trilogy, noting the concern with ecology and an interest in the archetypal structure of the journey to the underworld. 'Double Unit' indicates a similar set of concerns, in the schematic nature of the story, its dense plotting and pairs of contrasting characters. Walls shows how echoes of Lyndahl Gee's stories may be seen in Gee's writing for children, and notes in particular the repeated use of pairs of characters in the *O* trilogy. Echoes of Lyndahl Gee's writing are discernible in Maurice Gee's adult novels, too: Walls draws particular attention to the character of Meg in his *Plumb* trilogy who, like Lyndahl Gee, struggles to balance family and writing. Finally, Walls argues that Meg – and other appearances of Lyndahl Gee in his fiction, such as the mothers in *The Champion* and *Orchard Street* – show some of Gee's ambivalence towards his mother's work, as well as the delicacy and density of influence in Gee's work.

In his Margaret Mahy Medal Award lecture 'Creeks and kitchens', Gee explained the distinction he made between styles of writing: 'writing horizontally' – a term he applies to a 'surface' style of story, with action and adventure, such as the two earliest fantasy novels; and 'writing vertically', which he applies to a deeper analysis of character and motive. Louise Clark in chapter 5 explores the application of these terms to the portal fantasy *The World Around the Corner* and the realist *Hostel Girl*. She explores the idea of surface and depth, and considers it in relation to the imagery of looking that is seen in both novels: both have heroines who are required to look very carefully into things, for different reasons. Clark suggests that Gee's distinction between the two styles of writing is too simple to apply wholesale to his work; that even in the simplest of his stories, he is dissatisfied with staying on the surface.

Vivien van Rij shows in chapter 6 how literary, film and historical influences affect the design of two of the realist novels, *The Champion* and *The Fat Man*. She argues that each novel masquerades as a simple adventure story but contains a wide variety of influences as diverse as Laurel and Hardy and Al Capone, the stories of Frank Sargeson and Zane Grey, and the battlefields of Kettle Creek in the American War of Independence and Guadalcanal in World War II. Gee's use of intertwined intertextual and historical references layers resonant details over the action of his stories, and is part of a larger pattern of exchange in the stories' structures. Heroes and villains exchange places, as do adults and children (children behaving more like adults and vice versa). The seeming simplicity of these novels belies a rich complexity of influence and structure.

In the final chapter, Elizabeth Hale explores Gee's representations of responsible actions across two novels – *Under the Mountain* and *The Fat Man* – that reveal the challenges inherent in writing for young readers. Both novels received acclaim; however, they also disturbed some readers. Gee's response to those readers reveals much about his determination to write responsibly for young audiences. Far from disturbing readers for the sake of it, Gee's mission is to expose young readers to dark and difficult issues that are part of real life.

Conclusion

This volume aims to show the range and depth of Gee's works for young readers. There will inevitably be overlaps among the essays; indeed, we encouraged a sense of overlap by asking contributors to compare different works across the generic distinctions of fantasy and realism, and to consider how Gee's works speak to one another and to developments in his ideas about children's literature.

Gee's novels for young readers are notable for their evocative settings, compelling plots and thematic richness. Readers of the novels will be treated to some deep thinking about the nature of heroism and its burdens, the corrupting nature of power, the necessity of protecting the environment, and the consequences of repression and racism. They will gain insight into the frailty of human life, the beauty and simplicity of childhood in contrast to adulthood, the importance of the life of the mind, and the joys of music, art and literature. They will learn of the price that comes with a happy ending, and they will consider the nature of good and evil. And they may come away from Gee's books with their imaginations enriched, and with a heightened awareness of the worlds that lurk around the corner of even the most ordinary part of New Zealand.

1 THE EARLY FANTASY NOVELS
'a kind of perturbation, held within the pages'
Claudia Marquis

The great instrument of moral good is the imagination.
—SHELLEY, *A Defence of Poetry*

Good must be won daily in the battle that never ends.
—GEE, *The Halfmen of O*

Maurice Gee 'is a remarkable man', Kevin Ireland tells us: 'He's a very pure person with a powerful interest in the darker side of other people's lives.'[1] Improbable though it may seem, this paradoxical interest is perhaps most evident in Gee's fantasies for children. In reading these stories, we are highly conscious of what he has acknowledged as a general obsession: 'the human capacity for cruelty and inflicting pain on others'. 'This is something I can't come to terms with properly. What human beings are capable of doing to one another, I return to it again and again.'[2] This view of human rapaciousness, angling into violence, extends into the worlds Gee imagines for children, in the fantasies as well as in the historical novels, and makes tough demands of his young readers. Gee's fantasy stories articulate a vision that seems common to all his work, yet, as he himself maintains, he takes up the genre in part because it is traditionally a site of pleasure, promising a good end. How dark can fantasy get?

Gee has written eight works of what he has termed 'fantasy/adventure' for young readers: five novels in the period 1979–85, including *Under the Mountain* and the *O* trilogy and, for a slightly younger audience, *The World Around the Corner*; then – after the historical realist novels written between 1986 and 1999 – the *Salt* trilogy in 2007–10.[3] This is a significant body of work; yet fantasy still seems to be something of an exception in Gee's fiction corpus. For all his insistence on his desire to entertain, and his clear recognition that fantasy offers exactly this order of pleasure, he has never written in this mode except for children. As Bill Manhire has noted: 'The interesting thing about Gee's work for children is the extent to which it has welcomed fantasy, a possibility the adult novels never seem to entertain.'[4] Gee himself has consistently played down the value of his fantasy adventures for children in relation to his adult fiction; he has acknowledged that the mix of impulses that led to his writing them included a belief that children's fiction offered greater financial rewards than writing for adults, as well as a simple pleasure in the writing itself. Where the adult novels involved 'explorations of guilt and delving into psyches',[5] the children's fantasies developed the power of 'a horizontal, straight-line sort of story-telling'.[6]

When writers choose to write for such apparently diverse audiences – adults and children – the choice almost invariably prompts the obvious question. Tolkien meets it by claiming that he writes for children of all ages; Gee claims less grandly that, in writing for children, the labour virtually disappears: 'It's fun for me and fun for the readers.'[7] It is worth noting that nothing quite like Gee's fiction for children had appeared in New Zealand writing when he set about writing his first novel, *Under the Mountain*, in 1974. When it was published some years later, Joy Cowley called it 'the best New Zealand book yet produced for readers nine years and over'.[8] In 2004, when Gee won the Gaelyn Gordon Award for a Much-loved Book for *Under the Mountain*, it had proved highly popular in New Zealand and internationally; it was in its fourteenth edition and had sold over 20,000 copies.[9]

My business in this chapter is partly to honour the brilliance of Gee's performance in these stories. My major concern, however, is to explore their unanticipated power to provoke thought and convey a sense of passionate interior life. In the interview from which the Gee epigraph to this chapter comes, he states his ambition for his adult fiction, 'the *Plumb* and *Prowlers* sort': 'I try to give a sense of life going on beyond the pages ... localised in a mind, it's a kind of perturbation, held within the pages.' It is precisely this perturbing inner/outer, local/textual character in his early fantasy adventures that makes them such rewarding experiences for child or adult reader – and critic.

The books and their readers

Gee's self-deprecation when commenting on the significance of his fantasy fiction for children seems to have been persuasive: although they are widely reviewed, the fantasies have received virtually no extended critical attention. Criticism has tended to be limited to comparisons with the work of other fantasists; or to discussions of his performance with respect to specific issues, in the context of New Zealand fiction writing. Diane Hebley's wide-ranging survey of imaginary topographies, *The Power of Place: Landscape in New Zealand children's fiction, 1970–1989*, is a case in point.[10] Another, more recent and much more ambitious study is the collection of essays edited by Anna Jackson, *A Made-Up Place: New Zealand in young adult fiction*, in which several contributors have taken up Gee's work, although none with a sustained concern for developing a critical account of his interest in a New Zealand fantasy.[11] Gee's writing for children has figured in a number of postgraduate theses. The most important, by Vivien van Rij, has led to an essay, 'The pursuit of wholeness in Maurice Gee's *O* trilogy', in which, leaning on Jung, van Rij makes a determined bid to define an ethical centre for the children's writing that relates closely to Gee's major concerns in his adult fiction.[12] This essay stands out as much for its singularity as for its insight: it is the only critical study of the early fantasies.[13]

In its ongoing reference to the adult fiction, van Rij's critical reading of the *O* trilogy offers a particularly forceful, considered example of modern criticism of Gee's fantasies, which in general places them in contexts determined by his life or his history as a novelist of national importance. In an interview with Colleen Reilly, Gee contributes to a flattening criticism of his writing for children, measured in broad contrasts between the differing objectives of his adult and children's fiction:

[Gee] ... I do a lot of straining and heaving.

[Reilly] *Does that include in the children's books?*

No, no, there the object is simply narrative clarity and narrative pace.

There is no element of what would be called 'fantasy' in the adult novels, yet the children's novels are full of fantasy.

> It's a different function altogether. I simply play games with the fantasy. I look on it as a kind of relaxation.
>
> *But there's no desire to include that in your adult work?*
>
> No, there's not.[14]

Gee's brilliance in '[playing] games with the fantasy' tends less to confirm the validity of the rather limiting views here expressed than to require testing them. In taking up that challenge in this chapter, I am concerned especially with *Under the Mountain* and the *O* trilogy – all aimed at young adolescent readers – but also, briefly, with his novel for children, *The World Around the Corner*. The peculiar value of the latter is that it underscores Gee's willingness to make testing demands of his young readers. It possesses marked narrative complexity, and it suggests compellingly that Gee makes no intellectual or ethical compromise in writing for this age group. All his fantasies, indeed, share an ethical drive alongside a commitment to fascinating and stirring their audiences by helter-skelter action.

Gee and the ends of fantasy

The ethical power in Gee's fantasies seems to have a good deal to do with his discovery of the formal resources of the fantasy/adventure genre. If there is not much to be gained from detailed comparisons with the work of other fantasists, it is instructive to know that Gee has acknowledged the stimulus he found in Alan Garner's *The Weirdstone of Brisingamen* when he first contemplated writing fantasy for children. Arguably, too, connections between his works and other major texts in the tradition such as C.S. Lewis's Narnia stories and Tolkien's Middle Earth epics are unmistakable. These creative relations do imply recognition of the characteristic moves of this kind of story. At least in part, however, the peculiar excellence of Gee's fantasies is grounded in a certain resistance to the genre, especially to the near invariable optimism of its conclusion. In Gee's stories the ending is never exactly happy, and that refusal of a fundamental narrative convention constitutes a challenge – and suggests one line of explanation of the felt power of his stories.

In 'Creeks and kitchens', his Margaret Mahy Award lecture, Gee defines with useful economy what he aimed to produce in writing his adventure fantasies: 'Put the emphasis on movement, develop narrative pace, tell a story pure and simple.' In Garner's novel he discovered the situational strategy that guaranteed the kind of narrative energy he desired: 'place the child characters in dreadful danger from some supernatural or monstrous thing, while leaving them in their natural everyday world with no way of making adults see the danger'.[15] Manifestly such a narrative is charged with tension for an audience of child readers, creating a dynamic relationship that impels the reader into identification with the hero. Reviewing his own childhood reading, Gee talks enthusiastically about a favourite collection of Robin Hood stories and recalls, pointedly, the impact of the 45 Zane Grey novels he read. He describes the picture they left of 'the sweat-stained man on the dusty horse, galloping into the badlands with the posse at his heels', and suggests it dramatically figures an ethical insight – 'that we are essentially alone, that we are in some sense fugitive'.[16] The difference that Garner introduces into this complex is that the hero no longer possesses an automatic superiority by virtue of his adulthood; rather, adult society all too often becomes at best the 'posse' in an ambivalent relation with the hero, often representing in fact the danger the child hero must face. If that intensifies the sympathy in a reader's identification with the protagonist, it also points up the social isolation with which such characters are threatened.

Much adventure writing for children, of course, depends on separating the child from his or her parents, but fantasy tends to remove the protagonist more absolutely from parents and normal society, even as it burdens this character with an added responsibility – to save not the aging horse threatened with slaughter but the entire parental world from threatening doom. The consequence is a developing sense of the importance of certain values: in Gee's five early fantasies, moral courage, duty and self-sacrifice are the heroic qualities that will ensure the continuation of a world under threat.

Colin Manlove notes that fantasy 'tends to be moral in character, depicting the different natures of good and evil, and centrally concerned with viewing conduct in ethical terms'.[17] Because fantasy works with polarities in organising the conflict between its central characters, the genre seems to have allowed Gee to project a sense of the threat of evil with great force and clarity. The hero/heroine shows dogged determination in extreme peril, faces difficult decisions, performs acts of spectacular heroism and self-sacrifice and finds the strength and purpose to persist in combat with threatening evil. Yet for Gee, the contest between good and evil never has a decisive outcome. The concept of an ever-recurring evil is central to his fantasy writing – developed most extensively in the *O* trilogy. Marna, who features only in the first book of the trilogy, is the closest we get in Gee's early fantasy novels to the figure of the wise woman of myth. She cautions her young visitors from Earth against complacency: 'Good must be won daily in the battle that never ends' (*HO* 77). This is a lesson that all of Gee's fantasies enforce in their different ways; it also justifies critical reluctance to credit the claim that Gee makes, not infrequently, that his stories succeed sufficiently if they succeed simply as fun, engrossing tales.

Nothing in Gee's own comments on these stories quite suggests he would deny their power to convey certain virtues or values. He himself recognises that the *O* trilogy, at least, points to certain lessons 'about the pollution and degradation of the environment and of natural things, about the danger of nuclear weapons, about the abuse of political power'.[18] It might indeed be argued that these books offer something quite as profound as the analysis of history and character Gee carries out in his adult fiction. Bill Manhire registers this force in Gee's fantasy writing: 'Magic and fantasy … are a means of exploring and intensifying life, not of evading it.'[19] Marna's advice mixes stoicism and pragmatism but, as we will see, it presents a vision of the good, locked in defining opposition to evil, that has immense cultural resonance – as an ideal of achieved integrity. What is remarkable is that however serious, however complex the vision of integrity, Gee's first ambition is to give expression to this sense not in lessons, but in histories.[20]

Something of this understated but undeniable seriousness can be seen in Gee's refusal to shield his youthful audience from fundamental realities:

> It seems to me that in so much children's literature the children go through terrifying adventures; they face great danger, they are heroic; they do all these things and come out the other end victorious. There is no price paid. No consequences. And life's not like that.[21]

In both *Under the Mountain* and the *O* trilogy, while good wins in the conflict with evil, there is a cost – arguably excessive. In *Under the Mountain* there is Ricky's death at the hands of the evil Wilberforces. Ricky is the cousin of the twins who are elected to take on the significant task the story relates. We are persuaded to like him, partly because he is a young man, full of vitality, and because he has protected his cousins from the Wilberforces. His death serves no narrative need but, perversely, answers Gee's larger purpose in creating a genuinely tragic awareness in the tale. For all his canny adaptation of fantasy's conventions, Gee here simply refuses to play the generic game; he is concerned primarily to demonstrate the fateful consequences of action, not to provide the consolation of a happy ending.[22]

Generic hybridity and ambiguous vision in *Under the Mountain* and *The World Around the Corner*

In the last pages of *Under the Mountain*, the 11-year-old twin protagonists Rachel and Theo save the Earth from annihilation by aliens. This moment is both haunting and horrendous, since the twins' triumph is achieved at a terrible price: devastation and the death of many – presumably including the twins' aunt and uncle, who stand in for their parents throughout the story. Furthermore, the explosion that brought about this ruin is unanticipated, the result of a moment's weakness, a lapse in concentration. Theo drops the magical stone he must use in the fight against the alien invaders, the wormlike Wilberforces; the stone is damaged, with catastrophic results: instead of being reduced to dust, the huge worms explode beneath the volcanoes where they lie sleeping, in a catastrophe that rocks the entire region. In such small failures, we recognise a general law that binds action to consequence – a greater law than the generic principle that mostly brings fantasy to a happy conclusion. We cannot help but take pleasure in the children's success in their combat with the Wilberforces, but the final sign of this triumph is less than glorious – the prospect that the children face is merely 'shelter from the wind and ash' (*UM* 155). Gee's play with scale, which sees children engaged in cosmic conflict, finally does not despatch reality from the textual world of the story, nor real-world expectations.

We might approach this issue differently: in writing his fantasy adventures, it could be argued, Gee equivocates with reality rather than wishing it away. The story manifestly contains numerous fantastic components, but the world it imagines is not fantastic in the slightest. The action takes place largely in the Auckland suburb of Takapuna; on Rangitoto, the volcanic island at the entrance to Auckland's harbour; and on Mount Eden, the most central of Auckland's volcanic cones. In a sense, the alien invaders who lodge in these volcanoes offer an animistic account of a natural phenomenon – volcanic eruption; except that sceptical adult society is to some extent hooked in to the twins' efforts to halt the worms' blitzkrieg attack on Earth. This, then, might be taken as the kind of fantasy we know as science fiction, somewhat like John Wyndham's influential horror classics of alien invasion. On the other hand the children, who are Earth's only defence, find their most important assistance, quite improbably, in the person of a 'loony'-like old man, Mr Jones – who, we discover, is no loony at all but a member of another ancient alien species, engaged for aeons in combat with the Wilberforces across the universe. If this sounds rather like the backstory to a television programme such as *Star Trek*, the children's other-world mentor possesses attributes that connect him with one of the central characters of fantasy, the guardian or helper – most dramatically in his identification with light. Fantasy characterisation takes an old man – whose oddness and obsession with the red-headed child twins might disturb the reader in a strictly realist fiction – and converts him into the representative of good, locked in symbolic conflict with evil.[23]

Gee aims for a type of moral characterisation that goes beyond concrete physical description: images associated with the aliens depersonalise them. The battle between good and evil as a conflict between light and dark is a familiar component of much fantasy writing, producing a set of programmed responses.[24] The Wilberforces are dark; Mr Jones is light. Even when he is most human, description reinforces the association: his hands 'flickered with light' (*UM* 107); he himself turns into 'a figure of light' (*UM* 90). His light-likeness functions not only on a metaphorical level: at several significant moments, as light, he imparts physical warmth and comfort; for example, when we first meet him in the prologue, protecting the three-year-old twins from death by exposure in the bush, he settles around them like a blanket of light. Furthermore, within this ambit, Gee has him mix magic with the real: 'we had learned to harness the powers of the mind. But magic is what we call it. And we simply tied the Wilberforces up, we dropped a net of magic over them' (*UM* 75). This ability may be spoken of as magical, since it is incomprehensible, invisible, the work of one mind on another. From John Ruskin's *The King of the Golden River* to *The Lord of the Rings* to *Harry Potter*, magic is the fantasy element that ensures the seemingly powerless can defeat the plainly more powerful. To invoke it here, where so much that looks improbable enters the lives of the child protagonists, is to haul an apparently realistic Auckland story into the field of fantasy.

The generic hybridity is so marked that the story does not work simply as fantasy, since all that is fantastic is assigned a possible place or function in a world we could know as ours; it demands to be taken as real. On the other hand, so much of what goes on can scarcely be understood if we view it as fact – even the kind of odd fact we know as hyper-real science fiction. In effect, the narrative invites the child reader to conspire with the author in imagining how our world is charged with the potential for happenings that our present rational systems of knowledge cannot accommodate. Then again, the story insists that the play of what we might term the imagination is by no means detached from reality – a site of entertainment – nor separable from full understanding of human experience. This loosening of the forms in which the logic of this world is displayed, since it nevertheless insists on being understood as reality, corresponds to what Tzvetan Todorov calls the 'fantastic' – against what we commonly call fantasy.[25] Todorov has proposed that the structural character of 'le fantastique' is determined in effect by a set of moves within the text, the result of which is that the reader, outside the text, shares with its primary narrator a state of uncertainty about where reality lies: in this world, or that. The consequence is twofold: the narrative of events at some level gives way to a narrative of perception; and secondly, this double action ranges across two fictional worlds, one that corresponds to reality as the reader would normally view it and as the narrator/protagonist expects to find it, and a second that is disturbingly different from ours but which makes imperious claims to be understood as reality itself. An insistent ambiguity typifies this genre: 'the fantastic is a particular case of the more general category of the "ambiguous vision"'.[26] Todorov's fantastic is defined not so much by its contents as by its differences from other narratives that present action in a world other than our commonly accepted reality. It does not fit within the narrative of what Todorov terms the marvellous, since action in such a text admits of no doubt that this world is anything but itself; for the time of the fiction, it is reality. On the other hand, the fantastic fits no more properly within the textual category of those fictions that present some other world as reality, but sooner or later dissolve its differences from ours as the issue of some condition that is relatively familiar in our world – a dream, perhaps, or an instance of the weird and 'uncanny'. We may not understand what is happening, but the force of the narrative eventually is to confirm for us that, odd though the experience may be, it may be explained.

Such narratives leave us – and their characters – uncertain about the epistemological status of the world of the fiction, at least; they frequently play with perception and dramatise the construction of subjectivity, in a manner more or less subversive of rationality. In effect, in *Under the Mountain*, Gee's adult reader is probably going to resolve the conflict between fantasy and the real as the children's perception of the world around them; for the time of the reading, we – as children – accept the reality of their experience. Paradoxically, for the local reader, the topography of the story-world is so familiar that the fantastic order of narrative events is underpinned by the real: Wilberforce worms on the one hand; but, on the other, North Head, Mount Victoria, One Tree Hill, Mount Wellington, Mount Eden, Rangitoto and Lake Pupuke.

The second of Gee's fantasies, *The World Around the Corner*, is intended for a younger audience than Gee might have expected to be interested in *Under the Mountain*, but, as we have already noted, that does not seem to lessen the seriousness of its founding concerns. The book's premise, once more, is that good must battle continually to keep evil at bay; and, again, only partial solutions are available. Although *The World Around the Corner* is set in our world, it would scarcely be a story at all if it were not for the sudden occurrences of the marvellous that it reports. There is no sharp transition from primary to alternative or secondary world; rather the marvellous is an element of a secondary world that seems to slide under ours and for a short time intersect with it. In that sense, although it misses the tensions of the gothic narratives that Todorov explores, this story, like *Under the Mountain*, is something other than the kind of fantasy Todorov associates with romance; it is, again, more like his 'fantastic'. There is no super-abundance of marvels to change the narrative course from the governing realism set up in the opening pages. Most of the action takes place in our world and the secondary world is somewhere out there, kept at a distance, glimpsed fleetingly, mostly through a dream vision of the main protagonist. Perception is a more central issue in both narrative and thematic terms than in *Under the Mountain*, although once more oddness of perception has much to do with the character of the child protagonist and, to that extent, invites being read tamely – as anecdotal evidence of the vital childish imagination.

Caroline, the eight-year-old protagonist, gains the ability to see another world when she saves a pair of glasses with 'a crack in the left-hand lens' (*WAC* 8) from the villainous adults who are hunting for them. She has her special hiding place in the loft of the antiques shop owned by her father, from where she can observe the behaviour of the various people who come to buy and sell old treasures. When she discovers several pairs of glasses hidden beneath some old books brought in for auction by an old woman, the adventure begins. It becomes clear to Caroline that there is more to the old woman than is immediately apparent when she discovers that the pair of glasses with the cracked lens enables her to view the world with remarkable clarity: 'Everything was brighter. Everything had a sharp clean edge. She looked at her hands. They were pink as candy floss. Her finger nails shone like jewels. Little golden hairs grew on her wrists' (*WAC* 8). To wear the glasses, to look through the cracked lens, is to be made instantly conscious of the beauty of the ordinary; the world is suddenly clearer, more splendid, becomes as brilliant and desirable as fairyland.

This is not all a fantastic play with the child's perception, however. In the later fantasy of the *O* trilogy, similarly, fractured perception takes the form of contrasting colour-sensitivity: the halfmen – human, but debased – are unable to see the colours of their own world, even though those colours are perfectly visible to other beings who have not suffered the same moral collapse. In *The World Around the Corner*, perception likewise plays an active role in the contest to which the story introduces us – if in very different terms. The old woman, like the cracked glasses, is more than she seems: she proves to be an elf, fleeing from the villainous Grimbles, who are goblins in disguise. The glasses turn out to be weaponry – a magical aid used by young elfin warriors who must yearly fight the goblins' dragon to save elf land. If the elf warrior should fail to defeat the dragon, elf land will be captured by the goblins, and a pleasant land of wood and glades, flowers and trees will be turned into a desert, reduced to the sort of nothingness the goblins love. The goblins, after all, live in 'great walled cities', a kind of military–industrial wasteland:

> Their world is one of smoke and poison and darkness. They have factories making weapons. They fight among themselves. And they have burrowed under the mountains into our half of the world. They want to turn that into desert too. That is their way. (*WAC* 38)

The desperate fragility of the good, besieged by darkness, is painted in the contrasting picture of the elf warrior – 'a waif, with her thin arms and legs' (*WAC* 61) – in battle with a dragon that 'towered like a mushroom cloud' over her (*WAC* 69). These vivid images are designed to produce a set of responses – sympathy and loathing – like those we feel towards the opposing forces of good and evil in *Under the Mountain* and the *O* trilogy.

In the world Caroline glimpses 'around the corner', as with the worlds of O and the universe the Wilberforces would create in consuming ours, there is no apparent destinal agency or providential plan; but there is an undeniable moral centre, however undefined. This ethical code is readily linked to current concerns with ecology, and with the implications of scientific and technological development when harnessed to the will to power.[27] The geographical landscape of the Grimble goblins is remarkably similar to the landscape of the halfmen in the later *O* series. Gee's villains all employ machinery of one kind or another to enslave others and destroy nature. In *The World Around the Corner*, the corrupting effects of materialism and lust for power are realised by Gee in what can be seen as a parable of the confusion and suffering that accompany technological development. The struggle is between natural, creative good and destructive or de-creative evil.

Likewise, in *Under the Mountain*, although the children's experience is grounded in our world, it takes on symbolic force from the patterning of the imagery, once they are implicated in the conflict between Mr Jones and the Wilberforces. The contest of light and dark, as figure for the conflict between good and evil, marks the difference between the two alien species that come to shape Earth's future. The Wilberforces' natural form combines parasitic, mobile intelligences with 'huge worm-like creatures' (*UM* 73). As worms they bring sterility upon the universe through which they move, by a dreadful, up-ending irony transforming all existence into a wasteland in which nothing can flourish. They seem archetypal evil:

> The ships landed, the blind worms wriggled out, each ridden by its brain. Devastation, death. And from the huge factories that sprang up there trundled fantastic machines that chewed each planet to mud. On and on it went, across a whole arm of the galaxy. The planets turned from green to brown to grey. (*UM* 74)

This account is visionary, since Mr Jones places it in the children's minds; but it becomes directly symbolic: every aspect of the Wilberforces contributes to a kind of moral portrait. We get a sense of their character, their lack of imaginative thought or intelligence. A sense of the symbolic is no less true of the opposed portrait of virtue, when Mr Jones allows the children a glimpse of his own home-world: 'Yet they had a sense of life flickering in those cities, moving like blue and yellow flames, swiftly and lightly' (*UM* 75). The scene is animated and every word invokes a sense of the good.

Finally, the radical difference between these alien life forms crystallises in names that cannot be voiced, but that represent their species-determined character: the Wilberforces are 'People of the mud, who conquer and multiply', while the Joneses are 'The People who understand' (*UM* 74, 75). Understanding, in the context of this novel, itself suggests compassion; it excludes conquest or appropriation and carries with it suggestions of imaginative sympathy with others. 'The great instrument of moral good,' Shelley tells us, 'is the imagination.' The work to which this instrument is put is inherently creative, supporting a fantasy that calls material ambitions into question and accords value instead to harmonious relations between this world's peoples, and between this world's peoples and their world.

Changing views and changing worlds: portal/quest narrative in the *O* trilogy

Like *Under the Mountain* and *The World Around the Corner*, Gee's *O* trilogy seems born of an intensely suspicious relation to modern society. While it is tied to the real world by its framing moments, however, it is much more fully a work of fantasy in that action is switched to an alternative world. As he has often stated, Gee early developed a strong distaste for war and violence; he recalls that, as a 17-year-old student at Avondale College in Auckland, he began a pacifist novel designed to end war on this planet forever.[28] It was never completed, but it points to a lifelong concern with human cruelty and violence against others and against the natural world. The adult Gee may have realised the impossibility of the utopian dream of his first novel, but now, in the *O* trilogy, writes another fantastic parable, a serial cautionary tale capable of rooting an attitude, at least, in the minds of a youthful audience. Reality, in this case, is no longer confined to the local scene – Nelson or Auckland's North Shore – but appears in an entirely other world, where it takes on greater force as this world's questions are raised with increased urgency.

The pleasurable fantastic text performs ideological work, presenting a vision of the world just as surely as realistic fiction does. Peter Hunt's point, 'the one thing that can rarely be said about fantasy is that it has nothing to do with reality',[29] holds good for these stories. The genre may possess a distinct philosophical and social force as parable, allowing the writer to make observations about society without commenting directly on specific incidents or events in what Tolkien termed the 'Primary World'.[30] Pleasure, in such a case, stems largely from the indirection of the narrative statement; the narrative is a glass through which we delight in seeing the world darkly. If pure, secondary world fantasy is most difficult, as a work of invention, for many writers it is the most satisfying to create and the most compelling, for readers, as narrative art. Tolkien refers to it as 'Enchantment', 'a kind of elvish craft'.[31] He claims the status of 'sub-creator' for the writer of such fiction; sub-creative art he considers natural to humankind, but in a sense it imitates the work of the divine creator in which it also participates, capable of affording us 'fleeting glimpses of Joy, Joy beyond the walls of the world, poignant as grief'.[32] Furthermore, for all the invention, at least the primary world may be brought into focus more sharply, allowing 'a sudden glimpse of the underlying reality or truth'.[33] Tolkien terms this capacity 'Recovery'. It especially occurs when fantasy's 'arresting strangeness',[34] its power to shatter over-familiarity with things, causes the reader to regain 'a clear view' of the world: '"seeing things as we are (or were) meant to see them" – as things apart from ourselves'.[35]

Like any effective fantasy or fairy tale, then, the alternative world dimension of Gee's fantasy has the force to recharge perception and ethical positioning in this world, producing 'a clear view'. The more powerful of these stories aspire to do more – that measure of enchantment that Tolkien calls 'Primary Belief', where there is no disputing the reality presented by the writer. Gee is acute about this in comments on his own stories of fantasy/adventure:

> I loved writing them. But there's a danger in this sort of writing – the danger of over-invention, of making too much happen, and too much that's strange. The anchoring of such stories is the challenge. They proceed by invention, they're anchored by the imagination, the thing that produces recognition in the reader as his or her world connects with the invented world.[36]

In the *O* trilogy, while we are left in no doubt as to Gee's attitude to war and his distrust of political rhetoric, this distrust is so deep in the actions and words of his warring characters that it drives our engagement in the fiction itself. Gee downplays the importance of what he actually thinks – he is no philosopher. Rather, he places strong emphasis on the textual form and structure his ideas take, or perhaps enable: 'But I regard all my speculation in these areas as banal ... the furniture of a writer's mind isn't necessarily interesting, it's the way he arranges it that has the interest.'[37] His emphasis, in talking about his fiction, constantly falls on the 'imagination' at its connective work, often performed by 'something down to earth', 'humdrum' or, in tracing the movements of a character's thoughts and feelings, 'quiet moments', 'where the writer's language has to be exact yet reverberative'.[38]

In comments on the first of his historical novels for children, *The Fat Man*, which is connected to events that are deep in his memory, Gee noted he wrote 'with full commitment', adding, 'It's fully imagined.'[39] This is his achievement in the *O* trilogy, too: these novels are no less fully imagined – although they are imagined otherwise, as many textual moments allow us to see. Authorial 'commitment' to the world of the story is registered sharply, for instance, in the passage between Gee's primary world (Collingwood) and his secondary world, the world of O (Wildwood), especially when, in line with his schoolboy–scientist disposition, young Nick offers Susan – Gee's major character in the series – a quasi-scientific explanation for their mind-bending translation from one world to the other:

> 'Is this world a dream?'
>
> 'No. It's real all right. The planet O. I haven't worked it out yet. I thought it might be some sort of alternate world – but the moon is different, and the stars. So we must have travelled out somewhere into the Milky Way.'
>
> 'How did you get here?'
>
> 'I pinched Jimmy Jasper's bottle and had a sniff. I think what happens is – they've got some sort of force-field in there, in the mineshaft. When you sniff that stuff it drags you in. Then it breaks you down somehow, into molecules maybe, or impulses, and you go through a warp. It puts you together again when you come out the other side. I'd sooner travel by train.' (*HO* 61)

There is fantastic 'invention' here, obviously, but the imagination is exact not only in the detail, but in phrasing and idiom. This is dialogue that has a history in both O and Nelson, in genre and in social relations, but above all it is an entirely situated, sure conversation.

Part of the fully imagined dimension of the narrative that runs from *The Halfmen of O* to *Motherstone* is the generic logic by which it operates – but which it also transcends. The basic condition of this kind of adventurous narrative has been aptly described by Todorov as a passage from equilibrium to disequilibrium, completed by a return to equilibrium. The shift from one world to another – where a testing sequence of events occurs that restores social and psychic balance, permitting a return to the primary world – effectively realises the power of this kind of dynamic.[40] In Gee's trilogy, of course, the shift happens not once but three times, which gives the series more shape and more sequential significance than, say, C.S. Lewis's linked Narnia stories. At the same time, the necessity to return to O actually subverts (or transcends) the apparent coherence of the preceding story, generating scope for development, but also instability: the repeated need to return renders the achievement of order on O provisional and problematic. Action is locked up by the designs of the rulers who pursue power and seek to control their societies through violence and/or war. The trilogy does not end in wholesale ruin like that which devastates Auckland in *Under the Mountain*; yet the resolution to its history of unceasing human hostilities is somehow even more devastating and demands even sterner insistence on ultimate good. The end of the series, in fact, brings to mind Terry Pratchett's comment about fantasy: 'the *real* concerns of fantasy ought to be about not having battles'.[41] The huge number of deaths should surprise no one who is acquainted with fantasy, of course, since in this genre violence between parties, however much the work of heroes, tends to be a clash of apocalyptic dimensions. Famous instances, including the last of all battles in Lewis's Narnia tales, or the battle before Sauron's gate in *The Lord of the Rings*, do indeed seem to be modelled on the biblical *Revelations*, so that loss paradoxically contains a promise of restoration: from destruction will come a new beginning.

Ethics, endings and evolution on O

It is here, though, that Gee parts company with his predecessors: he does not accept the apocalyptic ending of fantasy – even if he invokes it, when he has mage-like Freeman Wells speak of the time of these stories as the 'last days' (*M* 120). In the course of three books, over three regimes, humankind on O proves to be so far beyond redemption that the species must be returned to an early stage in its evolution, relatively helpless, lacking much in the way of clothing or tools and incapable of speech: 'Their language was a grunt, an exclamation,' Nick says, when he sees them after this event, 'back with the monkeys' (*M* 180). Freeman Wells explains that human violence stems from an evolutionary history so erratic and rapid that humankind had never had time to develop a balanced disposition: 'Theirs was a headlong rush through the tale of kinds' (*M* 122). Humankind's 'Law' has become the will to dominate, which places the whole planet at risk. Returning humankind to its infancy, as it were, may give the species – and the planet – a 'second chance', the possibility of revising evolution, through generations, into 'something different', more in tune with the harmonious world that human appetites have almost destroyed. Evil is shackled for the time being. Some small hope resides in the possibility that evolution will this time show intelligent design, when humankind is placed in the care of the Woodlanders – adoptive 'parents' – with a view to nourishing an understanding of the nature of good and evil and acknowledging the balanced differences that transcend them.

In the first book of the trilogy, Susan Ferris is the visitor from Earth, marked at birth by Freeman Wells as the chosen one, the saviour of O. Different geographical landscapes and variously rational inhabitants constitute this fantastic, complex world as something like the Golden Age, when men, birds and beasts spoke to each other in a common language. Each species – Woodlanders, Birdfolk, Stonefolk, Seafolk and Humankind – has its own domain, culture and history, 'And each its dispensation' (*HO* 74). This may be 'humdrum', 'Primary' world stuff, like the seals' knowledge of kelp and mussels; it may give to O's domains a different order of significance, as when the limits set on the Birdfolk's power to range connects to an earlier history of destructive rapacity; it may derive from symbolic but material divisions between the inert and the animate, presented in the Stonefolk's dispensation, which sees them incapable of surviving the light. None is promoted as the embodiment of a transcendent social ideal, although the Woodlanders come closest, perhaps, in their compassion and especially in their denial of violence, their refusal to kill. The sense of a world structure of domains is the stronger because of the absolute identity of history with the passage of time registered from a human point of view; humans are never completely themselves for long, but persist as Halfmen, or as Mixies, always at odds with each other, always seeking a gain for themselves at the cost of others, including other species. The two stones that figure the divided condition of humanity are consigned to the guardianship of the Birdfolk and the Stonefolk; guardianship of humankind passes to the Woodlanders at the end of this triple history. At the start of the series, humankind lives in Darkland, once a city known as Manhome, but now decaying ruins; at the end of the story, Darkland is no longer even a memory and man's home is unimaginable: 'It'll be thousands of years before humans learn to have homes.' (*M* 181) The route to this point is circuitous, marked by false prospects and dead ends as well as journeys and homecomings. The tragedy of the history Gee constructs is that so often the journeying takes us past the same places, in demonstration that good is necessarily engaged daily in a battle that never ends.

Many of the social and political problems that Gee sees as damaging to our society are explored in his secondary world; the destructive nature of power especially. So, in *The Halfmen of O*, we hear of the transformation of Otis Hand, 'a golden boy, brilliant and beautiful', (*HO* 77) to Otis Claw.

> He had tasted power, and the seed of evil grew in him, and swelled in him, until he was nothing but a smiling face, a fair exterior, fitted over evil. He saw the land of O, he saw the world, and wanted it for his. He saw humankind, and saw the seas and Wildwood and the mountains, and their Folk, and saw that everything was free. That he could not bear, so he plotted to enslave them and possess them. (*HO* 76–77)

As with Milton's Satan in *Paradise Lost*, the desire for power must be recognised for what it is and controlled, or it will destroy the man or woman who lusts after it. With its demanding context of power, ambition, cruelty and violence, action in *The Halfmen of O* appears concerned above all with choice.[42] Nineteen years before Susan and Nick's arrival on O, humankind had been split into 'half' creatures by Otis Hand, who forced humanity to make a binding choice between good and evil. The reverberations of this choice give this event biblical proportions, as if it were an Edenic fall; Susan's arrival, in answer to Freeman Wells' call, tends to confirm the pattern by sketching in the possibility of redemption. At the very end of this fantastic history when, in accordance with Wells' design, humankind is reduced to its lengthy sleep, the logic of his judgement again registers choice and its consequences: 'They were chosen – but they chose' (*M* 180). Chose ill.

Gee's language again turns startlingly Miltonic, as Marna, Freeman Wells' wife, looks back on recent human history on O, in which the natural balance has been destroyed and a Manichean conflict between good and evil initiated:

> [I]n every man and woman in O, good had fought with evil, one last fight, until one or the other was driven out. We had no doubt which would be the strong. We knew that down in Manhome, Darkland now, Darkland from that instant, the hordes in whom Evil had triumphed hunted down and murdered the unresisting Good. We were good. I say it with no pride. There is no pride in being half. Good must be won daily in the battle that never ends. (*HO* 77)

Temptation and choice – humankind must choose at every step of the way. Milton believed that, in giving reason to humankind, God (a good God) gave him the capacity to choose his own way, 'for reason is but choosing'.[43] Gee's argument has a different orientation from Milton's. Whether God is or is not, the vision identified with and by Freeman Wells – who may or may not be God's agent – forms a defining principle of the good that needs no God to underwrite it. Gee's deeply felt conviction, like Milton's, is that the freedom to choose is a defining aspect of our humanity, since otherwise living would be little more than soulless, mechanistic activity.

The first book ends with Susan restoring the balance between good and evil, thus reinstating, for a time, the capacity to choose. In the second book of the series, *The Priests of Ferris* (1984), she is summoned back to O because it is again in crisis. This time, her mission is to destroy the repressive religious cult that has been instituted in her name and has taken root in the decades following the destruction of Otis Claw and his Halfmen disciples. Gods have no agents on O, despite Susan's election as this world's saviour. Religion, as Gee depicts it in *The Priests of Ferris*, however, finds close parallels in earthly human history, with respect to the damage done in the name of 'god' and faith: enemies of the 'cult of Ferris' are identified as non-human and vilified as 'vermin' (*PF* 31), including those humans who turn heretical in questioning the cult's governing beliefs and actions. Arguably, Gee's deeply entrenched liberalism becomes visible at this point in the novel, just as his abhorrence of militarism, nuclear weaponry and pollution are glaringly obvious throughout the trilogy.[44] The cult's High Priest uses religion as a means of maintaining his power. He knows the founding tenets of the cult constitute a lie, but they are useful: belief is employed to manipulate the people into killing and torturing in Susan's name. The young girl Soona, who is scheduled for sacrifice, makes the point to Susan very plainly: 'This isn't a religion, it's a government. The High Priest is a king. He's not interested in Ferris bones and religious rites. He's interested in staying on his throne, staying in power' (*PF* 126). Later, when Susan faces the priest, she protests at death done for cultic ends, and his response is swift as an executioner's blade:

'You're mad,' Susan whispered. 'You're all mad.'

'No,' smiled the High Priest, 'we are sane. We are the State. We are truth and life and order.' (*PF* 136–37)

Susan succeeds in putting an end to the High Priest's reign, despite the priestly grip on the social imagination of humankind on O. She shatters any notion of the cult's legitimacy, but is not so successful in eliminating the human capacity to commit evil, or the dominance of society by a self-interested political elite.

In the last book of the series, *Motherstone*, Susan is obliged to undertake this final mission, even before she completes the return journey to Earth that she and Nick intended. Osro, one of seven 'Candidates' chosen and trained as possible successor to the High Priest, quickly moves to fill the power vacuum left by the priest's sudden fall and death. He has the means, manpower, intelligence and megalomaniac will to build a weapon with which he can subjugate all life forms on O. Any who oppose him 'will burn like a field of dry corn. And the Birds will flare in the sky like paper kites' (*M* 23). This weapon will enable Osro to bend all living beings (even the Stonefolk) to his will; he will be King and 'rule by fear and might – because I desire it and because I know the way' (*M* 11). Susan's renewed quest is to find a way to save O from the evil designs of its human inhabitants once more, restoring the balance between all living creatures.

Critics of fantasy often feel under pressure to read the *O* trilogy in allegorical terms: the names of the various regions in O persuade all but the most trusting reader to feel that, however fully imagined it is, this long narrative is patterned so strongly that it just will not do to treat it as an imaginary history. Allegorical directions in the names and the allegorical nature of its narrative conflicts seem unmistakable. In the most fully articulated instance of an allegorical reading of the trilogy, Vivien van Rij argues that Gee 'encompasses the particular, political, and universal; and the present, the past, and the primal' in the O narratives.[45] Central to her reading is her sense that Gee is committed to the explanatory power of Jungian psychology. In consequence, the sweep of history finally proves to be 'psychic', a 'journey' in which Susan proves exemplary of mankind in her achievement of a fully integrated personality; the wholeness is represented symbolically in the completed Motherstone.[46] The trilogy does indeed seem to comprise tales mapped out to bring the reader to an understanding of the divided nature of humankind and motivated by a concern for wholeness and a countervailing obsession with violence and the absoluteness of evil. It seems to me, however, that for all their unblinking gaze into the face of evil, say, these are not stories that simply translate into a set of ideas that may be said to command the narrative and justify it. It might well be argued, in fact, that, as earlier suggested, the term parable is preferable for a narrative that seems determined to reach into daily lives, even if it plainly deals in the symbolic. The term suggests a tale engaged in the business of illumination by means of exemplarity, but one that tends to be formally spare in its detailing – which seems to accord with Gee's notion of the general character of effective children's fiction. Gee's well-attested interest in the craft of writing for children puts us under pressure to think not only of themes but also of structures and forms of narrative expression.[47]

Given the undoubted spareness of these stories, it is useful perhaps to consider again the question of characterisation, with van Rij's arguments for exemplary wholeness in mind, especially in light of Bill Manhire's claim that 'character creation' is the 'greatest' among Gee's gifts as a writer. Manhire likens Gee in this respect to Dickens; yet he rather slights characterisation in the fantasy tales, claiming that the children are given little more than traits of a general kind, presumably in order to keep the plot going.⁴⁸ It seems useful, nevertheless, to keep in mind Gee's comments about localisation: 'I wanted settings New Zealand children would recognise, with New Zealand the most important place in the world, as it is for the children who live here.'⁴⁹ This determined orientation suggests that these fantasies may work by a rather remarkable ventriloquism, where the assured, adult, third-person narration is projected in tones that suggest his lexicon or register draws on the language – and lore – of the New Zealand child. The High Priest's guards did not flank the temple dais protectively, but 'scrummed' about it (*PF* 168). Again, when Susan lies in the dark at the beginning of *The Halfmen of O*, totally alone, after being captured by Otis Claw and his minions, her desolation is shaped by New Zealand memories: 'Now and then distant animal cries came from the forest. Once a bird like a morepork sounded close. Tears ran down her face. She would never hear real moreporks again, or see fantails, or see her mother and father or her dopey cousin, Nicholas Quinn' (*HO* 52). The morepork then converts from bird into a bird call, as language used by a child – in this case her 'dopey cousin' – to let her know that he had followed her into O: '"Morepork." A long pause. "Morepork"' (*HO* 53). More tellingly, perhaps, because the local becomes personal, Otis Claw, the other world's evil leader, is unnervingly grotesque until the moment when, for Susan, he subsides into her memories of a tubby, aging former schoolmaster. Gee's application of a domestic New Zealand context to frightening other-world figures is worth noting. In this case, it is reasonable to take another look at characterisation of the leading alien figures – the three who visit O from Earth.

O: A New Zealand story

For a start, O's New Zealanders possess what virtually nobody else does on O, even after Susan and Nick's team have set this world to rights – a complete humanity, however imbalanced. In an interview, Colleen Reilly talked to Gee about the question of evil in his work, *Plumb* especially:

[Reilly] *Yet, for me, what Plumb gets from his 'vision' of evil ... is not the ability to withstand evil necessarily but a more whole human self.*

[Gee] Yes, exactly. I guess *The Halfmen of O* spells it out.[50]

It does indeed, in the history of humankind on O, but especially in the differing dispositions and judgements of the three earthly characters, significantly named 'Mixies'. External signs represent an internal reality when Susan is identified as the bearer of a salvational power, marked by the image of the halves on her wrist.

> 'Light and dark contended and held each other in a deep embrace. Yes Susan, that is it, you have the mark on you. There on your wrist. See how the light bends into the dark, see how dark leans into the light. They hold each other, good and evil. And see, if you look close, in the light there is a spot of dark, and in the dark there is a spot of light.'
>
> The children looked. 'I see,' Nick whispered.
>
> 'Yes,' Susan said. 'And together they make a perfect circle.'
>
> 'That is Man. That is Freeman's Law.' (*HO* 75)

Marna speaks here with all the authority of her wisdom and grief over the loss of wholeness on O. What is read here as a sign of human nature is about to take on material existence in the Halves that must be retrieved and reformed into a whole. It constructs, indeed, an index of psychic and emotional health and a ready figure for the action of the entire trilogy: plotting sets good and evil in constant, repeated conflict yet, over the course of the series, grapples them together.

Neither good nor evil, it seems, can triumph conclusively over the other. Each has its place in the human mix. The constant exercise of choice becomes, therefore, the defining nature of humankind – without it, we would be mere puppets, instruments of another's will, like the Wilberforce worms. Manhire suggests that the child characters are reducible to traits – 'one child is dreamy, the other practical'; but perhaps, despite the dichotomies that his comment properly emphasises, characterisation tends rather to be worked in terms of this principle: the human capacity to weigh good and evil, and to choose.

Perhaps the most graphic exemplification of this agency is Jimmy Jaspers, whose initial brutality is the stuff of any child's nightmare but who quickly discovers his humanity once he is exposed to the force of undiluted evil, becoming every kid's favourite old great-uncle. In this he is conclusively differentiated from the Clings and Claws of O, halfmen by self-definition.[51] Gee fashions this mix in Jimmy not only by giving him a history like nobody else's – adult but, more especially, reprobate – but also by granting him a much appreciated impropriety of behaviour and expression. When we first meet him, he impresses himself upon us, as on the youthful heroes of the story, as a local grotesque (to Nick, he is 'some old loony'); his rough, singular history is disclosed for us when he apologises for his part in Susan's abduction:

> 'Girl ... I'm sorry. I done some pretty hairy things in me time. Jumped a claim. Stole a horse from me mate. Smash-an-grabbed a jeweller's shop once. Did time for that one too. But sellin' kids. That's the bloody worst. I'll never do that again.' (*HO* 72)

At a primary level, in line with familiar generic character patterns, he is simply the hero's 'helper'; this role is combined in the first story with another, as the one who 'calls' the hero to her mission/adventure – however unaware Jimmy may be that he is serving Freeman Wells' purpose in this, rather than Otis Claw's. His idiosyncracies, however, make him individual and hugely attractive – although we should note that the unconventional helper is a minor convention in fantasy, from George MacDonald's *The Princess and Curdie* to George Lucas's *Star Wars*. Jimmy defies general decorum, not just in his unregenerate passion for physical violence but also in his irreverence and his scabrous, indeed scatological wit.

> 'I'm Jimmy Jaspers,' he yelled. 'I'm the bloke yer been callin' the Terrible One. So lissen ter me, yer bunch of bloddy no-hopers. Yer Temple's done for. Finished! Kaput! Yer High Priest's finished. We'll give 'im a job cleanin' dunnies. That's all e's good for. So keep yer bums on yer seats. One move out of you lot an' them Birds up there is gunner let yer have it.' (*PF* 168)

Jimmy, then, almost invariably acts according to type, but his type is eccentric rather than strictly conventional; and nobody serves better to keep New Zealand in the story. Nick carries nothing like the same load of mixed cultural luggage, even if he is very local – not only is he an other-world visitor, like Jimmy and Susan; he is also visiting from out of town, an Auckland relation, picking up former connections to his

Collingwood cousin Susan, who is both a bit odd and a little bit older than he. For some time at least, in O, his relations with Susan seem inflected with the awkwardness of such family facts – and, of course, it is to family matters that he and Susan will return in the last sentences of the trilogy. He is unquestionably practical, like Theo in *Under the Mountain*. He is the one who has the wit to build the kites that enable Susan and her small fellowship to escape their Halfie pursuers and to sail into the city, thereby fixing them in O's cultural memory – with such mixed consequences. Yet there are generic elements in his character, too: he is the most constant of Susan's helpers; indeed, like the hobbits who accompany Frodo, he links with other characters to form a kind of collective hero, a fellowship. Above all, however, he is just Nick, possessed of the typical arrogance of the Aucklander and the adolescent male ('He was still a know-all, still believed he knew more than anyone else' (*PF* 7)), but still anxious about his cousin and increasingly protective of her. And there is more to Nick, perhaps: he does seem to grow up. He certainly becomes more responsible for devising and carrying out much of the important business in the last book of the trilogy.

In this regard, what is really interesting is the way in which notions that could not be allowed to determine action in earlier stories come into their own in this later fantasy. Recurrent situations allow Gee to revisit common problems, but to elaborate a different point of view. In particular, we might well conclude that Gee takes up in *O* the imaginative sympathy Rachel feels for any living thing in *Under the Mountain*. A sharp contrast is drawn between her attitude, which the reader is invited to endorse, and the monomaniacal quest of the Wilberforces. Rachel, the dreamer or seer, questions the right to destroy any living creature, especially if it involves the annihilation of a race. The question is raised precisely to mark the sharp distinction between two principles at work in the novel's action – negotiation or justified violence – although finally the force of the story works against allowing evil to continue unchecked. Her suggestion that humans could talk to the Wilberforces and 'persuade them to go away' is pushed aside by Theo, but no less by Mr Jones, who emphasises their destructive force and appetite. Rachel's unease, however, goes to the core of our humanity: imaginative sympathy and compassion is the more human response. If her response is naïve, it nevertheless seems more truly adult than Theo's. It is significant, furthermore, that it is her stones that work, not his. We have to concede she is wrong here because the Wilberforces are implacably evil, but hers is a mature voice, speaking one kind of truth, perhaps superior. It is her instinct for negotiation and her desire for peaceful coexistence with other species that are taken up in the *O* series in Nick, surprisingly – even if they prove no less problematic.

Ursula Le Guin, in her 1973 National Book Award acceptance speech, argues fantasy's capacity for serious exploration of society, and makes a powerful claim for the force of the imagination: 'For after all, as great scientists have said and as all children know, it is above all by the imagination that we achieve perception, compassion, and hope.'[52] Nick's failed but resolute efforts to talk the opposed hosts into negotiation and compromise in *Motherstone* may well not have happened at all if he had not grown into the compassion and trust Rachel tentatively voiced in the earlier story.

At the beginning of *The Priests of Ferris*, when one hundred turns have taken place in the O calendar, Nick is back in Collingwood for his family's annual visit and Susan smiles at his ebullient show of know-all-ness, concluding that a year has made little difference in him:

> It had made a difference in her. She was no longer a child. She'd started growing up on O, and a year of remembering had turned her into a woman. Child/woman, her mother called her. It would be stretching things, she thought, to describe Nick as boy/man. (*PF* 7)

In the long story that follows over the second and third books of the trilogy, Nick does do some growing up, as mentioned earlier. It is interesting, then, to ask where the story takes Susan. It is worth noting, for a start, how far she is from Gee's other female heroes. It is exceedingly interesting, indeed, that the elect company of Gee's fantasy heroes are mostly girls. If gender figures in these stories, sexuality barely surfaces. On the other hand, it clearly is important in Gee's later *Limping Man* trilogy, where its function is wholly familiar (love and reproduction), despite the fact that this trilogy is a true alternative world fantasy. In a sense, it normalises a fantastic history by construing it in terms of nature and natural generations, rather than in O's loose chronology of 'turns' interrupted by catastrophic visits from Earth. Yet, although sexuality never surfaces directly on O, it does have some force. It can be measured across the generations when, in Susan's mission to renew the Halves on the Motherstone, her last and most threatening opponents are the older women in the city, its guardians.

> She swung round to face the women, these hideous priestesses of their god, and held up her hand. 'Stop!' They were ten paces back, pressing in their hundreds, and setting up at last a soft anticipatory cackle. But they stopped, and leaned towards her, and pulsed and breathed like a single organism. (*M* 170)

Susan, then, is rightly viewed both in her combat with violent men and in comparisons with other women on O – she is not to be understood just as a dreamer, in need of the complementary gifts of the practical boy who is her companion. Derek Brewer's useful discussion of what he calls symbolic stories – fairy tale, fantasy and romance – recognises in them a common concern with liminal, threshold moments and the universal processes of maturation.[53] In symbolic terms, the triumphant return home after a testing adventure abroad signals the passage from youth to adulthood. To cross from one world to another – Collingwood to O – manages this kind of development; it is forecast, anticipated or first played out on O, in O's terms, but understood as somehow taking place materially in Nelson.

It is difficult to get beyond the heroic pattern Gee elaborates: Susan is never less than singular, since she is the one who is called to carry through an enormous cultural renovation, not once, but three times. She is fused to the demands of her mission, just as Frodo is bound to his, so that personal characteristics seem somehow irrelevant. When we first meet her, we learn that her own family has thought of her as odd and that they are disposed to track this oddness to the curious events of her infancy, when Freeman Wells singled her out, as she lay in her cradle, and marked her on the wrist. What they see as a disturbing birthmark, the story soon reveals as the sign of a mission she has always waited for – even if she has no idea when she will be called, or to what. Once her mission is under way, oddness lingers only in the isolation that not infrequently separates her from her companions. At the same time, by the logic of the mission, her status within the story increases as the stories advance. If she has personal characteristics – sympathy, belief and an extraordinary gift for focusing on the business in hand – all that is somehow subsumed into the larger wholeness of nature that is the end-point of the undertaking she has necessarily accepted, at the call from Freeman Wells. She has the complete humanity that is represented in the figure on her wrist, and which she has to establish as Humankind's Law, in place of the passion for self-interest and self-gratification that renders humankind so dangerously less than itself.

In an interview with Brian Boyd, Gee makes an interesting comment on the familiar reviewers' judgement of his novels as marked by pessimism:

> I mean to entertain and it puzzles me when reviewers accuse me of pessimism. The movement in my novels is always towards knowledge – self-knowledge in the characters, and they get there, they have their natures, all of them, and a vast amount of entertainment is had along the way.[54]

In the very last pages of *Motherstone*, Susan seems to have moved on to a stillness she has not before possessed, and that seems proper, since this time the mission is truly completed. But if Gee's comment applies to the children's fiction as well as to his adult novels, it is fair enough to ask what self-knowledge – or, more plausibly, sense of self – does Susan come to? We will not necessarily find it by analysing her as we might a figure in a realistic novel, even if it is precisely that order of fictive being she must finally return to. This is a fantasy, a symbolic story, so the more fitting conclusion is that, while Susan is secure in her knowledge of her mixed human nature, the final action of this story, in setting her against the women guardians of the Motherstone, brings her symbolically to the threshold of this future, too: her future as a woman.

Knowing something of the place for the first time

None of Gee's fantastic works quite achieves the eucatastrophe or happy ending noted by Tolkien as a necessary ingredient of fantasy; no 'lifting of the heart' that he requires, no 'Consolation of the Happy Ending'. This is as true of the later *Limping Man* stories as it is of *Under the*

Mountain, *The World Around the Corner* and the *O* trilogy. What Gee aims for in the five fantastic narratives written between 1979 and 1986, however, is perhaps something closer to the vision by which, he says, his own life was 'changed', at 16, when he first met 'the Dickens world' – 'that huge and violent and tragic and heroic and comic and swarming world of the imagination'. This encounter would also have served to introduce him into a 'moral universe', enlarging understanding.[55] This does not translate into any sense of a divine purpose at work in the world of O, or Auckland, as grasped in Gee's fantastic narratives; but, if there is no explicit articulation of a seriously religious faith, a definite philosophical and moral sense does radiate through these novels, and does somehow seem supported by their final events. Choice made at this point demands serious courage; courage becomes serious when it is ethically anchored.

What is peculiarly interesting in each of the early fantasies, but most markedly in the *O* trilogy, is a dynamic that depends on the capacity of symbolic stories to catch the trajectory of maturation; in each of these stories, the child heroes grow up and, in doing so, are made special by growing into a kind of wisdom. At the end of *Motherstone*, Soona and Aenlocht, reduced by the final cataclysmic judgement on O's humankind to the most rudimentary, language-less existence, do enjoy the promise of reproduction, sex's longer prospect, as Nick recognises: 'He supposed they would start having children soon. That was a good thing – a new generation' (*M* 180). So, no triumphal conclusion, personal or social – but, however problematically, O is 'saved': 'They had a second chance' (*M* 181). For Nick and Susan, the happiness of a good ending is even less noisy. They will go back to the day they started from, yet there will be disconcerting changes in their appearance and behaviour – as happens in the adolescence into which they now enter – and folk will notice: 'We're different people' (*M* 184). This time, returning as heroes of a fantastic tale, even if they are not believed they will tell their 'truth'. Which is perhaps the best future adolescence can offer – idealism to steer one's actions.

2 THE GOOD, THE BAD – AND IRONIC REVERSALS
Moralscape in Gee's realist historical quintet for young readers

Diane Hebley

Between 1986 and 1999, Maurice Gee wrote a quintet of realistic historical novels for young readers: *The Fire-Raiser* (1986), *The Champion* (1989), *The Fat Man* (1994), *Orchard Street* (1998), and *Hostel Girl* (1999). Set in New Zealand in different periods of history ranging from World War I to the 1950s, these novels are remarkable for their investigation of the morality of the country. They are probably unintentionally a quintet, since Gee did not use the intertextual references or family continuity that distinguish his *Plumb* trilogy. Nevertheless, the coming together of landscape and moral concepts links them all. Indeed, through these novels, Gee devises a New Zealand moralscape that reveals for young readers the recurring destructive consequences of racism, classism, bullying, revenge, and predation in the past, ongoing by implication to the present day.

For his portrayal of small-town or suburban New Zealand, Gee draws largely on his boyhood experiences as outlined in 'Beginnings' and 'Creeks and kitchens'.[1] He establishes a range of variable family types – from the nuclear 'normal', made up of two parents with one or more children, to the 'deviant', made up of an unstable solo parent or grandparent with a child – to portray the different moral stances and crises in the novels. Unlike some children's novels where parents are mostly in the background, the parents in Gee's quintet are of major importance. Nevertheless, as befits the tradition in children's books, Gee keeps mainly to the perspective of his young protagonists, who are influenced in their own development by reflecting on the behaviour of their parents and other adults in a position of authority. Gee is adept in his use of the 'parrot' technique, a device where children repeat information and attitudes of their elders to cover what they do not understand or experience for themselves, and yet are influenced by what they see and hear. Thus Gee's layered narration explores the white, the black and the many shades of grey in his moralscape.

Racism and revenge in *The Fire-Raiser*

The first of Gee's historical novels, *The Fire-Raiser* (1986), is set in Jessop – a fictionalised small-town Nelson – during World War I, when racism inevitably, even understandably, was rife in the community because of the death of many young New Zealand soldiers fighting in Europe. Gee refers to historical events, such as the attack on a German butcher in Gisborne on the eve of 1915, to verify racism in his fictional world. In his exploration of racism and revenge in this novel, he lays out different moral stances schematically through different sets of parents who exhibit a range of attitudes to family and society, and who act according to their beliefs without question. They are morally 'good' or 'bad'; the latter includes 'weak' and 'damaged'.

An arsonist is terrorising Jessop, and four children – Kitty and Noel Wix, Irene Chalmers and Phil Miller – are intent on unmasking him. Of the four, the first two have 'good' parents who are mainly benevolent and middle class. Indeed, though Mrs Wix resorts to physical punishment to ensure her children learn acceptable behaviour, the 'nuclear' Wixes come closest to an ideal balanced family. In this quintet of historical novels, baker George Wix is the first of Gee's admirable tradesmen fathers, based on Gee's own father. Jovial and ebullient, he lets the children make pies and eat them (which endears him to hungry Phil). Moreover, he is one of Gee's notable adults who are fond of quoting poetry to suit the circumstances. Quick and practical in fighting fires, he supports the boys when they entrust him with their suspicions. Most importantly, however, both Wix parents stand out against the prevailing racism of the town. The implication is that George's poetic interests have led to increased moral perception. Despite danger, the Wixes unhesitatingly translate their antiracist attitudes into action when they rescue and protect Frau Lotte Stauffel from the racist rabble.

In contrast, Irene's parents have pretensions towards English gentility and social superiority but do not display moral leadership, nor a balance in their own relationship. Mrs Anne Chalmers, although she aspires to give Irene the best education, is a snob and a racist with the power to 'damage people' (48). She looks down on schoolmaster Thomas Hedges as 'a tradesman' (47), and criticises her servant, ex-schoolgirl Nancy, for breathing loudly (62). She rejects any criticism of the 'good' Marwick family, who used to have 'garden parties. And a duke and duchess to stay' (102). Yet despite her lofty airs, she carries out her own destruction of European cultural inheritance through her racist stance: she sells her gifted daughter's German piano and cancels her lessons with Frau Stauffel, whom she reviles as a Hun. Mayor Francis Chalmers is pompous in his official role and capable in his importing business, but ineffectual in controlling the rabble of xenophobic bullies intent on attacking one harmless and cultured woman – a far from noble, or even patriotic act. In private, he is dominated by his wife and manipulated by his daughter. His love for the latter, however, is his finest quality. Eventually it gives him enough nerve to stand up to his wife in his daughter's best interests, such as supporting her friendship with the 'rather common' but intelligent Kitty (77).

Phil comes from a working-class family. His widowed father Charlie is forced to seek work out of town, leaving Phil in need and having to fend for himself. At 12, Phil is close to becoming a thief. Gee's indictment here is of a society so structured that this situation could occur. Charlie, however, is good at heart and shows, like other parents, aspirations for the clever son he has recently neglected through circumstances. Charlie is glad when Phil is offered opportunities, through education and an interest in astronomy, to rise from working-class levels, and he is glad when the generous Wix parents agree to take Phil into their home in the meantime.

The most eccentric and 'damaged' solo parent in *The Fire-Raiser* is English-born Julia Marwick, who lives her dysfunctional life with her middle-aged son Edgar in a large, once-elegant farmhouse just out of town. Her 'witch and spider', Miss Havisham-style behaviour, which gives her 'power, and secret knowledge' (35), is eventually explained. Thirty-five years previously, her eight-year-old daughter Lucy was drowned – for which Edgar was blamed – and her husband died soon after. Grief turned her into a reclusive widow, 'an ancient, dry-boned, beak-nosed queen' (71), who used to punish Edgar by shutting him in a dark cupboard. Unhinged enough to think temporarily that Kitty Wix is Lucy restored to her, she then reverts to the cruelty of shutting a child – the trespassing Kitty – in a dark cupboard, and instructs Edgar not to hurt the boys 'too much' (87). Although both cruel to and protective of Edgar, especially when the police come to ask questions, she shows real grief for Lucy, enough to engender in the reader some sympathy for her. Her grief is costly, however. It leads to more grief, not just for Edgar but for all those in Jessop who suffer from his revenge. Whether she will ever recover mentally from her own near-drowning is left in doubt.

Gee gains narrative power from the contrast in the moral dynamics driving four different family units: the comfortable nuclear Wix family with good principles; the rich but snobbish and unhappy Chalmers family with poor principles; the poor but plucky solo father who tries his best; and the warped and wealthy solo mother who causes damage to all around her. None of the adults questions their moral stance. It is one of Gee's ironies that, in a kind of reverse snobbism, the lower-class families behave according to higher moral principles than the wealthier 'better'-class families.

The other group of Gee's influential adults comprises the teachers, and he draws them with greater complexity and in a more ironic light than he draws the parents. Gee suggests that teachers should be the very ones concerned with passing on knowledge and culture, and should be perceptive and compassionate. Not so Mrs Bolton in *The Fire-Raiser*. She exemplifies what Gee calls his obsession with 'the human capacity for cruelty and inflicting pain on others', an obsession he returns to repeatedly in his fiction, as he indicates to Cate Brett in 'The Gee genius'.[2] Mrs Bolton displays an unbalanced, overly rigid subservience to received wisdom, which results in unthinking, racist treatment of her pupils. Her only redeeming qualities are her willingness to raise money for the Belgium Relief Fund and her own, if warped, view of education as important. She insists – by bullying – that her pupils use refined speech and behave genteelly. She even demands propriety when Mrs Marwick is feared drowned.

Mrs Bolton rejects both Maori Wipaki and working-class Phil as unsuitable for the role of representing New Zealand in her pageant. She accepts Phil eventually, but only with disdain. She exemplifies what

Brian Boyd, writing about Gee's early adult fiction, refers to as the 'negative force' of being judgemental.³ She cannot see that excessive nationalism leads to xenophobic harm, and that her pageant will stir a jingoistic response from the MP, Mr Jobling: 'Who doesn't want to go out and shoot a Hun right now?' (118). This tirade inflames the Jessop rabble to carry out the same sort of destruction that the Germans are perpetrating in Europe and that, ironically, the Allies believe they are fighting to prevent.⁴ Led by unstable Edgar, the rabble attacks one defenceless woman, Frau Stauffel, smashing and burning her house and her piano – a symbol of what is good in European culture. They would have killed her, too, if she hadn't been rescued by the children and Thomas ('Clippy') Hedges.

In contrast to Mrs Bolton, Clippy Hedges represents the maverick creative intellectual – another recurring figure in Gee's fiction. Based on a gifted headmaster who lived in Nelson in the early days,⁵ Clippy is the main exception in Gee's sorry line-up of teachers, and a much more complex character than the other adults in *The Fire-Raiser*. He is ugly in appearance but generous of spirit, and he has what Gee sees as important for his 'good' characters to have: 'an intelligent life, things that interest them'.⁶ Clippy entertains his classes with stories and information to stretch their minds. He refers to the 'new science' of psychology (25), to Milton and Keats, and passes on his passion for astronomy to Phil, hoping to interest him in higher education as the only way out of poverty. He even proposes to the Wix family that they should look after Phil until he, Clippy, can take over, once he has married Lotte Stauffel and created a stable home for a child. Already an outsider in Jessop's wartime community, Clippy has no time for rabid nationalism and racism. His moral stance allows no dilemma about attitude or action, yet he pauses to consider: 'Beethoven was a German, and so was Bismarck, and so's the Kaiser. And Shakespeare was English, but so was Butcher Cumberland' (109). So he establishes that racism is not restricted to any one race.

However, Clippy has a major flaw in his character: his temper. This, he says, is driven by that 'crocodile' part of the human brain that leads thugs to fight and nations to war (32, 109). Mainly he controls it – but not when Edgar Marwick puts the children in danger by trying to stop them swimming in the river. Clippy's fight with Marwick shames him into feeling 'like a crocodile', and he acknowledges it 'won't solve anything' (130). Indeed, the fight and then the near-drowning of Mrs Marwick combine to enrage Marwick further, leading to his final act of revenge on the school.

Against this background of community 'good' and 'bad' attitudes, with racism heightened in wartime, an unidentified arsonist intensifies the community dynamics. Gee's title and masterly opening chapter point to the crucial moral question that drives the novel: who is really the arsonist in Jessop? In terms of the main mystery of the novel, Edgar Marwick becomes the obvious culprit. Gee's third-person narrative, which allows for a wider point of view than just the children's, intimately reveals Marwick's tortured need to light fires to drive out the darkness in his mind, to burn living things to death, and to take revenge on those who anger him, including Clippy Hedges and the children. Although physically big and strong, he is impelled to seek power and pleasure through the glory of light and flame (7, 8). His behaviour is undeniably bad and deviant, sometimes purposefully so, as when he chops a tree down into the pool where children are swimming. But he had been from childhood 'damaged in ways that could not be repaired' (39). Yet he still loves the mother who damaged him. The lasting image from this novel is one of ironic pathos as Marwick, once the exulting, terrifying, revengeful wielder of fire-raising power, is led away, powerless and mentally broken. And it is additionally ironic that a skeleton, used by Clippy Hedges for comedy and education, is finally responsible for unhinging Marwick.

Other characters are obviously damaging fire-raisers too: Mrs Marwick because of the destructive way she treated her son; Anne Chalmers because of her denigration of German culture and her demeaning treatment of all around her, including her daughter; Mrs Bolton because of her racism, her classism, and her inflammatory pageant; Mr Jobling – who is, briefly, one of Gee's political 'total bastards' – because of his raving; and the Jessop rabble because they behave as destroyers, not builders in society.[7]

On the other hand, Gee gives a most important twist to the fire-raising analogy. Clippy Hedges also lights fires, but his are the fires of enlightenment. He belongs to that group of Gee's most interesting characters who 'strive to develop themselves'.[8] In doing so, through his eclectic knowledge and enthusiasms, he sparks a strong response in his students. Likewise, Lotte nurtures the passion she and Irene share for great music. George Wix shares his passion for baking with the children. Of all those in the community on whom the arsonist and the ensuing sequence of events have bearing, those who gain the most are Clippy and Lotte, who can now go forward in their marriage, and Phil, whose life now holds better prospects through support and education.

Of course, the other major group involved in Gee's schematics of moral attitudes comprises the children themselves. They are, as always, subject to their environment at home and at school. Not surprisingly, the less important child characters spout the racist attitudes of their parents, and several girls enjoy taunting Irene. None seems to gain any wisdom from their experiences in the community. However, Gee gives the main four children intelligence enough to think for themselves and strength enough to make good moral choices, to recognise and to stand against the injustice of racism and bullying carried out by children and adults. Kitty, who 'saw through adults easily, but could not shake off her feeling of being ruled' (31), stands up to her classmates when Irene is taunted, and wants to help Irene continue her music lessons with Frau Stauffel. Kitty actively dislikes Mrs Chalmers for her treatment of Nancy as a servant, and through her ordeal in Mrs Marwick's house, she gains a new awareness of moralscape: '[She] felt very sad, and frightened too, at the danger and dreadfulness of life, and the mystery of time passing by and making things old, and things that happened long ago staying alive and turning people into different shapes' (102). Her brother Noel, though he dislikes Phil (whose clothes stink), sees the cruelty in Mrs Bolton's choice of Phil as the Kaiser in her pageant, and volunteers to take the role himself. He never hesitates to stand against the racism of the crowd. Irene, quiet in general but fierce when thwarted, 'loathes' Mrs Bolton's favouritism and her values system that reduces music to the level of good manners (27). She fights against her mother's racist behaviour towards Lotte Stauffel. Phil, after a 'crocodile-brained' fight with Noel which Clippy ends (32), for a while still resorts to taunting Irene and is puzzled by Clippy's moral stance against racism, but he accepts opportunities to join in Wix family activities. All four children are resilient and persistent in searching for the fire-raiser and in rescuing Lotte Stauffel. Although they take pleasure in the romanticised pageant on stage – almost to the point of being carried along with their peers by the jingoism and fervour to show 'patriotism' – at the crucial moment in real life they spurn the racist attitudes of Jessop's adults and take action to help save Frau Stauffel.

Though the four children do not appear to influence their classmates by their more enlightened understanding and behaviour in dealing with racism and classism, in their moral strength lies some hope for the community. As adults, they may find opportunities to spread the enlightenment they have gained from the examples, good and bad, of their parents and teachers.

Racism and revenge in another war: *The Champion*

Hope for a New Zealand community free of racism, bullying and revenge is, however, dented in *The Champion* (1989). Gee sets this novel in 1943 in Kettle Creek, a fictionalised version of Henderson (then a small town, now a suburb of Waitakere in West Auckland), where he spent his childhood. Here he turns his schematic focus on three main families: the 'normal' nuclear Pascoe family, the solo grandmother with her part-Maori granddaughter, and the solo father of Dalmatian origin with his two sons. Here Gee extends his focus to include grandparents. This gives him the opportunity to explore again the moralscape of classism and racism, as well as wartime notions of heroism. In addition, he achieves much of his power to underline the moral stance of his characters by using humour unexpectedly in difficult situations.

Jackson Coop, a black American soldier, comes to stay with the Pascoe family to recuperate from injuries sustained in action in the Pacific region. His visit is only two weeks in length, but acts as a lightning rod for the racism inherent in the community. The story is told in retrospect by Rex Pascoe, 12 years old at the time of the action, forcing him to confront his own limited assumptions about race and the nature of heroism. However, the racism that drives much of the novel's action is not part of Rex's family's attitude to life. Like the Wixes (*FR*), the Pascoes are a praiseworthy family. Rex's mother Bernice is one of Gee's most admirable poetry-loving characters. She has developed a high moral code, with warmth and kindness: 'Mum couldn't be cruel if she tried' (9). An admirer of Paul Robeson, she invites Jack to recuperate with her family because she guesses no one else would, and she makes him feel welcome. Rex's sister Gloria follows their mother's example in her attitude towards Jack, and towards the young man she is dating, Dalmatian Matty Yukich.

Barber Alf – another apparently worthy Gee tradesman-father – is kind, too. He outlaws racist behaviour in his barbershop, and is proud that racism is not institutionalised in New Zealand as in the United States: 'We don't have any colour bar' (86). In a delightful comic episode to defuse tension, he outwits the two racist American Ozark soldiers when they try to have Constable Davies, a Maori, removed from the barber's chair. Yet Alf is 'full of contradictions' (19) and flaws. Rex disapproves of his father's black-marketing and bookmaking activities, into which he is drawn as a runner. According to Alf's moral code, though, he is simply supplying people 'with some fun in their lives ... a social service, for morale' (28–29): the driving force in Alf's life is to make money without doing harm to others.

To complete the family goodness, Bernice's parents are kind, wonderfully unconventional for 1943, and non-racist. Grandpa Crombie welcomes Jack's help in developing an extraordinary amphibian machine, which proves crucial in the dénouement. Grandma sunbathes nude in her garden, makes organic fertiliser, rides a motorbike and brews parsnip wine. Without any sense of superiority or racist attitudes, she helps where possible her neighbour Mrs Stewart and her part-Maori granddaughter Dawn. Later, both Grandma and Bernice even act against the law in order to follow a higher moral imperative: they help their friend Jack, deserter though he is, to escape from the military police so that he has the chance to find freedom.

The second family in *The Champion* is controlled by the damagingly racist widowed Mrs Stewart, a 'tough grey stringy lady' (58). As with the intimidating Mrs Marwick in *The Fire-Raiser*, Gee establishes mitigating reasons for Mrs Stewart's bitterness. In her struggle to run her heavily mortgaged farm, she had 'lost' her daughter Rose, who ran away from hard work on the farm and from her mother's antagonism to her sweetheart, Maori Jimmy, whom she then married. When Jimmy later dies, Rose leaves her baby Dawn to her mother to bring up. Although Mrs Stewart keeps Dawn (12) clean and well dressed and fed, and without whippings (unusual in contemporary terms), she is unfair in her psychologically harsh, loveless treatment of her granddaughter. She even burns money that Rose on one occasion sends to Dawn. Mrs Stewart's bitterness drives her to take revenge on the people of Kettle Creek by watering down their milk. Still, Gee engages the reader's sympathy for this unattractive old struggler who cuts herself off emotionally from the one person who could bring love into her life – her granddaughter Dawn.

As for Rose, who makes only a brief appearance in this story, she is portrayed as a pretty, good-time girl who prefers the softer life in town to that on the farm. Nevertheless, she leaves her daughter in the very same environment from which she wants to escape. Rose's attitude may be understandable, given the difficulties of being a solo mother in those days, but it is hardly admirable and adds to her daughter's misery and feeling of rejection.

The third family in *The Champion* is the Yukich family: Stipan and his two sons, Matty and Leo (aged 12). Leo becomes increasingly important as the story evolves. The family manage quite well with their vineyard, and play their part in the community, though some call them 'Dallies' and 'squareheads' (95), but in a mild rather than vicious racist way. Stipan is accepted fairly as the winner of the mallet game on Gala Day, and applauded for breaking up a fight. He is more principled than Alf. When Alf offers him illegal sugar to use for his sherry, he rejects the offer.

Of the two figures of authority in Kettle Creek – Constable Davies and the teacher Miss Betts – it is the policeman who is more principled in his protection of the community. The most interesting of Gee's policemen, he carries out his duties with due diligence and fairness without racial bias. He is not prepared to tolerate the American soldiers Marv and Herb's racist-driven fight against Jack. Nor will he follow up on the evidence produced under dubious circumstances by Miss Betts that Mrs Stewart has been adulterating the town's milk supply. However, he regards himself as honour-bound to catch Rex's father Alf in some of his illegal dealings, such as selling black-market sugar or acting as a bookie. He pursues Alf with cat-and-mouse determination for legal reasons, and is greatly irked by his lack of success.

The worst aspects of inherent racist attitudes of the community are concentrated in the other figure of authority, the teacher Miss Lorna Betts, who is a younger, more vicious version of Mrs Bolton (*FR*). Again, as a public role model in moral behaviour, the teacher fails dismally. Although Rex thinks she is 'good' at instilling knowledge into students, she seems 'to enjoy hurting people' (24). She vents her racist cruelty on Leo Yukich by regularly calling him a squarehead, ridiculing him for his climbing ability and strapping him harshly on any pretence. She treats Dawn badly by repeatedly claiming Dawn's brains are made of wood and she should be back in the pa. When Jack comes to school to talk to Rex's class, she embarrasses him too. However, when she refers to the 'darkies' being 'equal' and being 'treated very well since Abraham Lincoln' (53), Gee turns her racist slurs into a comic scene to intensify her cruelty:

> Jack gave a watermelon grin. 'Ye-es ma'am.' Oh that 'yes', I hear it still, mellow, rich, submissive, marvellously false. 'We's happy folks, us darkies.' ... He shuffled his feet and started to dance. He turned himself into a golliwog ... He went round Miss Betts in that way, floppy arms and legs but fast feet, and that sugar smile on his face ... The fury and bewilderment of her! She could not find a way to stop him. (53–54)

Her insulting term 'darkie' is all the more ironic since Alf had previously used it in a friendly way when he welcomed Jack with a beer (39). Then dithery headmaster Mr Dent arrives, applauds Jack's performance, and takes him off to entertain his class, hence adding to the irony. And, as if Gee wants to confound the idea of goodness being part of his poetry-loving characters, he gives Miss Betts an interest in writing poetry, though what she writes is doggerel rather than poetry with 'good feeling' (24). Despite her cruelty, however, Rex perceives that Miss Betts is driven by anger and unhappiness in life – a reason, but not an excuse for her poor moral behaviour.

In contrast to other more complex characters such as Rex or Miss Betts, Gee depicts a stark kind of racism in the two Ozark soldiers from the US army who, like Jack, are recuperating in Kettle Creek. They are among the few characters in the quintet to be drawn with no redeeming attributes or motivations, other than that their attitude is 'the way an American from the South would see [the Maori] Bob Davies' (29). Their revenge on Jack later, in fights that ultimately send him AWOL, adds to the ugliness of their attitude. Says Marv: 'I'll show you folks how we deal with nigras' (99). That means chasing 'niggers in their cars for fun' (42). Such behaviour, Jack says, led a mob to kick and kill his father in a Chicago alley. There is no police protection for black people there, whereas in Kettle Creek Constable Davies aims to stop all fights.

Jack himself, a product of Chicago's cruel slums, is the antithesis of would-be superior Miss Betts. He is kind and courteous, sensitive with Dawn, and loyal to the Pascoes, who nurture him. In another comic interlude, he saves Alf from being caught by Davies with two sacks of black-market sugar in his hearse: 'I couldn't let [Alf] get caught. He's been good to me' (78). In a poignant moment before he sets out on what will be the last event of his life, Jack affirms that 'Kettle Creek's the best thing that ever happened to me' (150). His moral code extends to worrying about involving the children in his bid to escape, about stealing necessary tools and spark plugs, and about wanting to treat people fairly in a world where there 'ain't no justice' (129). Above all, he enables Rex to understand that the real value of friendship goes beyond the bounds of race, age and culture.

When it comes to negotiating the moralscape of Kettle Creek, however, of all the characters in this novel, Rex has the furthest to go in moral development. By establishing him as a retrospective first-person narrator, Gee gives Rex the benefit of hindsight in his interpretation of the many twists and turns leading to his enlightenment. Gee can thus follow Rex's development more closely than with the children in *The Fire-Raiser*. And by delaying Rex's enlightenment, Gee not only increases tension in his story, but indicates just how hard it is for this boy – and many others like him – to set aside prejudice and accept friendship from someone of a different race.

Initially, Rex has romantic notions of heroism, fuelled in particular by the exploits of RAF pilots in his favourite comic, *The Champion*. He looks down on 'Dally' Leo, until Leo impresses him by his 'heroic' pole-climbing feat (23). Rex then seeks friendship with Leo and, later, with Dawn. Although he falters at times, Rex's developing friendship with Leo and Dawn becomes important in his progress towards enlightenment. Rex has to learn his judgement is not always sound, and his romantic notions of heroism have little to do with the realism of war. When Jack arrives and shakes hands, Rex, unlike his non-racist parents, responds automatically and shamefully by wiping his hand on his trouser leg. He has to learn to see Jack not with a 'kind of horror' nor as 'Private Monkeyface' (40), but as no less human for being scared of war (55). He must accept that a black American private can be as deserving of a Purple Heart as a pilot. Yet, after Jack has bested Miss Betts, Rex still hankers for his imagined hero, Lootenant Buddy Storm. To his surprise, however, he feels 'left out' when the family and Dawn and Leo all become Jack's friends (70). Soon, because of Jack's persistent friendliness, Rex begins to feel 'possessive' (70), protective and accepting (72). And as Jack explains how his own father was killed in the slums of Chicago, Rex realises that, in a 'night of mobs and Marvs and rats as big as dogs', he would run away too (87).

Nevertheless, Rex still feels confused that he likes Jack so much, and that his old Rockfist Rogan hero now seems unreal. What's more, when Jack returns AWOL to Kettle Creek and admits again that he is scared of the war (126), Rex is angry at Jack's lack of heroism. It takes Leo's forceful lecture on friendship to stop Rex reporting Jack to the MPs. Rex finally accepts the role of friendship, and becomes as keen as Dawn and Leo to help Jack escape. Rex and Leo paddle valiantly in the amphibian – a leaking joke of a craft – and rescue Dawn from being drowned in the estuary, but not her grandmother nor Jack. That Gee can inject a darkly comic element into such a dire moment of pathos is another twist in a moralscape that encompasses the good but cowardly Jack and the not-so-good, bitter Mrs Stewart. Both try to escape – Jack from the living hell of military retribution and a return to war, and Mrs Stewart from her loveless, endless struggle. Both drown. Mrs Stewart's body is found on the bar; Jack's never. A small romantic touch lingers in Rex's last musings: 'And I sometimes wonder if he … somehow managed to survive' (173).

Here, then, is the tragedy of a young man who, Gee makes clear, does not deserve to die. However, Gee does not want his novels to be like other adventures stories for children in which there is 'no price paid. No consequences. And life's not like that.'[9] The price of friendship and Rex's enlightenment are played out against a moralscape that shows the consequences of different levels of racism in action, ranging from the mean to the harmful and viciously dangerous.

Bullying and revenge in *The Fat Man*

Not racism, but the terrible consequences of bullying and revenge are the focus of the moralscape in Gee's uncompromising next novel, *The Fat Man* (1994). In a third-person narrative, Gee filters events through the perceptions of Colin Potter, the 11-year-old protagonist. Colin and his family come under the control of Herbert Muskie, who has returned home after many years abroad to inflict revenge on those who tormented him in his childhood. Muskie is a repulsive figure. By the end of the novel, however, he attains a degree of sympathy as Gee reveals the trauma behind his behaviour, though Gee does not condone Muskie's acts of cruelty.

The Fat Man is set in 1933 in the small town of Loomis, another version of Henderson, and Gee uses the economic hardships of the time to intensify the moral issues under scrutiny. Hunger is the major driving force and the Achilles heel of the main characters: hunger for food, money, or revenge. At a time of great poverty brought about by little available work and little money, his victims mostly find it impossible to resist temptation. Through his weakness for chocolate, Colin Potter, always hungry and skinny, falls into the power of the sadistic Muskie when he returns to Loomis to hide out from the law and carry out his plans. Muskie wants to track down his former bullying classmates, especially Colin's parents. Colin comes across Muskie by chance at the dark waterhole in the creek, which, with its slime, eels in the deeps, weeds rank and overgrown, is symbolically the source of horrors and the place where accidents happen. When Muskie discovers who Colin's parents are, he tricks Colin into becoming his accomplice, thus drawing him into a world of moral dilemmas.

In a moralistic world where people should pay for their sins, Colin's parents Laurie and Maisie could be considered due to pay for their bullying of Muskie some 20 years ago. Led by Laurie, a group of classmates spat in Muskie's sandwiches, ensured he was blamed and caned daily for their own antisocial farting, and held him under water till he nearly drowned. Maisie, like the other girls, laughed at Muskie and generally supported the boys in their bullying. Yet both Laurie and Maisie have grown up to become mainly good citizens, good marriage partners, and good parents – which is some mitigation for their past (though not in Muskie's eyes).

Muskie's hunger for revenge and power drives him to play on the weaknesses of others. Laurie's hunger to do almost anything not illegal to take him off the unemployment relief payments of 1933 leads him to accept Muskie's terms of work. His emotional attachment to his boxing competition cups, which Maisie had sold to raise money and which Muskie buys back for him, means that he feels gratitude to Muskie, not revulsion. He cannot know that Muskie's money is tainted, gained previously from theft, bootlegging and murder in the United States and Canada. Muskie is, indeed, as 'cruel, selfish, manipulative and unscrupulous' as the businessmen in Gee's adult fiction.[10] And to align Muskie with that other group of Gee-detested people – politicians, particularly the New Zealand prime minister in the 1980s, Robert Muldoon – Gee extends Muskie's mouth in a sinister, worm-like scar that curls up into his cheek, a reference to Muldoon's dimple. Even so, Laurie does not see until almost too late that Muskie wants to embroil him in illegal activities, eventually kill him, and marry Maisie. She has been wooed through her weakness for oranges – rare things in Depression days – although she is not fully taken in. She says of Muskie, 'There's something wrong with him. He was cruel to that girl' (71).

Again, as in *The Champion*, a boy has to come of age in his perceptions of heroism. Colin admires his ex-boxer, carpenter father Laurie. He likes working with him and playing gunfights – Sheriff and Black Jack, like in the westerns. To his dismay, he begins to see weaknesses in Laurie's heroic persona. Gradually he realises that Laurie was a bully at school and a wimp, who bawled when he was beaten by his own father for almost drowning Muskie at a picnic. Throughout the novel Colin sees Laurie lose ground to Muskie mentally and physically, and feels his father 'shrink to something small and dark inside him' (134).

As well, Laurie's parents, Colin's beloved grandparents, although they are not Muskie's main targets and have given him no cause for revenge, become embroiled in Muskie's plans. As characters, they serve to reveal the extent of Muskie's wickedness and lust for power. Because they are part of the Potter family, they have to suffer too. They run a boarding house where Muskie stays until he gains control of his family home. Naturally, as a gourmand, he enjoys Grandma's cooking while he tightens his hold on Colin and Colin's family. He even exploits the moral weakness in Colin's beer-loving and easily-led Grandpa by encouraging him to run a sly-grog shop in 'dry' Loomis, for which Grandpa later has to serve a month in prison.

Muskie, then, is one of Gee's classic outsider figures – the damaged product of childhood experiences who wreaks revenge on a 'normal' family and on his own dysfunctional family. His mother is another of Gee's eccentric elderly women, like Mrs Marwick (*FR*) and Mrs Stewart (*TC*). Not that a Gee eccentric is necessarily unpleasant or cruel, as Grandma Crombie (*TC*) demonstrates, but Mrs Muskie was just as incompetent a mother as was Mrs Marwick. She denied her son 'love and understanding' as a child. She was unable, or perhaps unwilling, to save him from bullying at school and beatings from his father at home – beatings his siblings never had to endure (58). So she has become another target in Muskie's vengeful sights.

Once the head of an important family who owned most of the town, semi-demented Mrs Muskie now lives in a state of decay – smell, dust and dirt – symbolic of her dysfunctional relationships with her four daughters, whom she has rejected and who have neglected her. Although her elder son Clyde lives with her and runs the family mill at a loss, it is the return of her youngest child she hungers for, waiting every day for the train to bring him home. Muskie soon has all her affairs entrusted to him, thus completing his revenge against his siblings. Moreover, by stealing his mother's gold sovereigns, he ensures that her madness increases as she searches for them in vain. Yet when she is found drowned – almost certainly by Muskie's hand – in an unexpected twist he becomes a weeping mess of a man, a classic example of the rejected child who loves and hates the mother who rejects him. In another love–hate spurt of fury before he makes his last escape, he shatters the stained-glass, multicoloured rose window above the staircase with a hammer, because it symbolises the wonder in life that he was deprived of as a child.

Last, as part of his hunger for revenge, Muskie inflicts a kind of cruel parody of family life on two people who had not hurt him in the past. He marries an impoverished widow, Bette, who is understandably driven into Muskie's net by hunger for money. She thinks he will protect her and her daughter Verna, but he treats them with violence and humiliation. To Verna, who is the least deserving of all of Muskie's victims, Muskie is particularly cruel. In a reenactment of the bullying he had endured, when Verna loses her hair from scarlet fever, Muskie hacks off the new growth to make her ugly – particularly in Colin's eyes. This backfires. Colin and Verna develop an innocent friendship and love, one that contrasts very clearly with the power play of Muskie's relationship with Bette, and Muskie's latent sexual desire for Verna. Ultimately, Bette, who has been under Muskie's thumb for most of the book, finds the courage to protect her daughter and is able to warn Colin's family of Muskie's evil intentions. This desire to protect her daughter becomes a higher moral imperative, overriding hunger and fear.

In the moralscape of Loomis, however, it is hard for children to escape bullying, for it is institutionalised in the school where the teachers are the very ones who were part of Muskie's, Laurie's and Maisie's childhood. Mr Edgar (Itchy) and Miss Burgess use corporal punishment rather than moral example to control their pupils. Itchy in particular takes pleasure in giving the children the strap, and he encourages the boys to torment Muskie. When the children go too far – they nearly drown Muskie in a local pool; or, in the 1933 action, they cover Verna with slime – investigations are perfunctory and no real action is taken against the bullies. In short, Loomis is a place in which bullying is condoned and perpetuated within the community, and is in some degree responsible for Muskie's sadism. Somewhat surprisingly, Muskie doesn't seek revenge on his former teachers. Instead, he concentrates on the families and on harming the community through burglary and other activities such as receiving stolen goods.

The final irony in the moralscape of this novel lies in the relationship between Colin and Muskie. Muskie overpowers Colin through intimidation and by making him his accomplice in the theft of his mother's sovereigns. Nevertheless, he is not able to corrupt Colin's moral sense. Although Colin wonders if he will ever feel brave again, he learns how to act for others, especially Verna, risking his social status with his classmates to help her as an outcast. He learns how to read Muskie, and to understand the fears of Muskie's victims. He realises his own fear for his parents as they fall into Muskie's power, just as he learns uncomfortable truths about their past weaknesses. Yet his compassion grows for the tormented boy he can see in the crazed adult Muskie.

Colin comes of age in this novel, particularly in his ability to hold contradictory perceptions in balance. The culmination of all these perceptions enables him as a hostage to follow Muskie's orders once more. He cuts the rope to send the flying fox (a fitting symbol for the cunning avenger) sweeping across the ravine, with Muskie in the wooden cage (another fitting image) still hoping to escape from the police but facing almost certain death. Colin, the avenger's forced apprentice, turns into his master's executioner. He is redeemed, though, because he is obeying a higher imperative of love and sympathy to release Verna from Muskie's power. Colin goes through the process of developing from the greedy, hungry boy who succumbs to Muskie's control, to the horrified boy who observes Muskie's manipulation of his parents' weaknesses and Muskie's cruelty towards all he is involved with, and who notes the failure of his teachers to lead by moral examples. So Colin comes to understand what drives even wicked people like Muskie. In Gee's moralscape, then, Colin turns into a worthy character through his empathy and moral growth – all the more admirable because of the terrifying experiences that Muskie forces him to endure.

Politics, religion and bullying in *Orchard Street*

Set once again in Loomis/Henderson, this time during the social crisis of the 1951 waterfront dispute, *Orchard Street* (1998) features new twists in Gee's recurring concerns in his moralscape. Bullying shows a political face; intolerance and notions of superiority are based not on race but on religion; and adolescent love pushes sexual boundaries and drives predation – an offshoot of revenge – to be resolved in a bathetic act of heroism.

Gee broadens the sweep of this novel to consider a range of families, and the adolescents within them. Again, the central family includes an admirable tradesman-father and poetry-loving mother, Eddie and Lil Dye, who have two sons, including Austin, the 14-year-old protagonist of the novel. Down the street live other family groups – the Catholic Collymore family which comprises the parents, four daughters and two sons; a supportive grandfather figure, his married daughter and her inspiring husband; and the eccentric Pike family, whose son is a would-be heroic gunslinger. The novel is seen through the eyes of Austin (called Ossie or Dinky) Dye. Ossie is skilled at spying on adults (something all Gee's main child characters do without compunction).[11] Through his spying, he learns much about the complex behaviour of people and about events involving parents, older siblings and neighbours in the community. What he learns provides the novel with a less sensational and vicious moralscape than the others in the quintet. Ossie's first-person retrospective narrative increases the reflective nature of the novel, and the events of the novel encourage what he calls a 'sad familiarity' concerning time and place (7).

Gee's boyhood experiences again provide much of the novel's material, such as the official use of guns by bank clerks. However, 20 years on from *The Fat Man*, Loomis hardly seems the same Gee town: a completely new set of characters takes centre stage, and there is little to do with the river that is central to drama and drownings in the three previous novels. Nevertheless, the moralscape concerning community issues in *Orchard Street* is familiar Gee territory. The community is divided by the waterfront dispute of 1951. Some people support the wharfies, others the shipowners. Since newspapers are not permitted to print letters against the government, his parents secretly print and distribute pamphlets for the wharfies' cause, and construct a special hideout under the house for their illegal printing activities. Ossie approves of his parents' moral stand in support of the wharfies and helps them distribute pamphlets.

Like Rex in *The Champion*, Ossie absorbs himself in books and fantasises to manage his fears. Unlike Rex and Colin in *The Fat Man*, though, Ossie maintains his admiration for his parents. He is merely bemused that his mother Lil, who supports the workers, should aspire to gentility: 'Polite behaviour ... Elevated thoughts' (34). He even sees her as a snob, if a mild one. She remains convinced of the moral rightness of the wharfies' cause and of the need to defy the ban on printing their pamphlets, although her fear of jail and her tiredness from late-night typing shorten her temper. Likewise, Ossie's printer father Eddie is sure of his moral stance – to begin with. He has to undergo a change in moral perception not of the cause itself, but of the bullying way aspects of it are carried out. An 'ardent union man' (10), he went to fight Hitler to get rid of the sort of fascist oppression he sees the government using to break the strike. Nevertheless, he dislikes the emerging ugly side of unionism. Although he saw too much killing in the war to tolerate talk of shooting Prime Minister Sid Holland as Ossie's older brother Les advocates (51), he is disturbed by the 'flat beer lists' and the 'rolls of dishonour' (69) that the wharfies use to try to stop their members from breaking ranks. The ordinary men, Eddie says, may be 'weaklings, but they're just trying to keep their families fed' (69). Ossie listens to his father but, without losing any respect for him, ponders on the distinctions between what is legally and morally right or wrong in this class struggle between workers and the bosses supported by politicians. Thus Ossie, like most children, begins his moral and political awareness by observing his parents.

Ossie's development continues through his interaction with other adults. Parroting his parents, he tells neighbours Mr Worley and his son-in-law Mr Redknapp that his family are 'Labour Party', not communists (71). Mr Worley and Mr Redknapp, however, consider both lots – the unions led by Barnes, and the bosses supported by Prime Minister Holland – 'a pack of scoundrels' (72). Thus they partially redress the balance for Ossie between his Labour-supporting parents and the equally ardent, but eccentric Pike family, who live across the road and who belong to 'a strange religion called Radiant Living' (21). Mrs Pike is a nutritional extremist in practice; Mr Pike is a communist-hating extremist in opinion.

Through their interest in books and astronomy, Mr Worley and Mr Redknapp make their contribution to Ossie's education. Mr Worley leads him to Zane Grey and the escape Ossie needs in adventure stories, and then to the enriching world of Dickens – though Ossie tells us it took years for him to appreciate 'the value of Mr Worley's gift. It was almost as wonderful as Mr Redknapp's Jupiter' (105). Mr Redknapp inspires Ossie – as much as schoolmaster Clippy Hedges inspires Phil in *The Fire-Raiser* – with a first lesson in astronomy 'on a night that changed my life' (18), and with his last-minute gift of a telescope before he heads north after his ill wife. As alternative teachers, these two men show an admirable sort of moral fibre in their care and consideration for Ossie.

Ossie is embroiled in a complex moral situation when his brother Les goes to paint anti-government slogans on Mr Pike's garage door. Les is nearly caught by Mr Pike, and rushes across the paddock where Ossie has joined Mr Redknapp in watching Jupiter through a telescope. Mr Redknapp, realising Les would lose his job as a bank clerk if he was caught, goes against his own moral code by lying to protect him. Bike Pike, too, lets Les escape because 'Les and me are friends. Sort of ...' (99). Ossie, uncomfortable now with Mr Redknapp and annoyed with Les for ruining his stargazing, realises Les is stupid in his bravura and not acting just 'for Dad' (98). Yet in these circumstances Ossie still considers it morally acceptable to tell lies. As well, Mr Redknapp gives Ossie the tip-off for his dad Eddie to increase the blackout cover over the windows where he keeps his Gestetner – another good gesture. In contrast, Mr Pike takes copies of the pamphlets to the police – a legal action seen as wrong in neighbourly terms. The moralscape of the community takes on an additional complexity from an unexpected source, much appreciated by Ossie's family. The local policeman, Constable Pearson, shows divided loyalty and sympathy for the wharfies' cause. While ostensibly supporting the law, he quietly advises Lil to destroy incriminating evidence before the police search.

Ossie observes surprising behaviour from various quarters, including that of his bookish neighbour Mr Redknapp, and his own mother Lil. The families have been neighbours for years with little contact, but when the Redknapps are about to leave Loomis, they have a farewell dinner. At that dinner, Lionel Redknapp and Lil begin a flirtatious literary conversation in which Lil reveals the depth of her enjoyment of literature and creativity. Ossie recalls, 'I had never seen her sparkle like this before' (107). While Mr Redknapp 'was turning into someone he once had been', Lil was 'letting out things she hadn't known she still possessed' (108). Ossie learns from this that Lil has held things back in her relationship with the less-educated Eddie. He wonders if she will run away with Mr Redknapp. Later he observes Lil reassuring Eddie. Seeing the complexity of adult relationships like this, Ossie concludes: 'I don't know any time when I've been so pleased for her, or so sad' (108).

At this dinner party Ossie becomes aware, too, of the quiet tragedies of suburban life, brought to the fore in a discussion about religion. Lil, as spokesperson for the atheist Dye family, declares, 'No such place [as hell] exists.' Quietly, Lionel Redknapp contradicts: 'Oh it exists ... It's just not where the preachers say' (106). His keen pleasure in the farewell dinner stands in stark contrast to his sad private life. He was gassed during World War I, leaving him with severe chest troubles, and Mrs Redknapp had given birth to a stillborn girl. Her consequent depression and misery isolate the Redknapps, and this is further compounded by a community that judges without enquiring as to the reasons why.

Despite being poetic and creative, Lil has a superior attitude and she disapproves of the Collymore family at the other end of Orchard Street. Frank Collymore is a poor figure of a father. His wife is terminally ill, and after her death he struggles to look after his family. It is left to his younger daughter Teresa, even more than the older Eileen, to do the cooking and caring for her young tearaway brothers. Frank runs a cartage business and, unofficially, like Alf Pascoe in *The Champion,* he is a bookmaker. Against Lil's wishes, Eddie cheerfully sends Ossie with his bets to Frank, and both her sons socialise with the Collymore girls.

Les, almost 19, dates Eileen, who is nearly 18. Ossie has a growing interest in Teresa. To comfort Teresa after her mother's death (the full impact of which is left unexplored), Ossie shows her his father's secret printing room under the house. However, Ossie's pride leads to Eddie's downfall. When the police arrive to raid Frank's house after a tip-off, Teresa escapes with his betting records and runs to Eddie's hideout. The police follow her. Both fathers are arrested. Both teenagers acknowledge their guilt in ruining Eddie's cover. Ossie is furious with Teresa for acting stupidly, but knows he is partly to blame (119) – he was wrong to break faith with his parents by revealing the hideout to another person. He also feels guilty that he and Teresa enjoy sitting in the cinema eating chocboms the day both their fathers are arrested. These smaller moments of betrayal are forgiven, however – part of the rhythm of *Orchard Street* involves minor transgressions, apologies and forgiveness.

Much of the narrative tension in *Orchard Street* comes from its exploration of the love affair between Les and Eileen. (Ossie and Teresa's relationship is uncomplicated and innocent.) Eileen agonises about whether to have sex with Les: 'It's not wrong when you are in love' (66). Neither realises that Bike Pike, tall, gangly, athletic and older, is growing obsessed with Eileen and sees himself as her saviour from Les's desires. Having decided to play the hero and rescue Eileen from doing 'bad things' with Les (99), Bike tries one night to shoot Les and then himself. He accidentally shoots Eileen, leaving her with a permanently scarred face. Unexpectedly, the wisdom of Mr Redknapp averts further tragedy. He climbs up the tree to talk to Bike – as Bike later tells Ossie – about his own war experiences, about facing up to the consequences of one's actions, and about having to go on in life regardless. The way Lionel Redknapp resolves issues and uncomplainingly endures what life deals to him makes him the unsung hero in this complex focus on daily suburban life.

In contrast to the previous novels discussed in this chapter, the consequences of the various wrongdoings in *Orchard Street* are less severe. Frank and Eddie – who remain appealing characters in their individual ways – are fined, not imprisoned for their illegal gambling and printing activities. Frank grows morally; he gives up bookmaking in order to concentrate on his cartage business. Eddie establishes a thriving printing company – although he never gives up gambling on horses. Bike's would-be-heroic shooting leads to a prison sentence, but then, having paid his debt to society, he marries well and has a successful career. Ossie, wiser about life though not fundamentally changed, only hints at the outcome for himself and Teresa. He says simply that further information is 'a private matter' and 'I became an astronomer. She became a dietitian' (137). Thus young readers are left with the impression that it is still generally wiser to follow good moral examples for a happier outcome in life.

Classism, predation and sexual desire in *Hostel Girl*

In *Hostel Girl* (1998), for the first time in this quintet of historical novels, Gee chooses a female protagonist, and he moves the setting to the Hutt Valley, a suburban part of Wellington. The historical event that gives impetus to aspects of adolescent – and adult – relationships is not war nor depression nor political strife, but a document that in 1955 rocked New Zealand society, especially in Wellington. The Mazengarb Report, as Gee explains briefly, followed a government inquiry into newspaper scare stories about rampant sexual immorality among teenagers at Hutt Valley High School. Themes in *Hostel Girl* revolve around issues of classism and sexual predation, set against an urban backdrop where amateur theatricals and B-grade movies blur the lines between moral and immoral behaviour.

Again in his moralscape Gee places different families. Ailsa McGowan and her hard-working, admirable, single-parent mother provide a contrast to the dysfunctional, affluent nuclear family of her boyfriend, Calum Page. Three other individual characters have a profound influence on the moral issues of the story: Ailsa's hostel roommate, Gloria; a maverick teacher, Mrs Nimmo; and a predatory neighbour, Errol Parkinson.

Fourteen-year-old Ailsa lives with her widowed mother, who works by day as a wages clerk and by night as matron of a YWCA hostel for trainee dental nurses. She does her very best for the girls in her charge, including her daughter – especially since Ailsa's father had been killed in Crete before she was born. Although she struggles financially, she decides to protect Ailsa from the issues raised in the Mazengarb Report by sending her to Willowbank, a private, single-sex church school. Ironically, this move leads Ailsa into dangerous encounters. Ailsa has a good relationship with her mother; she often wishes she could confide in her and 'not be responsible any more' for what is happening in her life (108).

More influential in the story, however, is the Page family. Ailsa's classmate Helen invites her home to play tennis, and there she meets Helen's 16-year-old brother Calum. A polio survivor with a painful crippled leg, Calum walks with a limp and often resorts to a wheelchair – but he can ride a bike. Understandably, he lacks interest in life, but he agrees to coach Ailsa in tennis for a bet, so that she can beat Helen. Their friendship develops through tennis, bike rides and visits to the local milkbar and the pictures.

Ailsa becomes aware of the 'good' and 'bad' qualities in Calum's parents. Mr Page, a wealthy partner in his old family law firm, is friendly if somewhat distant as a father. He wants to build a yacht and 'sail solo round the world' (52). Surprisingly, he is the parent who approves of Ailsa: 'I quite like her. At least she's brought him back to life' (109). In contrast, Calum's mother, willowy and languid, is too driven by snobbishness and pretensions to be a 'good' mother. She dislikes her own son, as Calum explains, for classist reasons – 'People like us don't get polio, it's working class' (51) – and she maintains that '[Ailsa is] straight out of the Mazengarb Report … I'd sooner he stayed in a wheelchair than run around with girls of that sort' (109). As for his wife, Mr Page berates himself for marrying for looks: 'Well, dumb-ox, you married her' (31). Mrs Page obsessively pursues amateur theatricals in the company of their creepy neighbour, Errol Parkinson, whom she often meets in town at tearooms (86). Certainly, the Pages have such different values that they 'hardly ever talk to each other', says Calum (52).

Ailsa's other store of information about relationships comes from her roommate at the hostel, Gloria Wood, who is trying to cope with sex and its consequences (19). Gloria has escaped from a miserable childhood at the hands of her physically abusive father, and is now glamorous and extremely attractive to men. Having given in to the demands of a bullying boyfriend, she is afraid she is pregnant.

In seeking help for Gloria's problem, Ailsa turns to Mrs Nimmo, one of Gee's unconventional but supportive teachers, who is an outspoken fiery communist. Ailsa likes 'the contrast between her haystack hair and baggy skirts and politics and her voice like Lady Bracknell's (59). Indeed, she is not the sort of staff member one would expect at Willowbank. Ailsa trusts her enough to ask for help for a friend who is pregnant. Mrs Nimmo returns the trust, at risk to herself, by whispering that she could try stilboestrol, but Gloria, who is Catholic, refuses to consider taking something that can induce abortion. All three realise the need for moral support and secrecy. They cannot openly discuss abortion if Mrs Nimmo is to keep her job and Gloria is to keep her place in the hostel. It is part of Ailsa's moral code not to break promises of secrecy. She wants to protect her teacher and her roommate, whose friendship she values highly. Yet by her silence she increases the dangers facing Gloria.

Gloria, meanwhile, is receiving threats from a disguised predatory stalker who sends anonymous, increasingly sexual messages written in coloured pen and derived, not from poetry, but from popular songs that emphasise purity. Ailsa tries to persuade Gloria to tell about the letters so that the police can discover the stalker's identity. Gloria gives out some information, but not all. Ailsa attempts to find proof of his identity: she spies on him and bikes after him to see where he lives. He then pursues her, and she experiences how sinister his intent is. With some help from Calum, she discovers he is the Page family's neighbour, Errol Parkinson, who had previously used his fearsome Alsatian to intimidate her when she climbed over the wall to retrieve a tennis ball. As Herbert Muskie haunts Colin's mind in *The Fat Man*, so Errol Parkinson haunts Ailsa's. In his dark, predatory power, he is an amalgam of Marwick (*FR*), Muskie (*FM*), and Bike Pike (*OS*), a power that, as Mark Williams comments about Gee's adult novels, 'springs from a level in the human mind that precedes the construction of social order'.[12]

That Errol Parkinson is a clever, complex fantasist adds to his menace. Gee allows him little justification for his obsession with teenage girls, only a hint of dysfunction and unfulfilment in his married life. Before his wife's illness and death, he had indulged in theatrical fantasies of heroic, B-grade movie rescues, modelling himself on his namesake Errol Flynn, making him a somewhat artificial, even phony character. However, his intentions are deadly. By the time Ailsa and Calum break into his house to look for disguises to confirm his identity, he has already prepared an exotic, boarded-up bedroom displaying a pink pillow embroidered with Gloria's name. Clearly, his terrifying purpose is to imprison Gloria there.

Gee shows his flair for making a darkly comic scene out of a moment of high tension when, at a gathering at the Pages' home after Errol's wife's funeral, Ailsa decides that, even if she goes against her own moral code and breaks a secret, she must try to destroy his infatuation by declaring that Gloria thinks she is pregnant, but taking stilboestrol will not work:

'She's going to try gin and hot baths next.'

Errol Parkinson's cup rattled so hard it seemed that his saucer would break. Tea spilled in his lap. It burned him and he made a sharp sound, half yelp, half hiss.
... Some instinct kept him acting, but he could not control his eyes – they seemed to jump and rattle, as brittle as his cup ...

Mr Page was grinning. 'You really fixed him.' (115)

This, of course, only further inflames Errol. He steps up his campaign against Gloria, who, he claims in his next note, has 'betrayed' him (117). According to his warped moral code, this betrayal gives him the right to exact revenge.

Meanwhile, in stark contrast to Errol, Ron Stack, the boiler man at the hostel, develops an innocent crush on Gloria. 'A bit simple ... but a good worker' (19), he just wants to adore, not to control her. With no immoral designs, he keeps watch on her room, hoping to catch and unmask the stalker. When Errol pounces, Ron succeeds in frustrating his attempts to drive away with Gloria, holding a knife at her throat. The car crashes, Errol escapes, and Ron chases him down towards the railway line. Other men follow and pull the men apart – so Ron can fancy himself as a hero without being burdened with the crime of murder. Errol Parkinson is killed instead when he is hit by a train.

Gloria thereby escapes another sort of death: that of being enshrined in a windowless room under Errol's power. Moreover, it turns out she isn't pregnant. Thus she escapes for a third time being dominated by a man: father, boyfriend or obsessive predator. She can look forward to greater happiness by going to Auckland to join her mother and sister, who have also fled their bullying husband and father.

So the novel, which begins with many theatrical elements and connections, ends in a melodramatic way. Only in the last page does it come back to the gentle relationship between Ailsa and Calum. In their love, where they promise not to go further than kissing and holding hands, lies the most ironic twist of all. The 'immorality' at the heart of the Mazengarb Report on adolescent sexual misbehaviour is reflected more exactly in the sexual desires and behaviour of the adults in the community than in the life of the adolescents.

Hostel Girl, like Gee's other four realistic novels for young readers, demonstrates the qualities that Mark Williams attributes in full measure to Gee's adult fiction: 'Gee's pictures of New Zealand life are exact and comprehensive. His novels are extraordinarily rich in both social and psychological observation. His historical range is extensive and minutely detailed.'[13] As early as 1986, Gee himself defines his aim as a novelist: 'My concern though is to tell an exciting story, not to point a moral.'[14] This sounds simple, but his historical quintet shows how complex his fiction really is. It is certainly exciting, and full of tension, gripping action, dangerous moments and surprising challenges for his characters. Humour often adds delight to his storytelling. All this ensures that he avoids overt or didactic moralising. However, by rooting his moralscape in New Zealand communities at a different time of crisis in each novel – whether war or depression, political strike or social scandal – Gee makes us aware of ongoing moral issues in our daily lives. He reminds us of our historical inheritance. He extends our moral imagination. His characters constantly confront – or perpetrate – the disastrous consequences of recurring racism, classism, bullying, revenge and predation. If they think and act according to good principles, they develop perception and moral enlightenment. Gee's schematic contrasts in family dynamics add to this richness, and his ironic twists increase understanding. By exploring the good, the bad, and the many shades of grey in his moralscape, Maurice Gee has produced a valuable and remarkable historical quintet for young readers of today.

3 MINING GEE
Salt, Gool and *The Limping Man*
Elizabeth Hale

In 2007, Maurice Gee returned to fantasy writing for young readers with the first of a trilogy of novels set in a fully realised, unnamed world. In *Salt* (2007), *Gool* (2008) and *The Limping Man* (2010), he also returned to the themes that have run through his novels for young readers, be they fantasy or realist novels. These themes centre on the division in human nature between good and evil, and are explored in the *Salt* trilogy through a series of conflicts between good, communally-minded country dwellers who live in harmony with nature, and wicked, power- and hierarchy-driven city-based institutions that exploit the people and the land. In each novel, a different kind of evil (corporate, governmental or religious) is overcome by pairs of young protagonists – teenage boys and girls – who use their complementary abilities for the good of the community. As they do so, they come of age, in the terms required of young adult fiction, whether fantasy or realism. They learn to control their impulses and powers, they reflect on the ethical implications of their actions, they find love and they find their place in the world. More than merely repeating preoccupying concerns, however, the *Salt* trilogy mines Gee's own oeuvre, calling up, or recalling, familiar figures of good and evil and drawing together the concerns of both fantasy and realist approaches to fiction for young readers.

The novels

All of the novels are set in an unnamed world, which might be post-apocalyptic and is certainly dystopian. In this world is a large continent on which a ruined city, Belong, is situated, surrounded by Country and Sea. In *Salt* (2007) Hari, a poor boy from a part of Belong named Blood Burrow, is looking for his father Tarl, who has been forced into labour by the tyrannical Company that runs the city from Compound, high above the Burrows. Pearl, daughter of a wealthy Company man, is fleeing Compound and an arranged marriage with Ottmar, Company's chief executive. She is fleeing with her maid Tealeaf, who is a Dweller from Country and has telepathic powers. Eventually the three join up and travel together towards Sea and Saltport, the Company mining town and the home of the Dwellers. Hari and Danatok, a young Dweller, venture into the deepest of the mines, Deep Salt, where Ottmar has discovered a radioactive substance that he uses for weapons and where he has sent Tarl, one of the strongest of the Blood Burrow men, to work. They rescue Tarl, but their tasks are not over. Hari and Pearl must return to Belong to challenge Ottmar using their innate psychic abilities. After a series of confrontations and disasters, they cause Ottmar and his evil son Kyle-Ott to be hurled off the battlements of Compound. Tarl is lost to Hari, having used his own innate psychic abilities to join with a pack of wild dogs. He retreats to the forest depths and becomes the Dog King. Hari and Pearl, who have by now fallen in love, return to Stone Creek where they start a family.

The action of *Gool* picks up 16 years later. Hari and Pearl's children Xantee and Lo have inherited their parents' psychic abilities. One day, Hari is attacked by a 'gool', a voiceless and inexplicable creature from another planet, which seizes him by the throat. Using their psychic abilities, the Dwellers find out that the gool is one of many offspring of an alien mother, a figure of pure evil fuelled by hatred, whom they must find and confront in order to loose its hold on Hari. The mother gool, it emerges, is living – trapped, perhaps – under the ruined city of Belong, which has fallen further into darkness since the overthrow of Company. Xantee, Lo and their friend Duro go to Belong, under the guidance of Danatok and with some limited assistance from Tarl. Belong is now riven by factions: the old Company is run by a bureaucrat named Clerk, and the Burrows are led by a hard man called Keech. Both men have psychic powers and control the minds of their followers. Their vicious fighting is powered by evil, emanating from the mother gool; and in turn, their fighting gives her further power. Eventually Xantee, Lo and Duro penetrate the labyrinth beneath the city, where Xantee confronts the mother gool. Realising that hatred and violence only fuel the gool further, Xantee enters her mind, finds a way to pity her – and it is pity that destroys this alien force and, with her, the child gools, including the one that is killing Hari. Lo is badly affected by the fighting and retreats to the jungle, leaving Xantee and Duro to begin a relationship.

The Limping Man, the final book in the trilogy, begins another 16 years later. Belong has fallen into the clutches of yet another kind of evil: this time, it is religious manipulation by the 'Limping Man', a High Priest named Vosper who, it emerges, has the power of mind control over the people. He has gained this power through a symbiotic partnership with an evil toad concealed in his headdress. He is ruthless in his treatment of the people: women are persecuted if they exceed their limited roles of sex and breeding. The novel opens with the suicide of the protagonist Hana's mother – a healer – rather than face ritual execution. Hana flees the city, pursued by Vosper's henchmen. In the forest she comes into contact with Danatok, the Dweller who had helped Hari and Pearl. Now an old man, he teaches her survival skills and shows her how to access her psychic powers. She pairs her mind with a bird, Hawk, who has been circling nearby, and they join with Xantee and Lo's community. There she meets Ben, the son of Lo, who has been sent by his father to live in the community rather than share his reclusive forest ways. The community is under threat from Vosper, who rightly fears their psychic abilities and whose greed for power is voracious. Hana, Ben and other members of the community go to Belong by different paths and confront the Limping Man. All seems lost, so strong is Vosper's power and control over the people of Belong; but Hana, who has observed the pillaging behaviour of a group of warrior ants controlled by parasitic mites, discovers the secret of Vosper's partnership with the toad and communicates it to Hawk. Hawk attacks Vosper and removes his headdress, detaching and killing the toad and destroying their power. Before they go home, the villagers and Dwellers use their powers to influence the disoriented people of Belong, now freed of the Limping Man's control. They advise them to leave the city and to live in small communities in harmony with nature.

Patterns of good and evil

In each novel of the *Salt* trilogy a pair of protagonists with contrasting experiences and complementary abilities come together to fight evil.

They do so as representatives of small 'good' communities who are living in harmony with nature and with one another. Some are possessed of psychic abilities. The evil they fight is large in scale; it is located in the city and within corrupt institutions. Usually those institutions have fallen into the power of evil men (white, middle-aged) who lust for power and who exploit other humans and nature without compunction. In *Salt*, evil lies in the will towards corporate power, as exemplified by Company and the wicked executive Ottmar. In *Gool*, it is the clash between bureaucratic power as represented by the Clerk and revolutionary street power, as exemplified by Keech. In *The Limping Man*, Vosper manipulates religious belief and superstition in order to gain power. Evil is hierarchical, not communal, Gee proposes. Humans are vulnerable to the control of hierarchical organisations and the wicked individuals who manipulate those organisations for their own gain. If a solution is possible, it lies in the dissolution of cities in favour of cooperative and communal agrarian life. Underscoring this pattern are the love stories in which pairs of girl and boy heroes – Pearl and Hari, Xantee and Duro and Hana and Ben – move towards creating new generations of ethical communities.

These patterns repeat not only in the *Salt* trilogy – they are found throughout Gee's work for young readers. Anyone familiar with the corpus of his children's and young adult novels will recognise his emphasis on the need for heroes to work in good company; the pairs of boy and girl protagonists who back one another up with complementary abilities and modes of being – the division of heroic labour into channelled aggression (mostly male) and the power of empathy (mostly female). They will recognise the emphasis on enlightened action for the power of good as a key part of coming of age for young protagonists. Ultimately, victory over evil requires heroic effort on the part of the protagonists – in particular the ability to understand and empathise with enemies, even as they destroy them. It also comes at a great cost – the seeming destruction of civilisation. However, that destruction results in a new world order that rejects hierarchical social structures in favour of living simply in harmony with nature.

Most of Gee's books involve a pair of heroes, a boy and girl in early adolescence, who track down a villain and are responsible for the villain's demise.[1] In *Under the Mountain*, they are the twins Theo and Rachel, who bring down the evil alien worms, the Wilberforces, before they can destroy the world. In the *O* trilogy, they are cousins, Nick and Susan, who defeat Otis Claw in *The Halfmen of O* and return to restore balance in later books. In *The Fat Man*, they are the hero Colin and Verna, the stepdaughter of the Fat Man, Herbert Muskie, who are witness to his final moments. In *Orchard Street* they are Ossie and Teresa, boyfriend and girlfriend, who witness the demented violence of Bike Pike; and in *Hostel Girl* they are friends Ailsa and Callum (who will fall in love during the action), who track down the stalker Errol Parkinson and lead him to his death. This is the case, too, in the *Salt* trilogy. In *Salt*, it is Pearl and Hari, a boy and girl from different social strata, who rescue Hari's father from the Deep Salt Mines and overthrow Ottmar. In *Gool*, it is Hari and Pearl's daughter Xantee and her friend Duro, who rescue Hari by overcoming Keech, Clerk and the mother gool. In *The Limping Man*, Hana from the Burrows joins forces with Ben, the son of Xantee's brother, Lo, to overcome Vosper.

As Vivien van Rij has argued in this collection and elsewhere, through Gee's novels for young readers run sets of formal patterns: here, it is the binary pair of heroes, boy and girl, who combine gendered strengths of rationality, physical strength and guile (male), and intuition and empathy (female). For instance, in *Salt*, Hari has the physical strength and confidence to penetrate the mines at Deep Salt and to save himself and Pearl from the violence at Belong by diving into the ocean, whose tides he has calculated. Pearl, however, has the intuition and empathy required to use her gift of telepathy well and to manipulate the wicked Ottmar. Similarly, in *Gool*, it is Xantee's pity for the gool monster that destroys it: 'She knew, then, that pity had been a weapon. Where Duro's knife had failed and flame and poison and spears would fail, pity had pierced the gool and made it shriek.'[2] And in *The Limping Man*, Ben's aggression fails to protect him against Vosper's mind-control, while Hana's telepathic communication and teamwork with Hawk destroy Vosper.

Gee does not always divide the heroic work along gendered lines: girls are not always only intuitive and empathic, and boys are not always only rational. The actions of Xantee, Pearl, Hana, Duro, Ben and Hari do, however, reinforce a division of labour in heroic action: between spears and pity; between the rational and the emotive impulse. Thus they call to mind the division in *Under the Mountain* between the twins' approaches to the task of killing the Wilberforces: Theo's scientific rationalism (which gives way ultimately to grief and rage), and Rachel's empathy; and the styles of Nick and Susan in *The Halfmen of O* diverge along similar lines. Gee does not suggest that all boys are rational killers, however – see for instance Colin's actions in contributing to Herbert Muskie's death in *The Fat Man*. By splitting different approaches to understanding the world into boy and girl minds, Gee's books argue that, when brought together, these binaries are best for harmonising the world and ridding it from evil.

At the end of each of the three *Salt* novels, the pairs of protagonists become lovers and, it is implied, partners for life, who will produce children who will carry on their heroic roles. Here, another pattern emerges: the satisfying end for a heroic individual involves settling into, or making and settling into, a happy family. (This is, of course, a familiar pattern in much children's and other literature – a variant of the 'home–away–home' pattern that Perry Nodelman observes in which, either literally or figuratively, the hero leaves home, faces a challenge away from home and, having overcome that challenge, either returns home or finds a new home.)[3] For the most part, Gee likes to have his protagonist come from, or return to, 'good' families – usually nuclear families – of healthy parents with healthy relationships with one another and with their children. Occasionally, in the realist fiction, these relationships are questioned, as when Colin Potter and Ossie Dye realise the frailties of their fathers in *The Fat Man* and *Orchard Street* respectively. Some alternative relationship models are proposed, as, for instance, in *Hostel Girl*, in which Ailsa's single mother is a model of good sense and empathy. Often, Gee likes to have his bad characters come from damaged and warped family structures. In *The Fire-Raiser*, Edgar Marwick's domineering mother turns him into a vengeful lunatic; in *The Fat Man*, Herbert Muskie's dependence on his mother marks him out as different and frightening. A whole, rounded, traditional nuclear family seems to be the ultimate goal, and at the end of each novel in the *Salt* trilogy we see each pair of heroes moving towards creating new, healthy families in that mode. Pearl and Hari, for instance, have an idealised relationship, in contrast with the myriad problematic family relationships they leave behind them: Pearl leaves a family willing to exploit her for social and political gain by marrying her to a disgusting old man; Hari leaves an essentially supportive father, but one whose lonely aggression means he is a less than suitable role model. In finding each other, fighting successfully against corrupting forces and creating their own new family, they have a traditional and satisfying happy ending. Creating a new family is a logical extension and expression of the individual; it also intends hope for new and healthy societies.

The relationship between individual and society is uneasy in Gee's work. On the one hand, he promotes the value of individual thought, action and moral codes, especially when society at large is damaged. He includes a range of appealing and enlightened 'teacher' figures who encourage the young protagonists to think for themselves. On the other hand, his narrative structures valorise traditional family structures at the expense of other modes of living, and run the risk of demonising difference. In this regard, his novels are paradoxically radical and conservative.

Although Gee's work is often paradoxical, however, it is remarkably consistent. In his representation of evil, for instance, he explores a range of villains – individuals, families, species, corporations and institutions – whose motivating principles always come from greed and the desire for power. The *Salt* trilogy offers several types of wicked operators: the father–son duo of Ottmar and Kyle-Ott in *Salt*; the gool and her children in *Gool*; and the figure of Vosper and his brutal father in *The Limping Man*. Ottmar and Kyle-Ott are models of evil conservatism and greed. The gool and her children, as alien species, are unthinking and instinctually evil, feeding on the fury of human warfare. Vosper, on the other hand, was created out of brutality – his father's vicious beatings because of his deformity, which make him further deformed in spirit. And again, despite exploring a range of types of wickedness, from the corporate, to the alien, to the religious, to the individual, Gee's representations of evil are consistent.

In particular, deformity is a notable marker of evil in Gee's works for children. Dorothy Butler was not too far off the mark when she complained that *The Fat Man* 'neatly equated evil with physical imperfections'; and Gee's defence that he simply relies on his childhood imagination for his detailed depictions of Muskie's grotesqueness is not altogether convincing.[4] Nevertheless, his depictions of evil characters are memorably grotesque, and he uses many unpleasant bodily images to revolt his young readers. In *Salt*, Ottmar is a fat, power-craving man with a scar in his cheek. In his sluglike grotesqueness he recalls the Wilberforce worms of *Under the Mountain*, Otis Claw, the evil overlord in *The Halfmen of O*, and the Grimbles of *The World Around the Corner*, all of whose bloated bodies symbolise their desire for world domination. The scar in his cheek has much in common with the 'wormlike' scar twisting in Herbert Muskie's cheek (and which Vivien van Rij and Diane Hebley intriguingly suggest recalls the conservative prime minister Robert Muldoon, notoriously hot-tempered and considered a bully by his critics).[5] Fatness and deformity, then, go hand-in-hand with a deformity of outlook.

Bloated bodies go along with greedy minds, as we see again in *Gool*. There are many villains in *Gool*, including a range of despotic and brutal leaders of warring political factions. But it is the gool that lies beneath the city of Belong that urges them on and feeds on their rage. It too has a bloated and grotesque body:

> The gool had been born from an oily crack in the mountainside. It bulged from darkness into the morning light, undulating beneath its skin. The main part of its body lay on the slope down from the crack, spreading, flattening, busy at its edges with a thousand tiny mouths eating whatever they found. Except for that ant-like busyness and the organs turning under its skin, it was like a dead jellyfish on a beach, but a thousand times large than any jellyfish ever seen. (73)

The busy hunger of the gool's many mouths is not so different from the frantic greed of human villains such as Ottmar in *Salt* and his successors in *Gool*, Keech and Clerk; it recalls the Wilberforce worms in shape and in their essential deadness. The Wilberforces kill everything they touch and leave it covered in a noisome grey dust; the gool emits grey dust from a 'pit like a blowhole' (73). A final key similarity is in their shared alienness. The Wilberforces are aliens from another planet. The story of the gool suggests initially that they have come to the world of Belong from another planet, brought there by a red star and a white star; it emerges, however, that gools are even more alien, being creatures from 'outside nature' itself, drawn into existence in Belong by the rage of warfare – a warfare that in *Gool* takes shape in the battle between the Clerk as a representative of government gone bad, and Keech as a representative of people-power gone wrong.

Gool, then, are evil aliens that feed on evil and, as such, are an effective symbol of all that the heroic children are fighting against. In a characteristic twist at the end of *Gool*, Gee suggests that although these bloated monsters are to be feared and exterminated, they must also be pitied. So although Xantee's pity for the mother gool, described above, destroys her, the novel reiterates a key theme seen throughout the children's books: the nature of evil and the responsible actions of heroes in dealing with it. Evil is to be pitied, but that pity should not lead the hero to be lenient or merciful. The responsible hero will still destroy evil, even as they sympathise with it; and its destruction will be more effective because the hero tempers mercilessness with pity. *Gool* thus offers Gee's most explicit statement on this idea.

In using an abject image for the gool as an almost disembodied embodiment of evil, Gee suggests again that evil is not merely deformed – it is innate and it is visually identifiable. In the third novel, *The Limping Man*, this idea is focused on Vosper. His deformities are physical (his twisted leg) and mental (his twisted mind). Is his deformity innate? Certainly he has suffered abuse at the hands of his vicious father. His response to that abuse is to abuse others, to seek power over them and to kill and torture his parents. (A marker of evil is that evil families breed disloyalty and dysfunction.) Vosper is able to do this because of a symbiotic connection with magical toads, which secrete in them the ability of mind-control, and communicate that ability to Vosper. When he hides the toad in his headdress, he draws power from it and uses it to control the people. Without it, he is helpless. The choice of toads is, of course, deliberate: this is a relationship of the deformed, the abject and the evil, working together solely to gain power.

Here in this novel, which may well be the final one he writes for young readers, Gee asks us to consider whether evil (or the will to power) is concentrated only in abject humans and animals, and whether evil is not a fundamental part of the natural world. It occurs when Hana is journeying back to Belong to assist in taking on Vosper. Pausing for rest, she idly watches the play of insects around her feet. She is suddenly arrested by the spectacle of warfare among them.

> Small red ants, busy ants, hundreds of them. Suddenly a door opened in the packed earth at the base of the rock and a dozen larger insects erupted into sight. These were scaly creatures, half the length of Hana's finger ... They had claws like pond lobsters and tails with stings that curved over their backs. She watched, fascinated, as they attacked the ants, snipping them in half with their claws, scattering them with sweeps of their tails. They seemed to be infested with mites that ran across their backs as they worked and fitted into cracks in their armour and seemed to suck. Hana shivered. Everything seemed to feed on something else. The red ants were defeated, but some message had gone back into the nest, for suddenly warrior ants streamed out. They were larger, although not a tenth the size of the attackers. They moved so fast Hana could barely follow them and could not work out what they were doing, how they were driving the attackers away. Then she saw. They were not biting the large creatures but picking off the mites infesting them, crushing them in their jaws, dropping their bodies on the ground. Once the mites were dead the creatures they rode became helpless. They did not know where to turn or where to find the trapdoor of their nest. The warrior ants butchered them. Only one, ridden by a mite between its eyes, made it to the hole. It dived inside and pulled the door shut with a flick of its tail.
>
> Hana shivered again. How savage and bloody everything was. How dangerous.[6]

Evil is present in the world; in a variant of Tennyson's 'Nature, red in tooth and claw', Gee shows that there is always something willing to feed on something else. This passage establishes the essential brutality of the world – Hana reflects that not just the city, but Country and Sea have their pecking orders, their vicious and terrifying aspects. The Limping Man and his toad are simply carrying out a law of evil, working together for their separate ends. Evil, or the power-hungry, always have willing helpers and are always able to find weapons to do their worst. Is this simply depressing and chilling, or is it oddly reassuring? One reading might be to suggest that while the fight against evil must always be ongoing, it is not a fight that should be taken personally; it is simply part of a grand tradition and a grand pattern – a chilling pattern, however, for Hana.

This passage, of course, offers a major clue as to the source of Vosper's power. It underscores that survival depends on fighting back, on identifying the source of power and removing it. It also underscores the darkness of Gee's vision overall. As Claudia Marquis points out in her chapter on the early fantasy novels, there is something Miltonic about his approach to evil. The conclusion of *Under the Mountain*, with much of the city destroyed and the twin heroes Theo and Rachel seeking shelter from the ash, has something of the end of *Paradise Lost* about it – 'with wandering steps and slow through Eden took their solitary way'.[7] Paradise is not possible in Gee's world, just the real world: 'Life's not like that.'[8] For good to triumph over evil, then, requires heroic effort, effort that comes at a cost.

Digging deep and coming of age

The battle between good and evil is a key pattern in Gee's work, and through it many elements of his other books find their way into *Salt*, *Gool* and *The Limping Man*. Villains and heroes, families and advisors, figures of darkness and figures of enlightenment, the battle between the city and the country, a deep concern about corporate or governmental or religious control, a distaste for repression, a limited sympathy for the outsider, a preference for intellectuals and artists, and an emphasis on the frailties of humankind are all ideas woven into the overall patterns of Gee's oeuvre.

Coming of age is a key concept in literature for young readers – young adults in particular are concerned with the issues and challenges of growing up, negotiating the pressures of family and friendships, finding their way in society and developing their own moral codes, frameworks of understanding and individuality. As Roberta Seelinger Trites observes in *Disturbing the Universe*, most literature for young adults aims to help them negotiate these pressures and desires;[9] but for the most part such literature seems to prefer to indoctrinate young adults into accepting particular types of social mores, outlooks, lifestyle choices and modes of behaviour. Thus, while adolescence is seen as a time of rebellion, the literature for adolescents aims to contain that rebellion and to encourage them to enter adult society in a way that is socially acceptable: if they are violent, they learn to control their violence; if they are sexually active, they learn to be sexually continent; if they have a particular skill or talent, they learn to direct that skill into productive outlets and not to overthrow the status quo. Even if they learn to express themselves as individuals and think for themselves, they learn to 'fit in'.

Gee's approach to this is somewhat mixed. All of his young protagonists come of age in some way. They learn how to manage their own abilities and interests, they learn that parental and authority figures may not always be right and they learn that life is intensely flawed. This is one version of enlightenment – as entrance into the adult world. Largely because of the darkness of his vision, Gee's novels, realist or fantasy, are more radical than many other young adult novels. In his realist novels coming of age, instead of socialising teens into accepting the existing social order, means learning how to negotiate highly flawed institutional, social and familial structures in order to find a place in the world that permits them some measure of independence and individuality. For instance, in *The Champion*, Rex (narrating retrospectively as an adult) reflects on the hard lessons he has learned from encountering, participating in and ultimately rejecting racist behaviour when the black American soldier Jackson Coop arrives in his small town. These lessons are important, enabling him to understand the value of independent thought – the value of connecting with those of different races as individuals rather than as part of a collective, and the value of not acting as part of a collective oneself – particularly when the collective is wrong. *Salt*, *Gool* and *The Limping Man* reinforce this message using some of the conventions of the fantasy genre. Where the action of the historical novels is contained in small towns and in individual cases, the action of the fantasy novels is epic in sweep, occurring at a national, if not global, level. Pearl and Hari, Xantee, Lo, Duro, Hana and Ben act individually against a global evil, and do so as part of a small and enlightened community, on behalf of the world. Fantasy novels, more than realist ones, offer the dream of overthrowing corrupt, evil or wrong social structures. Here, Gee's fantasy writing shows its complexity and depth. As Claudia Marquis points out in her chapter, the *O* trilogy comes to the conclusion that no structures at all will work, that the only solution is taking the people of O back to the stone age. The *Salt* trilogy comes to a similar conclusion in *The Limping Man*, when Xantee and Duro use their telepathic powers to encourage the people of Belong to leave the city and to form small farming communities. Cities and mass cultures only encourage sheep-like behaviour, while small communities may permit people to develop as individuals. It is a slim hope, however, consistent with the overall dystopian emphasis of the trilogy. Coming of age, then, in Gee's work, is a key aspect of the narratives for young readers, in which they must see the essential darkness of the world. Even in the fantasy novels – a genre which could more easily offer false hope – Gee's vision is uncompromising.

This is especially the case in the *Salt* trilogy. Here Gee blends realism and fantasy particularly effectively in his representations of the coming of age of his protagonists, drawing together the individual reflection characteristic of the historical novels with the heroic action required of fantasy novels. Coming of age can mean a number of things; here, he balances the movement towards maturity with the acceptance of the heroic role. In this regard, the *Salt* novels demonstrate the sense of finality identified above: in associating the heroic protagonists with enlightened communities working for the good – in the face of great odds – and using the coming-of-age pattern of narrative, Gee works out his preoccupation with moral character and individuality.

Endings, beginnings, worlds and mining

Interestingly, in this trilogy, Gee gets right away from his usual specifically New Zealand setting, with the effect that he is able to work out some of these issues of moral character in a fantasy world with a deliberately universal quality. When we consider the natural settings of the novels, this is very clear. Gee's language is always spare and evocative, but even more so in this trilogy. For example, here is an early description of the landscape in *Salt*, seen from the perspective of the Company girl Pearl, who has left the city for the first time.

> The rock chimneys rose in front of her. They were less smooth than they had appeared from a distance and she found handholds in the tallest and climbed above the scrub by a metre or two. There were the mountains, close enough

it seemed to touch, their snowfields and ice walls gleaming in the sun. At once she felt cooler and at peace. Another night and they would be in the foothills and reach the mountains and the snow after that. Tongues of bush pushed into the plain, the nearest one across a gully edging the scrub patch where they were camped. Perhaps there was a stream there.[10]

The plainness of Gee's language here is noticeable; its pared-back quality contributes to a universal, even archetypal, appeal. With words like 'scrub', 'bush' and 'gully', Gee uses a vocabulary that will be familiar to young New Zealand readers but also recognisable internationally. Readers from New Zealand could see their own country in the world of *Salt*, but equally so could readers from other countries. This world might be our world – just radically altered by the many events of the future; it might also not be ours at all. It might be local; it might be universal. The ambiguity and universality are striking, given the specificity of Gee's other books for children.

Two alternative interpretations of Gee's fantasy world are possible. The simpler interpretation is that, after writing a series of novels in which the New Zealand setting is important, with these final novels Gee removes his narrative fantasy world from the local scene completely.

The second interpretation is a little more complicated. Instead of separating the realism of the local world and the fantastic of the 'other' world, Gee blends the two to create an entirely different world, one where the local and the universal and the fantastic so completely intertwine as to be indistinguishable. In the world of the *Salt* trilogy, then, he brings together the fully inhabited qualities of his historical fiction with the alien strangeness of his speculative fiction.

In Gee's oeuvre, we enter a version of New Zealand that is specific to Gee – a New Zealand in which supernatural events or alien visitations are possible; a New Zealand, too, in which a strong exploration of morality occurs. It is a version that might be explicable by Russian literary theorist Mikhail Bakhtin's term 'chronotope' – a peculiar combination of time and place, in which the time and place of both composition and setting come together to create a specific literary experience. Thus, when we read one of Gee's novels for young readers, in the quality of his depiction of setting (and of character and genre) we find ourselves in what we might consider a chronotope of time and place, a literary New Zealand, created by the combination of times and places where Gee has lived and written. It is a version of the world we might call 'Geeland'; and until the *Salt* trilogy, all his novels connect to that place, that chronotope.[11]

With the three novels of the *Salt* trilogy, Gee draws on the ideas that have flowed through his previous works: the portal fantasies of the *O* trilogy and *The World Around the Corner*, the alien invasion narrative of *Under the Mountain,* and the coming-of-age narratives of the realist historical fiction. Themes of violence, cruelty, family, sexuality and passion, set against larger historical, social or fantasy backdrops, all make their way into these three novels in varying forms. Some of those elements are traced here by focusing on the characterisation of good and evil, and by considering the coming-of-age story and the resonances of the New Zealand landscape.

In Gee's use of recurrent themes, patterns, images and ideas, *Salt*, *Gool* and *The Limping Man* possess a reflective, backward-looking quality that suggests that Gee's greatest inspiration is now his own earlier work. Like an experienced miner, he returns to a fertile seam of ore to dig up new but familiar treasures for his readers. The image of mining is used deliberately here; as other chapters in this book have noted, in Gee's 2002 Margaret Mahy Award lecture 'Creeks and kitchens' he referred to his writing for children and for adults as being different kinds of mining:

> I wanted to get away from the explorations of guilt and delving into psyches I'd been doing in my writing for adults. I wanted, for a time, to write horizontally rather than vertically – do open-cast mining, if I can put it another way, rather than deep-shaft mining. For that reason I decided to write what I call fantasy/ adventure – put the emphasis on movement, develop narrative pace, tell a story as story pure and simple.[12]

It should be clear by now that there's nothing pure and simple about Gee's work. It has a deceptive simplicity to it that can lure the unwary into endless explorations of pattern, meaning, reference and allusion. The fact that Gee's novels seldom deviate from the formal patterns (good vs evil; individual vs society; coming of age) does not mean merely that Gee has found a formula that works; rather, he is returning again and again to a productive mine, working a rewarding seam.

Appropriately, Gee's protagonists frequently descend into hidden depths. In *Under the Mountain*, Rachel and Theo travel into the caverns beneath Auckland through shafts created by the Wilberforce worms; in the *O* trilogy Susan and Nick travel through cracks in the earth to O; in *Salt*, Hari and Pearl go to the Deep Salt mine, where the radioactive salt is brought from the depths to the surface; and in *Gool*, Xantee and Lo penetrate the labyrinth beneath 'Belong' to fight the gool. On the other hand, Herbert Muskie in *The Fat Man* rises to the surface from beneath the water, and falls to his death in a ravine – suggesting that he has come to Loomis from the depths of hell and must be returned there. Subterranean journeys, then, offer a particular kind of movement for protagonists in encountering and conquering demons. Even when Gee consciously lays the emphasis on action rather than introspection, he retains the idea that things are lurking beneath the surface, hidden in the depths, threatening the continued happiness or survival of humans.

The young protagonists of Gee's novels have to penetrate the dark spaces where evil lives, whether physical – as in shaft, cavern, tunnel, cave, corridor or labyrinth – or psychological. Theo and Rachel literally travel along the Wilberforces' tunnels; Hari goes into Deep Salt. In contrast, Colin Potter metaphorically enters the mind of the fat man, Herbert Muskie; so too does Xantee enter the mind of the gool. As Louise Clark notes in her chapter, imagery of seeing, perception and vision pervades Caroline's confrontation with the wicked Grimbles in *The World Around the Corner*. Going into the darkness, whether it is literal, symbolic or psychological, thus suggests the need to track down evil and confront it, but also to understand it: this is another version of the pity that Gee describes when Rachel, Colin and Xantee fully confront evil.

Gee's books are fundamentally about the quest for understanding, and the protagonists' journeys down their different tunnels, shafts or paths enable them to reach some kind of enlightenment. In his repeated use of the imagery of surface and depth, of creek, of shaft, of ravine, of corridor and of cavern, Gee is pointing to his own repeated digging for enlightenment, mining his own work to find new truths (perhaps unconsciously).

The *Salt* trilogy is magnificent in many ways: in its almost mythic, universal qualities, and in its uncompromising efforts to confront evil and to consider the ethics of heroic action. As a final trilogy, a possible rounding off of Gee's literary career for young readers, the three works offer a place to stand from which to survey the remainder of his fiction. And when we consider *Salt*, *Gool* and *The Limping Man* alongside those other works, they not only offer a sense of finality and completeness; they show how widely and how deeply Gee has mined.

4 'WHAT I MUST STEER CLEAR OF'
The influence of his mother's stories on Maurice Gee[1]
Kathryn Walls

Maurice Gee clearly admired his mother as a person. But although he has often noted that she was (or wanted to be) a writer, he has always stopped short of praising her work; he treats it with brevity and critical reserve.[2] Commentators and columnists seem to have followed suit. While they frequently record Lyndahl Chapple Gee's aspirations – with the implication that they must have reinforced Maurice Gee's literary ambitions – they have consistently ignored her writings as such.[3]

Contrary to what we have been led to expect, Lyndahl's stories exerted a strong (though probably unconscious) influence on several of her son's novels. This influence seems to have worked in two quite different ways. It is mostly overt in some of the children's books of the 1980s – the *O* trilogy in particular (1982–85), and *The Champion* (1989). In the adult novel *Meg* (which was published in 1981 as the second of the novels in the *Plumb* trilogy), this influence is far from overt. It is, however, profound.

Mihi and the Last of the Moas: The adventures of Mihi, a little Maori boy, with the very last of the moas

Although Lyndahl Gee evidently wrote far more than she ever published (and may well have published more than we know of), this study is necessarily confined to the two stories I have been able to locate.[4] The first of these is the children's picture book, *Mihi and the Last of the Moas*. Maurice Gee would have been 11 or 12 when it was published in Auckland in 1943 (under the imprint of Oswald-Sealy New Zealand), but he may well have been exposed to an earlier version when he was considerably younger.[5] Obviously directed at younger children, the book is written in verse of the nursery-rhyme variety (paired quatrains in lines of somewhat irregular metre and length) and illustrated (by Lyndahl herself) with full-page coloured pictures and black and white drawings. In other respects it is, as we shall see, similar to Kipling's

Jungle Book (which would have been at the height of its popularity when Lyndahl was a child) but with a distinctly New Zealand flavour.

For most of the story there is only one human character, Mihi – 'a little Maori boy'. His story is set in a vaguely designated location in pre-European Aotearoa New Zealand. Mihi is orphaned when not only his immediate family but his whole community is wiped out by an invading tribe. Marooned on a watchtower, he sobs loudly enough to attract the attention of the trees and the birds. The birds vote in 'Council' to rescue him. Their plan is to use the Moa, down whose long neck Mihi would be able to slide. They charge the Morepork with the task of fetching this giant bird from its underground cavern, and the Morepork undertakes the necessary underground journey. The Moa is vulnerable because 'Every warrior's hand, up and down the land / Was raised for his capture grim'[6] (which is why he is the last of his kind). He nevertheless agrees to come to the rescue of Mihi. Having served his purpose, however, the Moa decides to kidnap the child; but Mihi takes pity on his childless captor and actually volunteers to become his foster son. To celebrate his decision, the birds hold a feast.

At this point a contrasting character, the Tuatara (a fairy godfather figure), appears on the scene. Having come to the feast 'by an underground lane' (18), he presents to both Mihi and the Moa the secret of longevity – after which he returns home through 'the maze of underground ways' (20). The fact that the secret at stake is sunlight is not revealed to the reader until the end of the story. In the meantime, Mihi saves the day by frightening off a party of moa hunters with his fierce yells. But the Moa, in his hurry to escape, is crippled. He languishes in his dark cave while Mihi sets off to learn from the wise Tuatara how to shift the giant bird into the light of day. The Moa, meanwhile, waits in his underground cave for Mihi's return. In the end, following the Tuatara's advice, Mihi uses a raft to bring the Moa along an underground river into the sunlight, which does indeed revive him. The storyteller ends with the traditional suggestion that both Mihi and the Moa may still be alive to this day, since 'all that you see is not all that can be / In The Land of the Long White Cloud!' (35).

It will be evident that Lyndahl Gee's narrative depends on the archetypal motif of the underground journey, which is reiterated a total of seven times. (This was before the publication – in 1949 – of Joseph Campbell's influential study of such motifs, *The Hero with a Thousand Faces*.) Ideologically, the story is of interest for its attribution of tribal conflict and ecological irresponsibility to pre-European Maori. It would invite interpretation along 'postcolonial' lines as designed to mask or excuse the grave consequences of European settlement – were it not for the fact that the latter-day arrival of the Pakeha is acknowledged and negatively represented as a warlike invasion in the very first stanza: 'No white man had come, with his musket and drum / To fight with the brown-skinned men' (5).

Mihi and the *O* trilogy

Maurice Gee had already established himself as a writer of short stories and novels for adults when he published his first children's book, *Under the Mountain* (dedicated to his daughters Emily and Abigail) in 1979; and his second, *The World Around the Corner* (dedicated to Emily) the following year. It was, we may guess, writing for children, and especially his own, that brought the material of his mother's long-forgotten story back into his mind – even while, as it would appear, he remained unconscious of its source. I shall begin by isolating the quite concrete ways in which the *O* trilogy echoes his mother's picturebook.

Generally speaking, *Mihi* anticipates not only the essential machinery of the *O* trilogy, but also its implicit commentary on the negative propensities of human nature. In *Motherstone* (the third and final volume in the trilogy) for instance, the human inhabitants of O separate into two camps and seem to be heading for mutually assured destruction, and throughout the trilogy they threaten the survival of other creatures. In *The Priests of Ferris* the Birdfolk tell Susan how the priests (of the planet O) 'come over the passes and shoot [them] from the sky with their cross-bows'.[7]

Particular details are more telling indications of influence, however. Close to the beginning of Gee's first otherworld fantasy, *The Halfmen of O*, the female hero Susan finds herself isolated in a way that is more than faintly reminiscent of the child Mihi's original predicament, once his father has been captured and he finds that 'No *mother*, no *father*, no friends were in sight, / In the trampled tribal pa' (7, added emphasis). Gee's Susan is, at 12, much older than Mihi (who is four when the story begins, and eight by the time he is shifting the Moa near the end). Nevertheless, when having transported herself to O Susan is more or less immediately taken captive by the evil Odo Cling and his men, Cling gloats over her separation from her family – even stressing the crucial terms '*mother*' and '*father*':

> 'You are dangerous, Mixie. You are the last enemy.'
> 'I don't know what you mean,' Susan said. 'I just want to go home.'
> 'Home?' Odo Cling laughed. 'Soon you will be saying *mother* and *father*. These words have no meaning.'[8]

Apart from the villain Odo and his men, the first beings Susan and her cousin Nick encounter are the Woodlanders. Dressed in green, and with names like Verna and Dale, they seem to be a cross between indigenous people and nature spirits: they consider the trees, even blades of grass, as their 'brothers and sisters' (*HO* 59). As such, they are reminiscent of Lyndahl Gee's 'listening trees':

> The trees in the forest hushed their whispering leaves,
> And listened from far and near;
> A tall ponga sighed, 'I cannot abide,
> Such a sobbing as I can hear!' (8)

The Woodlanders' natural affinity with plants is demonstrated when one of them fetches leaves of a particular variety in order to soothe the rope-burns that Susan has suffered when held captive by Cling's men (*HO* 62) – recalling Mihi's use of leaves to treat the sick Moa (*Mihi*, 25).

The Woodlanders' likeness to Lyndahl's talking trees pales into insignificance, however, when we consider Maurice Gee's Birdfolk – the next species encountered by Susan and Nick. Like Mihi's Moa, they are giant sized – Nick guesses their height to be three metres, and their wingspan seven metres (*HO* 103). Like all the birds in *Mihi*, these magnificent creatures are anthropomorphised: Susan sees them as 'neither bird nor man' – with the implication that they are both (*HO* 100). The Birdfolk are also reminiscent of Lyndahl Gee's birds in their proud rituals. They hold a feast, make formal speeches in Council and vote on whether to assist the heroine Susan (*HO* 10). Lyndahl's birds, when they voted to rescue Mihi, dropped leaves (those that are torn signifying support for Mihi) on a thorn. The actual word 'vote' is not used in the *Halfmen*, but every one of the Birdfolk shows their support for Susan by swooping down and offering her a feather.[9] The Birdfolk are crucial because they enable Susan to accomplish the first component of her quest, flying her (in a kind of hanging nest) to the high cave where she collects one half of the stone that she will use to redeem the human inhabitants of the planet.

Equally crucial (and equally indebted to *Mihi*) are the antithetical Stonefolk. Explicitly lizard-like, these beings are strongly reminiscent of Lyndahl Gee's Tuatara (a 'lizard so wise and old'). The children reach the Stonefolk by the 'Lizard Path' (*HO* 135); and when Susan is transfixed with terror on her underground journey in their company, the Stonefolk wait for her 'still as lizards' (*HO* 142). Two Stonefolk escort Susan on her gruelling journey into their home territory, which is underground. It is there, in an unidentified dark space, that she takes possession of the remaining 'half'. Gee's description of this underground world owes much to his mother's book:

> Many times she heard water. It dripped and roared and hissed. She heard it making a throaty boom deep in a gorge, and felt its spray on her face from a waterfall. (*HO* 144)
>
> There was more climbing, more booming of water, and an echoing cavern that sounded. (*HO* 145)
>
> [Susan and her Stonefolk guides] followed the River Stoneblood for a long while. It flowed along silkily, lapping idly – strange for a river with such a fierce name. (*HO* 145)
>
> She and Finder and Seeker [the guides] kept on through lonely caverns. At last Seeker said, 'Climb.' She felt her way up a sloping wall, slick with running water. 'Now down.' She went down another wall, dry this time. It plunged deep and seemed to turn under the river, into a honeycomb of passages. There were broken echoes and sudden reverberations. (*HO* 145)

It is not just the topography of *Mihi* (the cavern, the waterfall, the tunnel behind it) that is anticipated by Lyndahl. Gee recalls the very words his mother used ('drips', 'echo', 'passages'); he personifies the cavern as she did; and, again like her, he evokes underground water as something heard but not seen:

> Nearby the coast was the cavern deep,
> Its mouth showing black as dye;
> > Through its rocky lips, wet with water drips,
> > > Flew the owl with his 'Morepork' cry;
> Every echo awoke in the passages long,
> > And caught up the sound as it fell
> > > ('Morepork Goes to the Moa for Help', 12)

> Now the way you must go is important indeed,
> > So listen with both of your ears;
> Steer with a turn, to the waterfall's churn,
> > And into its silvery tears!
> Once through its curtain of falling drops
> > A long secret tunnel you'll find
> Hidden away, at the back of the spray,
> > It leads to an outlet behind.
> > > ('The Tuatara's Plan', 29)[10]

Nick and Susan are often the recipients of advice like the Tuatara's, and in *The Priests of Ferris* one of the Stonefolk delivers a set of instructions that, with its injunction to 'listen', as well as its contents and vocabulary, is particularly suggestive in this context: 'Listen to what I am telling Nick. After you have climbed you will come to a river. Walk by the side of it until it vanishes. You will hear it booming. Go down then through a turning passage, deep down, very deep, and you will come to a lake in a cavern' (*PF* 37).

A crucial complication in *The Priests of Ferris* – which is, of course, also set on the planet O – is supplied by the fact that the Birdfolk are prevented by an ancient 'Prohibition' from passing beyond the mountains that border their region: when they try to fly above the mountains, they weaken and fall back. Wanting the Birdfolk to come to Susan's assistance on the other side, Nick struggles to point out to them the significance of the terms of this prohibition: '*Unless ye be as Humble as the Worm, never shall ye fly outside the Mountains*' (*PF* 143, original italics). The giant birds must 'forget wings' and go underneath the mountain, 'crawling in the ground' (*PF* 148). Here Gee seems to recall Lyndahl Gee's representation of the Morepork taking itself underground to find the Moa in his cavern. It has to be said, however, that the Morepork is quite comfortable in his surroundings ('Well knowing each turn of the cavern long, / The Morepork followed his beak, / Till rounding a bend, he found journey's end, / And the bird he had come to seek. / 'Twas a wondrous cave ...', 13), while Gee memorably transforms the birds' underground journey into a (morally purposeful) agonising experience. As a child, listening as he surely did to his mother's story, he must have contemplated what it would feel like to be a bird journeying underground. He attaches such imagining to his character Nick, who, we are told, 'thought of the Birdfolk deep in the mountain under them, turning in caves, shuffling in passages, with their great wings useless by their sides' (*PF* 151–52). The journey is so difficult that some of the Birdfolk cannot bring themselves to make it, and others die in the attempt.

Mihi and *The Champion*

As we have seen, *Mihi* and the *O* trilogy are both fantasies, and much of what the latter owes to the former is fantastical. Like his mother before him, Maurice Gee combines the mythical component of the underground journey with a cast of anthropomorphised aspects of nature, including birds and other animals.[11] Lyndahl Gee's story also anticipates – in just one respect – Gee's realistic novel *The Champion*. This novel is narrated by Rex, looking back on his 12-year-old self in 1943 and remembering the impact made on him by a young black American soldier, Jackson Coop, who stayed with his family but was in the end tragically drowned in his attempt to evade the military police as they tried to foil his desertion. The novel ends with Rex's reflections on Jack's final fate:

> I often wonder what happened on the launch at the very end. Jack probably tried to save Mrs Stewart [an unhinged old lady who was also on board]. That is the sort of thing he'd do. And then perhaps he tried to swim ashore. He could dog-paddle, after all. He wouldn't give up. And sometimes I wonder if he made it – just kept on kicking, paddling, as we'd taught him. Reached the other shore and pulled himself through the mangroves there. Was that someone moving, someone slipping quietly away? And he hid in the bush, up the coast where

Dawn had shown him on her map; and somehow managed to survive ... He's in Chicago now, living happily ... It's a dream. Perhaps I don't need to dream it any more.[12]

The echoes of the end of *Mihi* are unmistakable:

> No doubt you will guess that the sun's warm caress
>   Made the Moa quite magically well!
> And indeed if it did, as 'tis right to suppose
>   The bird might be living still,
> And the Maori boy too, since he also knew
>   The secret that we never will!
>
> So if ever you go for a roam by the sea,
>   Or over far headland or range,
> Don't be afraid, if by seashore or glade,
>   You fancy you see something strange!
> It may be a cloud shadow slipping away
>   For they take most mysterious shapes,
> And flee with no sound, across water or ground,
>   Like witches in billowing capes!
>
> And again if 'tis there by the stream's fronded bend
>   Where a tall something stands in a veil,
> Be sure to look twice, or possibly thrice,
>   And you may see the end of this tale!
> Of course you may say with a toss of your head,
>   "'Tis only a tree-fern bowed!'
> Yet all that you see is not all that can be
>   In The Land of the Long White Cloud! (34–35)

We may note how Rex recalls Lyndahl Gee's wording ('slipping ... away'), and that he admits to having indulged – right into adulthood, it would seem – a similar fancy. This might be characterised as a projection of the spirit of reconciliation (exemplified by the reconciliation of the once-racist Rex with the black American Jack) onto the paradisal landscape in which it was – according to the story until this point – accomplished. Unlike his mother, Maurice Gee (through his narrator, the adult Rex) dismisses that fantasy, but he is ambivalent about doing so.

Distinguishing himself from those writers who are able to produce portfolios of childhood reading at the drop of a hat, Gee has frequently suggested that he did far more playing in the open than reading as a young child. But while (unlike Margaret Mahy) he may not have been deeply into Kipling, he seems to have known his mother's rather eccentric handling of the 'wild child' archetype pretty much off by heart.[13]

'Double Unit': Lyndahl Gee's short story for adults

The short story 'Double Unit', published in Frank Sargeson's 1947 anthology *Speaking for Ourselves*, is a different kettle of fish.[14] Where *Mihi* is highly coloured (even literally, thanks to Lyndahl's painted illustrations) and spaciously written, 'Double Unit' is schematic and so densely written (it occupies just eight pages) that it seems to be all plot. And where *Mihi* is written in a warmly optimistic spirit, 'Double Unit' is a deeply pessimistic story. It is like *Mihi,* however, in being a fable rather than a 'slice of life' – for all that it is set during World War II.

In the story, two women friends occupy a double unit – each living in one half of what would now be described as a duplex – while their husbands are serving overseas. One of the women is as flirtatious and promiscuous as the other is serious and faithful. The flirtatious woman suspects her absent husband of infidelity, while the faithful one trusts her husband. When the husbands return, a local busybody reports the flirt's promiscuity to her husband (who has himself been a model of fidelity during his time in Italy), while the faithful and trusting wife is shocked to discover photographic evidence of her husband's sexual dalliances in Egypt. The 'double unit' is thus an emblem of the story's outcome. (The good wife has, earlier, pondered the fact that the other side of the unit, though identical to her own, seems 'the wrong way round', recalling that her frivolous counterpart 'was fond of saying that the Government architects, when planning double units, simply drew half a plan in ink and doubled it over when wet').[15] The unfaithful wife and her faithful husband reflect as in a mirror (that is, 'the wrong way round') the faithful wife and her unfaithful husband.

It will be evident from the above that the plot of 'Double Unit' is almost obsessively symmetrical. Lyndahl Gee goes further: she provides each of her two women with a son born on the same day (only months before their fathers were conscripted). These sons constitute another contrasting pair, one being keen on war games and the other drawn to art and gardening. They contrast not only with each other, but with their respective fathers – the destructive 'bully' is the son of the good father (whose disillusionment with war is indicated by his refusal to discuss it), and the creative 'sissy' is the son of the philanderer (who won't stop talking about the enemy, aggressively referring to the Italians as the 'bloody Eyeties').[16] The story ends with the boys exchanging their fathers' presents, a set of Egyptian coins (gift of the contemplative father to his aggressive son) for a knife (gift of the aggressive father to his contemplative son): '"Hot diggety!" Jackie [the bully of the pair] said, unsheathing the knife. "I wish we could swop fathers too!"' (30).

'Double Unit' and the *O* Trilogy

As we have seen, Lyndahl Gee's story depends on the division of her characters into pairs of opposing types. This kind of division is the founding principle of Maurice Gee's *Halfmen of O* (and indeed of many of Gee's novels, including those written for adults).[17] The two children who join forces to play the role of hero – Susan the dreamy contemplative girl, and Nick the practical and logical boy – constitute the central example. Then there are Susan's two Stonefolk guides, whom she thinks of as 'Seeker' and 'Finder'. Sometimes described – that is, thought of – by Susan as a composite being ('Seeker or Finder', and even 'Seeker/Finder', 140–41), they are nevertheless very different: Seeker is the compassionate one, while Finder is critical and judgemental.[18] Gee's contrasting pairs extend beyond individuals to groups, too. Thus, in order to obtain the two interlocking stones that she needs to perform the ritual to redeem the planet O, Susan must be flown to a high place by the planet's Birdfolk, and then be guided through the bowels of O by the Birdfolk's opposite partners, the worm-like Stonefolk. The human inhabitants of O are in need of redemption precisely because they have divided themselves into two opposing types: the thoroughly evil (typified by the cruel Odo Cling and his all-powerful master, Otis Claw) and the thoroughly good (represented only by the wise old woman Marna). Odo and Marna, having renounced their good and evil side respectively, are both 'Halfies'. As Marna explains to Susan and Nick, the transformation of humans into Halfies dates from the time when she and her husband Freeman Wells abdicated their social responsibilities and retired to live in Wildwood. Wells' absence provided the secretly ambitious Otis Claw with his opportunity. The original ancestor of Freeman had preserved equilibrium by uniting the above-mentioned 'halves' on the 'motherstone'. Claw managed to remove these halves and pull them apart, thus ensuring that every human being would become the victim of an internal struggle that would result in the triumph of either absolute evil or perfect – and, in practical terms, futile – goodness. The separation of the halves is obviously as much an emblem of its effect as it is a cause, and the seemingly innocent retirement of Marna and Freeman – a retirement that leaves Otis Claw free to pursue his evil ends – similarly anticipates the polarisation it is invoked to explain.

Gee's overt message is that society is endangered when human beings embrace the extremes of 'evil' and 'good'. His first point – that pure evil is bad – is of course obvious; but his second point – that pure good is also bad – requires interpretation: it makes sense only if we associate goodness with a lack of egoism at a personal level, and with pacifism as a political stance. Although 'Double Unit' does not (as far as I can see) have a moral, the story does associate the one-sidedness of each character with the misery of all. And Lyndahl Gee's notions of good (personally loyal, politically pacifist) and evil (personally selfish, politically aggressive) clearly parallel those subsequently embodied by her son: they are present not only in the *O* trilogy but throughout Gee's work.

It is in their emblematic approach, however, that Lyndahl Gee and Maurice Gee are most strikingly similar. The architectural plan of the double unit (that seems to function as a ground-plan for the awful fates of its inhabitants) may be compared with the 'motherstone', the circular altar that seems to yearn for the halves that once covered it, and which are restored to it by Susan:

> They [Susan's allies] sheltered each other, and watched Susan in the light of the Motherstone reach out for the Halves, one in each hand, and fit them in their places. A tiny thread of light ran round them in a circle, through them in an S, fusing them in the Stone and to each other. (*HO* 196)

Maurice Gee's image, unlike his mother's, is a positive one. When Susan places the halves, the Halfies are given the opportunity of coming back 'in Balance' (196). In Lyndahl Gee's story, each character is doomed to living in a private hell on what, for each of them, must feel like the wrong side of the double unit. This may have been too bleak an ending for Maurice at 13. Writing for even younger readers in *Halfmen*, he has taken his mother's pair of confining boxes that meet along a depressingly straight and impermeable line of division, and replaced them with a circle whose contrasting halves meet along an S-shaped curve – the Taoist image of perfect balance that was interpreted by Jung as a symbol of the integrated self.[19]

'Double Unit', *Hostel Girl, The Champion*

Gee has recalled his mother's line of division once more (this time as a straight line) in his 1997 novel for teenagers, *Hostel Girl*. In that novel, set in the Hutt Valley, he attaches a strong symbolic value to the railway line that divides the region. At the beginning of the novel, the main character, Ailsa, contemplates it from the overbridge: 'She liked to linger on the bridge and look up and down the shining rails that cut the Hutt Valley into two halves, and in a way cut her life in half' (6). What Ailsa is observing here is the division between the wealthy (epitomised by her boyfriend) and the working class (epitomised by the residents of the hostel where she lives, and by her mother, who works in the hostel as the housekeeper). Other divisions apply, too. Ailsa's boyfriend is disabled; she is healthy. Ailsa's flatmate loses her virginity to a shallow, uncaring male; Ailsa remains a virgin and has a boyfriend who is worthy of her.

Like 'Double Unit', *The Champion* is set during World War II. Although Gee's representation of life in New Zealand at this time owes nothing in particular to his mother's, his characterisation of Rex has much in common with his mother's descriptions of Jackie, the aggressive son of the pacifist-tending father and flirtatious mother:

> Jackie Gladson, endowed with his mother's appetite for adventure, played 'soldiers' constantly. Sunny-Jim [the contrasting child], his lively imagination at work, would watch Jackie realistically bayonetting and bombing Japs and Germans until he had gooseflesh at the thought of so much blood. Then he would seek his mother and the magic circle of security she represented. (*TC* 25)

> Jackie, in true 'Flash Gordon' style, butted with his head and laid Sunny-Jim low; then, with his hands holding imaginary 'gats' [Gatling guns], he stood over his sobbing victim and drawled in imitation of his favourite comic-paper character, 'Waal, you've had it, son.' (*TC* 26)

Rex's favourite illustrated paper is *The Champion* (a boys' magazine of the time), and the character Rockfist Rogan who features there is, like Jackie's Flash Gordon, the man he thinks he would like to be: 'the one I most wanted to be was Rockfist Rogan of the RAF' (10). The story begins with Rex's war games:

> On the morning of the day Jackson arrived I was out on the back lawn in my pyjamas shooting Hitler and Tojo with my BB gun. (*TC* 8)

> Standing on the back gravel I shot Hitler and Tojo from a distance of twenty feet until only tatters of them were left. (*TC* 9)

> We played games of that sort in the war years, stalking Germans in the grass, bayonetting Japs – and dogfighting in Spitfires. (*TC* 9)

It is probable, however, that in this instance what might seem like evidence of Lyndahl Gee's influence on *The Champion* is at least partly attributable to the fact that both she and (the adult) Maurice are portraying the behaviour of Maurice as a child. In an interview with Marion McLeod in 1989, Gee recalled his love of Rockfist Rogan: '*The Champion* played a large role in my life, I think it was my first real reading ... I was devoted to Rockfist Rogan.' In the same interview, Gee recalled how he 'used to play violently anti-Japanese and anti-German games'.[20] The fictional Rex comes, through his encounter with Jack, to reject his childish understanding of courage and to approach the values, not of Jackie, but of Jackie's father. His trajectory echoes Gee's own.

Gee's rewriting of Lyndahl: *Meg*

Given that the influence of Lyndahl Gee's works on her son is so readily demonstrable, the fact that Maurice Gee has said rather little about them could seem surprising. His most extended comment – published comment, at least – is contained in 'Beginnings', the autobiographical essay he published in *Islands* in 1977.

> My mother was a writer. When her day's work was done and her husband and children in bed she sat with her feet in the range oven and wrote stories and poems in exercise books. She had natural gifts, but her circumstances were wrong. She needed to write hard, she needed practice. There was never sufficient time. She could not discover what it was she wanted to say. She did not really want foreman Jim to punch the swagger's jaw. She did not really care about Mihi the little Maori boy and his adventures with 'the very last of the Moas'. (289)

These remarks, though warmly sympathetic to his mother as a person, are dismissive of her as a writer.[21] Gee does goes on to modify his initial assessment: 'Now and then she came near to her subject. Frank Sargeson included her story "Double Unit" in his anthology *Speaking for Ourselves*. One can see she would have been a writer' (289). But Gee does not linger on the merits of 'Double Unit', returning immediately to his conviction that his mother's domestic responsibilities had absorbed the time she needed in order to succeed: 'There should have been other stories, better ones. But she did not have time. Her family swallowed her' (289). His personal concession – 'she came near to her subject' – is vague anyway; and Gee distances himself even from that by seeming to base it on the fact of Sargeson's acceptance rather than on any positive appraisal on his own part. He does offer a few positive comments on his mother's abilities as a storyteller in response to some shrewd questions posed by Thomas E. Tausky in 1991, but mostly in reference to her spoken reminiscences. When it comes to her writing as such – or, at least, the 'pieces [he has] at home' – he begins positively but, as in 'Beginnings', moves quickly to her failings:

> She was a marvellous phrase-maker, but she needed to know how to piece a story together and she needed to discover what she thought. Just as sentimentalism was a vice with Meg, it was to a certain extent with my mother, and she needed to write herself past that.[22]

How are we to understand the coexistence of (on the one hand) Gee's detachment from and ambivalence towards his mother's writings with (on the other) their marked imprint on his own work? Paradoxically, the answer may be that these coexisting characteristics are two sides of the same coin. In his seminal monograph *The Anxiety of Influence* (1973), Harold Bloom observed that there is a certain category of writers whose works seem to be determined by their quasi-Oedipal need or 'anxiety' to deny the very powerful influence of their precursors – their literary 'fathers'.[23] The influence of the precursor may always, according to Bloom, be detected – but only in spite of the intense efforts of the successor to disguise it. Quite apart from any more obvious evidence of influences, these efforts themselves, in their intensity, betray it – at least to the alert critic conversant with Bloom. A writer will, in other words, deny crucial influence by writing in such a way as to counter, to an exaggerated extent, the tendencies of their precursor. Thus, if we accept that Maurice Gee has been deeply influenced by the works of his biological mother – who is, by virtue of her influence, also his literary parent – we should not be surprised by the fact that Gee has distanced himself from her work when commenting directly on it. More importantly, we would expect his creative writing to be diametrically opposed to hers in some essential respects.

We have already observed in passing a number of points at which Gee's works exhibit a kind of filial resistance to his mother's, her influence notwithstanding. One such point is the conclusion to *The Champion*, which recalls the happy ending of *Mihi*, when the narrator Rex acknowledges that his fantasy of Jack's survival is just that. But in order to appreciate the depth of Gee's denial of his mother's influence, we need to consider his avowedly highest priority as a novelist – at least, as a novelist writing for adults: the creation of 'character' – by which he evidently means the credible depiction of credibly complex personalities.[24] 'Character' in this sense is very clearly subordinated to other values in Lyndahl Gee's published stories. Applying Bloom's theory, one might be inclined to interpret Gee's strongly proclaimed commitment to 'character' as his reaction against his mother's predilection for myth and fable, where characters are functions of the plot – if it were not for his children's fiction, in which the story is still the most important element. The children's stories may be the exception that proves the rule, however, in the light of the fact that Gee himself has been keen to represent his children's novels as an aberration on his part, 'a kind of relaxation' from his serious vocation of writing for adults, and 'far less satisfying'.[25]

Without quite saying that children are superficial and satisfied with less (less of what Gee, at least, values most), Gee has accounted for the style of his children's books by reference to the notion that children 'don't have the sort of inner life and the relationships that give meaning to adults'.[26] He has described them as one-dimensional narratives, shallow in comparison with his adult novels:

> The narrative pace is very fast: I think of them as horizontal stories. Adult's fiction is horizontal in the sense that time's arrow is going on, but there are doublings back and occasionally you stop and *sink a lateral shaft*. I hope that metaphor holds up![27]
>
> In writing for adults there is far more call upon the imagination. There are various points at which you have to *go down and look deep*.[28]

For a novel to have 'depth' in Gee's terms it must incorporate what Bill Manhire has described as his 'serious exploration of character'.[29] Thus, although Gee's children's writing does, in its prioritisation of plot over character, have a basic affinity with his mother's works, the fact that he has in a sense excluded his stories for children from his personal canon is telling.

But Gee's recoil from what he would see as the simplistic is embodied even within the children's novels that he has virtually classified as such. It is especially prominent in the *Halfmen of O*, although (or, as Bloom would argue, because) it is strongly indebted to 'Double Unit'. 'Double Unit' had committed what was to become, for Maurice Gee, the ultimate crime for a novelist: because its 'characters' are clearly and quite frankly 'types', they are not 'characters' at all in Gee's sense of the term. Their meaning lies only in simple distinctions (faithful as opposed to unfaithful, militaristic as opposed to pacifist, physically active as opposed to contemplative). In this respect they are the precursors of Gee's 'Halfies' – who are either thoroughly good or thoroughly evil. In a way paradoxically, however, Susan's goal in the

Halfmen is the transformation of these one-dimensional characters into 'Mixies' like herself. When, having obtained both 'halves,' she unites them on the motherstone, the Halfies go into a coma from which they will awaken 'in Balance': 'They will be what they should be. Probably more bad than good, that is the way with men. But good will have its chance. They will choose' (196). The story functions at one level as an allegory of the process of individuation, accomplished (according to Jung) when the buried contents of the unconscious are brought into the light of consciousness. But it also invites interpretation as an allegory of the kind of writing that Gee knew he had to abandon in order to write a fantasy story for children. Susan's journey into the earth to claim the evil half literalises Gee's own metaphors for the kind of attention to character that he thought was possible only in a novel for adults – 'sinking a shaft', and 'going down'. Similarly, the transformation of the Halfies into whole people literalises a metaphor used by Gee – or more accurately one of his characters, the would-be biographer Raymond Sole – to describe complex characterisation. Raymond has put his half-written biography aside, thanks to what he laments as his failure to create '*whole* round lives'.[30]

It is, however, in Gee's adult novel *Meg*, written in 1981 immediately before *The Halfmen of O*, that Gee's attempt to – metaphorically speaking – vanquish his mother is supremely evident. This novel is prefaced by a note: 'Although George and Edith Plumb owe something to my grandparents, the other characters in this novel are imaginary. No reference is intended to any person living or dead. M.G.'[31] Thus any connection we might want to draw between Lyndahl, daughter of Gee's grandparents, and Meg, daughter of their fictional equivalents, is disallowed. Ten years later, however, Gee was to tell Thomas Tausky that his mother was 'a kind of touchstone for Meg', and vouch for the 'accuracy of [his portrait]'.[32] Whether or not Meg is a portrait of Gee's mother as a person, the crucial fact about Meg – for the purposes of this discussion, at least – is that she is both a mother and a writer. There are of course many writers in Gee's fiction; and Meg is not the only mother among them. Meg stands out, however, because the novel (*Meg*) represents itself as her autobiography. We are made aware of this from the very first page where (in a passage discussed in some detail below) Meg resolves to check her propensity for fanciful metaphors and write plainly, and the fact that the novel is her autobiography remains evident throughout the volume. Meg's story comes (almost) to an end with the funeral of her beloved brother Robert and the departure afterwards of her friends and remaining family. What she seems to recall, in a complex passage that defies analysis, is a sense of isolation created not only by their departure but by the fact that she has virtually completed the autobiography we have been reading (although she is, quite evidently, still writing – about her writing). The departure of real friends and family after the funeral merges in her mind with the imminent departure of all the literally departed people who 'lived' again for her while she was writing about them.

> Well, I thought, I'm alone here now. I'll have to make the best of it.
>
> But I have not been alone, in my *furor scribendi*. I have had more company than I have known what to do with. They are leaving me. I wonder if it's true I am acquainted with myself. In a curious way I am both empty and full. The figure I see is an hour-glass. With Robert's burial the last of the sand trickled through. By an act of will (but an irresistible act) I up-ended myself. I let it all trickle back. The story ends.
>
> I want very much to be quit of that metaphor. So – I'll put down one more thing. Rebecca and her husband ... (*Meg* 250)

Thus we are reminded once again that the story we are reading is not merely an overheard consciousness, but a written recollection. This seems particularly significant in view of the fact that neither Meg's father Plumb nor her journalist son Raymond provides us with any comparable evidence of their authorial abilities. Thus, although we learn that Plumb wrote his autobiography in the last year of his life,[33] we never discover whether it was a success, for there is nothing – or at least nothing conclusive – to suggest that the novel *Plumb* is this autobiography.[34] Even more tellingly, in *Sole Survivor* (sequel to *Meg*), Raymond – who has been trying to write a biography of the tragic rugby hero Albie Marsick – confesses to his Aunt Felicity (in a passage quoted above) that he has put it aside, adding, 'The work's all done. But I can't bring it together', and admitting privately to himself, 'I could not make a whole round life. I lacked the stillness and the breadth; I lacked the measure' (*SS* 212). What the fictional son lacks is what the fictional mother Meg so evidently possesses.

This being so, one might be inclined to see *Meg* as Gee's tribute to his mother – except for the important fact that Meg's autobiography is completely unlike anything that Lyndahl Gee ever (as far as we know) wrote. (Gee's prefatory note, by denying any relationship between his real mother and the character Meg, could actually be taken to suggest this by a kind of analogy.) It is, instead, very like a novel by Maurice Gee. Indeed, it *is* a novel by Maurice Gee! Through *Meg*, then, Gee has created a fictional mother who, unlike Lyndahl, is equal to and literally indistinguishable from himself. It is in this sense that he overcomes her, fulfilling the Oedipal purpose of Bloom's 'strong poet' in relation to the literary father. It may be relevant that Maurice Gee's own initials, 'M. G.' (which are attached to his author's note and so actually face the first page of the novel) are suggestive of Meg's name.[35]

At the same time, Meg's autobiography reveals that she has had to change in order to become the writer whose work we are reading. This is not, I think, because her early writing as she recalls it was essentially flawed. Indeed, the writing she entered into 'passionately' when suffering from homesickness at school in California (her evocation of 'the traction engine, chugging across the paddock, pulling the cookhouse behind it', 35) is surely promising in terms of Maurice Gee's standards; while her juvenile poem from the same time, 'A Mother's Love' (36) – a poem that could be dismissed as derivative and sentimental – is convincingly interpreted by the mature Meg as a symbolic projection of the intense insecurity she was suffering when she wrote it. Meg's early limitations lay rather in her fatal tendency to mythologise reality (in her mind, that is, and not necessarily in anything she wrote) instead of registering it truly. Thus the mature Meg has come to abandon what she now derides as her 'Capitals' ('my Father as a Giant Among Men' and the like; *Meg* 15) – the mythologising that is evident in Lyndahl's published stories and which, according to Gee, also characterised her oral retellings of family history.[36] Meg's childish demonisation of her brother Oliver for going to war despite their father's pacifism was a symptom of that 'capitalisation':

> It remained for me to declare him no longer a Plumb, which I did, secretly, in my playhouse by the creek, kneeling in an Islamic pose, tinkling a little hand-bell three times and intoning words of banishment: 'Out into the Darkness Oliver Plumb, we banish thee from Light.' (*Meg* 42)

Here Meg anticipates George Plumb's sinful banishment of his son Alfred. Most damagingly for Meg's own life, she allowed Jackson Gregory's popular romance, *Bab of the Blackwoods*, to colour (falsely, of course) her relationship with Fergus, so that, thinking herself 'in love', she married him. The negative consequences of that marriage saturate the novel.[37] The fact that the mature Meg is a different person, with a very different point of view, is always evident in her accounts of her earlier self – and in her wry mental response to anything inauthentic in the behaviour of others, too. For instance, having recorded that (after Robert's burial) their brother Emerson 'scattered a handful of earth on the coffin', she adds, 'He had probably seen it done in the movies' (*Meg* 248). The writer who offers such a comment is very different from the girl who identified with Jackson Gregory's Bab. The reader is made witness to the displacement of someone with the mythologising instincts of Lyndahl by someone with the clear-sightedness of Maurice Gee.[38] The process is gradual and fraught. Meg's somewhat unsettled style ('I want very much to be quit of that metaphor') could be taken to suggest that the process is also incomplete – or, rather, that Maurice Gee's ideal does after all allow for a degree of stylistic inconsistency.[39]

In the third paragraph of *Meg* – where it first emerges that what we are reading is an autobiography – Meg remembers the criticisms to which her son Raymond has subjected her:

> I gathered my things and made them ready on the back verandah: sandsoap, brush, disinfectant, half a dozen cloths, window-cleaner, all in the bucket; mop at attention by the rail, with its fringe of sun-dried white hair on its brow. No – I must avoid these fancies, Raymond says they spoil me as a writer, he calls them coy and clever and tells me I must be plain or fall into self-regard and falsity. I'll leave this one (I rather like it, that's the puzzle) as an example of what I must steer clear of. (*Meg* 9)

In what her son sees as her 'falsity', Meg might be identified with Lyndahl Gee, while the son whose critical voice she remembers sounds like Lyndahl's son, Maurice Gee. It will emerge, however, that the critical Raymond is not a writer (or, at least, not a successful one), while Meg is – or, more accurately, has become – one. There is a sense in which the fictional scenario reverses, as in a mirror, its biographical counterpart. (One might even say that the fictional and true situations reflect each other like the two sides of Lyndahl Gee's own 'double unit'.) In reality, the writer is not the mother, but the son, Maurice Gee. And the voice that lingers so insistently in Maurice Gee's memory is (again, in reality) that of Maurice Gee's mother, Lyndahl Chapple Gee.[40]

5 WRITING HORIZONTALLY AND VERTICALLY
in *The World Around the Corner* and *Hostel Girl*

Louise Clark

When Maurice Gee began writing fiction for children in the 1970s, he made a deliberate decision to write something completely different from his adult novels:

> I wanted to get away from the explorations of guilt and delving into psyches I'd been doing in my writing for adults. I wanted, for a time, to write horizontally, rather than vertically – do open-cast mining, if I can put it another way, rather than deep-shaft mining. For that reason I decided to write what I call fantasy/adventure – put the emphasis on movement, develop narrative pace, tell a story as a story pure and simple.[1]

This statement from Gee's often quoted 2002 Margaret Mahy Medal acceptance speech (subsequently published as 'Creeks and kitchens') provides a useful approach to his children's books, as well as revealing his underlying assumptions about the nature of children's literature. Gee's views on the differences between fiction for adults and children were typical of those of the period, and they correspond closely to the 'generally accepted distinctions' identified by Myles McDowell in 1973:

> There are observable differences: children's books are generally shorter; they tend to favour an active rather than a passive treatment, with dialogue and incident rather than description and introspection; child protagonists are the rule; conventions are much used; the story develops within a clear-cut moral schematism which much adult fiction ignores; children's books tend to be optimistic rather than depressive; language is child-oriented; plots are of a distinctive order; probability is frequently disregarded; and one could go on endlessly talking of magic, and fantasy, and simplicity, and adventure.[2]

Gee's first five books for children – *Under the Mountain*, *The World Around the Corner* and the O trilogy: *The Halfmen of O*, *The Priests of Ferris* and *Motherstone* – are fantasy/adventure stories that clearly conform to Gee's definition of 'horizontal' writing, and the conventions noted by McDowell. The fantasy form appealed to Gee as being as far removed as possible from the serious realistic fiction he was producing for adults. (Virginia Haviland has referred to the 'obvious and arresting' fact that 'those authors for adults who have written an occasional – or one – book for children have quite generally turned to fantasy.')[3] The fact that fantasy was a popular and well-respected genre in children's literature, and that a number of distinguished contemporary children's authors were writing in this field, was possibly an added incentive for Gee to choose this form. The books of Alan Garner, Britain's foremost fantasy writer of the 1960s and 1970s, provided Gee with his initial inspiration, and he decided to transplant some of Garner's ideas to a New Zealand setting.

In his five early fantasies Gee followed many of the conventions of fantasy writing for children: the struggle between good and evil; the child protagonist/s who alone can avert a cosmic disaster of which adults remain unaware; comparatively shallow characterisation; and an emphasis on action and excitement. Gee's fantasy novels, in fact, exemplify the 'horizontal' style of storytelling, in that the emphasis is on narrative pace, the plots are straightforward, events are presented in chronological order and there is limited character development. This does not mean that the characters are bland or one-dimensional, merely that they are secondary to the plot and there is no 'delving into [their] psyches'. As Gee explained in an interview with Brian Boyd in 1991:

> My concern is to keep the narrative pace fast, to have events piling up, to put the characters into dangerous situations and then get them out, to have lots of chases and narrow escapes – and when a rest is needed I do a landscape. It's fun for me and fun for the readers. But this is a horizontal, straight-line sort of storytelling, nice and simple. For adults I do something different. I shift about in time, to begin with, I put part against part to generate tension and create balance ... I spend a lot of time in people's minds at different levels – so this is not horizontal, straight-line stuff, it's quite complex – the vertical shaft goes down, the narrative doubles back, the writer is open to everything and the possibilities are hugely extended. It's a basic difference. This sort of thing can be done for children too, but I'm not the person to do it.[4]

While *Under the Mountain, The World Around the Corner* and the *O* trilogy lack the complexity and psychological insights of the adult novels, Gee is being disingenuous in dismissing the storytelling as 'nice and simple', for the books are very tightly plotted, the 'dangerous situations, chases and narrow escapes' are skilfully crafted to create maximum tension, and the landscapes are expertly executed.

The publication of *The Fire-Raiser* in 1986, however, marked a change in direction for Gee, as this and his four subsequent children's books – *The Champion, The Fat Man, Orchard Street* and *Hostel Girl* – are realistic novels with a historical setting. They are closer to Gee's novels for adults in content and style; in other words, they are more 'vertical', and have become progressively more so with each book. Gee's most recent junior novels, the *Salt* trilogy (*Salt, Gool* and *The Limping Man*, published between 2007 and 2010), return to the fantasy genre of his earliest books for children but resemble the later realistic novels in that the protagonists are older and their characters are drawn in greater depth. In this chapter I want to investigate the notion of 'horizontal' and 'vertical' as it applies to Gee's books for children by examining two books: Gee's shortest and simplest fantasy, *The World Around the Corner*, published in 1980, the most 'horizontal' of his books; and *Hostel Girl*, which appeared in 1999 and was described by Gee as a 'psychological thriller'[5] for young adults, which is the most 'vertical'.

Writing horizontally: *The World Around the Corner*

The World Around the Corner, like its predecessor, *Under the Mountain*, is a fantasy, but it differs from that book – and indeed Gee's subsequent fiction for children – in being written for a much younger age group, around seven to 10 years. As such, the story is comparatively short (72 pages divided into nine brief chapters); the language is simpler; and it is the only one of Gee's books to be published with illustrations. The central character, Caroline, is eight, compared with the 11-year-old twins in *Under the Mountain,* 12-year-old Susan in *The Halfmen of O* (she is 13 in the two succeeding volumes of the *O* trilogy), and the teenage protagonists of Gee's later realistic books for children, who are aged 14 and older. The theme, as in Gee's other fantasies, is good versus evil, but it is a milder and less frightening version; Gee himself described it as 'a gentler tale'.⁶ While the villains of *Under the Mountain*, the terrifying and repulsive Wilberforces, are completely original creations, as are the Halfmen in the *O* trilogy, in *The World Around the Corner* Gee uses traditional fairy-tale characters – elves, goblins and dragons – which are presumably more familiar to young readers (and therefore possibly less frightening).

The story begins with Caroline's discovery of a battered old pair of glasses hidden in a box of books at her father's second-hand shop in Nelson. When she tries them on she realises at once that they are magic: they make everything look brighter and let her see things that are not normally visible. In fact, the glasses come from 'the world around the corner' – a parallel world which is divided between peaceful, nature-loving elves and aggressive goblins, the Grimbles. The elves' half of the world is a beautiful place of mountains, waterfalls, lakes and trees, while the Grimbles have turned their half into a desert: 'They have cut down all the tress, levelled the hills, dammed up all the rivers. They live in great walled cities. Their world is one of smoke and poison and darkness.'⁷ Each year the Grimbles send a dragon to try and break down the magic wall between the two halves, and the elves' champion, Moon-girl or Sun-boy, must fight it single-handed, with the aid of a pair of magic glasses, which alone enable them to see the invisible dragon. Each year, the glasses need to be brought to our world to be recharged by the warmth of the sun. Two elves, in the guise of an elderly couple, Mr and Mrs Gates, bring the glasses through a gateway situated on Nelson's Botanical Hill, but they are followed by two Grimbles who are desperate to destroy the glasses. Caroline undertakes to hide the glasses and deliver them to Moon-girl, a task which she accomplishes successfully, though not without some adventures on the way.

Gee does not allow Caroline to indulge in improbable heroics, and her activities are all quite plausible. Shadowing Mr Gates to find out why he is looking for the magic glasses, hiding the glasses in her hut, and escaping down the river in an inner tube when the Grimbles discover the hiding place and pursue her, may not compare with Theo and Rachel's terrifying encounters with the Wilberforces in terms of dramatic impact, but they are exciting adventures which are quite in keeping with the heroine's age (and the age of the intended readers) and with the demands of the plot. The plausibility of Caroline's actions balances the more improbable magical elements of the story.

The plot, while it is ingenious and exciting, lacks the tension and violence of the books for older children and the overall mood is more optimistic. In contrast to *Under the Mountain*, which preceded this story, the threat is not to Caroline's own world, but to the unseen 'world around the corner', and there will be no adverse effect on the 'real' world even if the Grimbles succeed in their quest. Nor is Caroline in any real danger from the Grimbles, who appear in the real world as a man and his rather dim-witted son; although they pursue her, they never catch her, and she manages to outwit them quite easily. Compared with the foul-smelling slug-shaped Wilberforces, Mr Grimble is positively benign, especially as he is described primarily in terms of food: 'A man came from the front of the shop, walking in an oozy sort of way, like flowing malt. He had an oily face and puffed out cheeks and eyes of a treacle colour' (12). Later he is described as having 'fat buttery hands' and a 'treacly voice', although he is obviously evil because, when Caroline observes him though the magic glasses, his eyes are no longer 'molasses colour' but blood-red, glowing like burning coals (16). The younger Grimble is described in similar terms, with eyes 'like fire and his skin yellow as butter' (56).

Gee had drawn much of his inspiration for *Under the Mountain* from Alan Garner's *The Weirdstone of Brisingamen*. In Garner's book the fantasy is grounded firmly in a recognisable Cheshire landscape, and Gee realised he could do something similar in a New Zealand setting:

> I thought I would like to attempt what Garner manages to do brilliantly in that book: place the child characters in dreadful danger from some supernatural or monstrous thing, while leaving them in their natural everyday world with no way of making adults see the danger. It's a situation that generates enormous tension, and generates story endlessly.[8]

After the success of *Under the Mountain*, Gee used this formula again in *The World Around the Corner*, and it seems likely that he drew as well on Garner's later fantasy *Elidor*, in which four children living in the 'real' world must guard magical objects that are crucial to the survival of another world. Garner was not the only influence, however;

the fantasy elements of *The World Around the Corner* bear more than a passing resemblance to *The Hobbit* and *The Lord of the Rings*. For example, the 'good' side is represented by green-clad tree-dwelling elves who live in a beautiful land of woods and waterfalls, while the 'baddies' are evil goblins who have already turned their half of the world into a polluted wilderness and seek to do the same to the elves' half. The elves are attacked by a dragon (which appears initially as a mushroom-shaped cloud of poisonous gas, a reference to nuclear weapons which Gee develops further in *Motherstone*). But these similarities to Tolkien are not overwhelming; and, unlike the heroes and heroines of other fantasies of this type, such as the Narnia books, *Elidor* and Gee's later *O* trilogy, Caroline does not go to the other world she has to save – she sees it only in a dream – so the emphasis is on the real world rather than the fantasy one.

In traditional high fantasy, the child protagonist must use a special weapon or talisman to overcome the forces of evil in the alternative world. Gee departs from tradition here, though, to the extent that it is not Caroline but Moon-girl who must use the magic object. The choice of object is original, too: rather than a ring of power, a grail or a sword, the magic weapon is a pair of battered glasses, old and rusty with a cracked lens. Once again Gee may have been influenced by *Elidor*, as in that book the magical spear, sword, bowl and golden stone that the children bring back from Elidor do not appear as heroic objects in the real world (the spear looks like a length of iron railing, the sword two laths nailed together, the bowl appears as an old cracked cup and the stone is a plain brick). The glasses Caroline finds may not look very special, but they appeal to her initially because they are child-sized and therefore fit her properly, unlike the other, more attractive pairs she finds in the box. Once she puts them on, it is obvious that they are magic, and everything she looks at is clear and brightly coloured. Possibly there is a parallel with *The Wizard of Oz*, where special glasses transform the Emerald City into a green and magical place. There is also a certain irony in the fact that glasses, which in the real world are often associated with weakness, are a source of power in the fantasy world; a sign of difference/disability becomes a sign of strength.

Because this is a fantasy, the good side naturally wins: Caroline saves the glasses from the Grimbles and gives them to Moon-girl, who defeats the dragon. *The World Around the Corner* is the only one of Gee's fantasies in which the victory is achieved without a cost. Gee believes that there is always a price to be paid and that characters should not emerge from their adventures unscathed – hence the deaths of Ricky in *Under the Mountain* and Marna in *The Halfmen of O*, and the return of humans to a primitive state in *Motherstone*.[9] In *The World Around the Corner*, possibly because of its younger target audience, Caroline's adventures have no negative consequences for her. However, Moon-girl's conquest of the dragon is not a final victory, as each year the dragon must be fought anew, and each year it is stronger and harder to kill. Evil, externalised as the dragon, may have been defeated, but it is only a temporary respite.

One of the distinguishing features of 'horizontal' writing identified by Gee is the relatively superficial characterisation of the protagonists; what he terms 'open-cast' rather than 'deep-shaft' mining. Although *The World Around the Corner* is told from Caroline's perspective, it does not analyse her thoughts and feelings; there is no 'delving into her psyche'. Caroline is presented as a solitary, bookish, daydreaming little girl, and though these may seem unlikely attributes for the heroine of an adventure story, it is these very qualities that enable her to recognise the magic glasses and deliver them safely to Moon-girl. Her imagination is furnished with stories about magic and fantasy quests – 'She dreamed of castles made of ivory and pearl, of flying carpets and genii and dwarfs and dragons and children lost in the wood' (*WAC* 12) – and she is able to draw on what she has read for guidance during her adventure. Gee establishes enough of Caroline's character – her imagination, her determination, her resourcefulness – to make her a plausible and likeable protagonist, but, as befits this type of story, the action takes precedence over character development and the writing remains horizontal.

The portrayal of Mr and Mrs Gates and the Grimbles is even more horizontal; they have no distinctive characteristics, and are merely representatives of 'good' and 'bad', which are depicted in this book as polar opposites. *The World Around the Corner* has the typical fantasy theme of a struggle between good and evil, and the division between the two is clearly marked. In the 'real' world, the good characters, Mr and Mrs Gates, live with their golden cats in a pretty cottage with a lovely garden and neatly furnished rooms filled with vases of flowers and wonderful paintings. The Grimbles, on the other hand, live in a house on rotting piles in a weedy section, they drive an ugly black car which smells like old mildewy clothes, and they have two black cats with 'hating eyes' (30), which receive messages from an ugly beetle and a rat. In the other world the contrast is even more marked: the beautiful landscape of 'mountains, waterfalls, lovely streams and valleys' (37) where peaceful elves live in tree houses on the shores of lakes, is contrasted with the desert world of 'smoke and poison and darkness' (38) where the Grimbles make weapons and breed their dragons.

One of the other features of 'horizontal' writing identified by Gee is to 'do a landscape whenever a rest is needed'. *The World Around the Corner* has a number of detailed descriptions of its Nelson setting, such as the view of the city from Caroline's house (accurately depicted in the accompanying drawing by Gary Hebley reproduced on the cover of this book), Queens Gardens, the Maitai River and the area around Botanical Hill. (These last two also feature prominently in Gee's other children's book with a Nelson setting, *The Fire-Raiser*.) Gee was living in Nelson at the time he wrote these books and it is clear that he is recreating familiar territory. One of his intentions in writing for children was to use 'settings New Zealand children would recognise, with New Zealand the most important place in the world, as it is for the children who live here'.[10] In *The World Around the Corner*, as in his other fiction for children, Gee provides young New Zealand readers with authentic and recognisable landscapes. The descriptions of the landscape are there not just to vary the narrative pace, however; the settings also have an important role in the plot. For example Botanical Hill – which, as Gee points out, is the geographic centre of New Zealand – is a suitably symbolic spot for a gateway between the worlds; and the river – which, as in all of Gee's books, signifies adventure and danger – provides an escape route for Caroline when she is being pursued by the Grimbles. The reality of the landscapes helps to anchor the fantasy elements of the story. Caroline may be wearing magic glasses made by elves, but the river she is being carried down in her inner tube is real and readily identifiable:

> Just as bad was the thought that she would be swept out to sea. She would race down under the bridges of the town, and out past the ships tied up at the wharves, and past the lighthouse and through the gap between the boulder bank and Haulashore Island, and be carried out to the open sea, where, she thought, a shark would probably eat her. (*WAC* 58)

Unlike several characters in *The Fire-Raiser*, who either drown or nearly drown in the Maitai River, Caroline survives her adventure unscathed.

Concrete details make it easy for young readers to visualise the scenery in which the action is taking place:

> She crawled under the branches of the fig tree and started down the track which led to her hut. She went through fennel and a forest of barberry trees and made herself thin to edge by their thorns. Then came the old-man's-beard, the creeper that was taking over the hillside ... She crawled under it as though under a blanket. (*WAC* 19)

Gee's descriptions of interiors are equally graphic, in particular Caroline's hut under the pine tree, and her father's shop – both the front part selling antiques, 'old and beautiful things made of brass and crystal and coloured glass and wood with grain like waves in the sea or clouds in the sky' (2), and the tatty part at the back selling junk and old furniture, 'old sofas with broken springs, and radios shaped like church doorways, and washing machines with bent lids; and tables and bed-ends and sewing machines and pick axes and rolls of hose and shelves of books' (3).

The imagined landscapes are vividly depicted too, particularly the brief but evocative description of the 'world around the corner' as Caroline sees it in her dream:

> There was a valley and a stream and a waterfall tumbling over mossy rocks. Slender trees with trunks mottled green and silver swayed in a breeze. Their leaves threw a light cool shade on the valley floor. Small houses perched in the branches. They were lacy and leafy, elf houses, green and blue and silver. (*WAC* 68)

The valley with the stream and trees is almost an idealised version of Caroline's real world, with her hut among the trees transformed into an elf house. However, Gee makes it appealing and magical by the use of connotative language – slender, cool, light, lacy, leafy. The colours of the elf houses, green and blue and silver, are cool and soothing shades that mirror the colour of the water and the trees. Gary Hebley's drawing faithfully reflects this scene, and his other illustrations (one to each chapter) help to establish the Nelson setting, and reinforce the fact that this is a book for younger readers.

Many of Gee's novels – for adults and for children – share common themes and motifs; as Gee has commented, 'It's inevitable that what I am and my beliefs will somehow get onto the page and be kind of a shadow behind the story.'[11] *The World Around the Corner* may be for young readers, but it shares some of the serious concerns of the other children's books and the adult novels, such as pollution and the quest for power. The predominant theme, however – and one which recurs in many of Gee's other books, notably *Meg*, *Prowlers* and *Blindsight* – is that of sight and seeing, embodied here in both Caroline's glasses which she must wear to correct her defective vision, and the magic glasses that allow the wearer to see things which would otherwise be invisible.

The description of the way the magic glasses transform the picture on the train book cover is one of the more memorable passages in *The World Around the Corner*:

> On the cover was a picture of a steam engine coming through a cutting. The driver was leaning out his window blowing a whistle. It was a faded old picture. The colours were bleached. The driver's face was just a blob. It was impossible to tell whether the passenger looking out the window was a little girl or an old woman.
>
> Caroline stared at it a moment. She memorised all the browns and greys of it, the faded greens and yellows. Then she put the glasses on. At once the colours came to life, the details took sharp edges. The black little engine, trimmed with green and numbered in shining brass 275, puffed through the yellow cutting sending up clouds of cottonwool steam. The smiling, red-cheeked driver leaned from his cab. His eyes were twinkling blue. The passenger in the carriage was a girl, wearing an old-fashioned blue bonnet tied with a ribbon under her chin. She was licking an ice-cream. There was even a rabbit Caroline had not seen before, sitting on the bank with one ear pricked up and one flopping down, watching the train go by. There was a mouse in the grass, and a blue and white butterfly on a

leaf. And far away, through the gap of the cutting, was a fair on a beach, children and donkeys and red and white tents, and small white waves breaking on the sand. A ship was far out at sea. (9)

Gee stresses the contrast between the drab and featureless picture visible to the naked eye and the vibrant colours and enticing details of the same picture seen though the magic glasses. The transformative power of the lens may be seen as metaphor for the way a writer uses the lens of imagination to transform seemingly ordinary aspects of the real world into story. Surely it is no coincidence that the details of the picture are archetypical storybook elements – the little black engine and its smiling, red-cheeked, twinkling-eyed driver; the little girl setting out on a journey; the friendly little animals (rabbit, mouse and butterfly); the beach; the fair with its red and white tents and donkeys; and the ship out at sea. Gee returned to the idea of glasses that reveal details visible only with their aid in later books; for example, the telescope that allows Phil to view the night sky and spy on the Marwicks in *The Fire-Raiser*; and the magnifying glass in *Prowlers*, which Tup Ogier calls 'my truth-teller'.[12]

The idea of glasses that show 'more than the eye could ever see' (*WAC* 9) is an appealing one, particularly to a child like Caroline who is visually impaired and has to wear glasses to see properly. Caroline's poor eyesight puts her out of sync with many of her peers, and with conventional adult ways of looking at the world; and her glasses operate as a useful image for the way she sees things differently from those around her. Caroline is an observant child who undoubtedly sees more of what is going on around her than the adults do. She is the only one who is aware of the good versus evil struggle taking place on a fantasy level, but even in the real world she sees things – such as Mr Grimble's attempt to steal the glasses, and the coercion of Mr Gates during the auction – which the other characters do not notice. Caroline's choice of vantage points that allow her to observe rather than participate, such as the mattress loft above the second-hand shop, and her hut with its view of the city and the river, has parallels in the adult novels. Russell Haley has commented on Gee's 'obsessive interest in a private place from which one can view, voyeuristically, the world', and sees it as 'an unconscious metaphor for the role of writer/observer'.[13]

Caroline does not rely entirely on her physical vision, however, with or without the magic glasses; she has an insight that enables her to see beneath the surface in an intellectual and emotional sense and to grasp things instinctively. There is a certain irony in the fact that, although she is visually dependent on her glasses, she can see perfectly well with her 'inner eye'. As soon as she discovers the rusty glasses in the box she knows instinctively that they are magic, and what to do with them. When she first sees Mr Grimble, for example, 'She knew at once he was after her glasses. Mrs Gates had hidden them, this man was trying to find them. She did not question it. There were things she just knew.' (12) Similarly, she 'just knows' that she has to look after the glasses for 'someone who needed them desperately' and that 'her job was to keep them safe'. (20) Luckily she also 'knows' about Mr Grimble – 'He was wicked, of course, but something told her he was not very clever' (21) – so she is able to cope with hiding the glasses and delivering them to Moon-girl without too much stress. It is fortunate that Caroline has this knowledge as, unlike Theo and Rachel in *Under the Mountain*, she has no Mr Jones telling her what to do, and most of the time she acts on her own initiative.

Reading, books and storytelling are other recurring motifs in Gee's books. Bill Manhire has noted that 'Gee's novels are full of "literature". His characters tell stories and listen to stories.'[14] Many of the adult novels are about characters telling stories, and the same is true of *The World Around the Corner*, which begins with Caroline imagining herself in a magic land, and ends with the sentence, 'She had a wonderful story for her friend.' (72) Gee's storytellers are generally readers as well, and Manhire refers to 'the many characters who retire to their dens – to lose themselves in reading or writing or thinking'.[15] Caroline, as already mentioned, is a keen reader, and both of her 'dens' – the mattress loft and her hut – contain books. She is depicted as an imaginative and well-read child (her mother is, after all, a librarian) and she entertains herself by thinking about her everyday life in storybook terms. The book opens with Caroline fantasising about a summer rain-shower: 'It was like being in some magic land, she thought, where rain was warm, and the trees had voices and the mountains went down into the ground instead of into the sky.' (1) When she goes into her father's shop the fantasy continues; she makes her way among the antiques 'like someone in a jungle filled with brightly-coloured poisonous snakes' (2), and her father in his office is 'like a pirate sitting in his cave of treasures' (3). Caroline is not particularly surprised, therefore, when she finds the glasses, and immediately suspects they 'might be magic glasses in disguise – the way in fairy stories princesses sometimes dressed up as beggar maids' (8). Significantly, her realisation that Mr Grimble is looking for the glasses is described in terms of books: 'There were things she just knew, they came to you like coloured pictures in a book you thought had only black and white ones' (12).

Other themes that continually reappear in Gee's books are the environment and the threat of pollution, as epitomised by the Grimbles who have 'cut down all the trees, levelled the hills, dammed up all the rivers' and turned their half of the world into a desert (38). It is hardly coincidental that Moon-girl, the elves' champion, is dressed all in green. The Grimbles' dragon takes the form of poisonous fog in the shape of a mushroom cloud, in an obvious reference to nuclear weapons. As Bill Manhire points out, for Gee: 'The pollution of the natural world – whether by mud-wallowing Wilberforces or factory-building halfmen [or, indeed, Grimbles] – is a recurring theme, and is often an outward sign of inner pollution.'[16] The 'inner pollution' of the Grimbles takes the form of aggression against the elves and a desire to conquer them. The quest for power and domination is another theme that Gee explores in later books, such as the *O* trilogy, *The Fat Man*, and some of his adult novels.

These themes, however, do not weigh down what is essentially a very entertaining story for young readers. Gee wrote *The World Around the Corner* 'quickly and easily and with great enjoyment',[17] and that enjoyment is evident in the writing. Gee's two daughters were young at the time, and he is surely writing for (and being inspired by) them, as the story abounds in details which little girls would love: Caroline's mattress cave, complete with 'half-a-dozen books and a torch to read by, and a bag of plums, and a mirror and comb set' (11); the sparkly glasses with the red and blue stones that Caroline finds again at the end of her adventures; and the contents of Caroline's treasure box:

> She lifted out the shell necklace from Tahiti, the stone troll with rope hair from Sweden, her first pair of specs in their case, her kaleidoscope, her red marker pen, the little prayer book that had belonged to her grandmother, with a sachet of lavender tied to its string book-mark. (20)

The World Around the Corner is the slightest of Gee's books, but its various elements – the fantasy conflict between good and evil; the realistic story about a likeable and imaginative young heroine; the vivid picture of a unique corner of New Zealand; and the underlying environmental concerns – come together in an expertly crafted story which satisfies on many levels.

Writing vertically: *Hostel Girl*

When Gee turned to realistic fiction for children he modified his way of writing, and his historical novels have gradually moved closer to the adult novels in structure and content, and have become more 'vertical'. Unlike the fantasies, which are child-centred and action-driven, Gee's realistic novels for children have become progressively more character-driven; plots are dependent on relationships, and adult characters assume a greater role. While these books still have narrative pace and dramatic events, character development and relationships have equal weight. In many cases, what is happening between the adult characters is more important than what the young protagonists are doing; and the child protagonists themselves have become progressively older. In his historical novels for children, Gee addresses a number of major social, moral and cultural issues in the context of realistically evoked historical and physical settings. Although he has achieved this without sacrificing plot or narrative pace, these elements are not as important as they were in his earlier books. Gee has described the historical novels as 'proper novels', and said that 'while writing them I was engaged, to some extent, in deep-shaft mining not open-cast mining'.[18] The extent to which the writing is 'vertical' rather than 'horizontal' distinguishes Gee's historical novels for children from the earlier fantasies. Gee himself acknowledges that these novels are much less concerned with simple narrative pace:

> While several of them can be described as thrillers, or even psychological thrillers, I don't think of them as being in that genre because there's a much fuller development of character in them, in the adult characters and the child alike. They're meant to involve on a deeper level.[19]

In Gee's fantasies, the emphasis is on action rather than character. Readers have access to the thoughts of the main child protagonists but not of the other characters, so they remain comparatively undeveloped. While the historical novels have strong elements of mystery and suspense and a skilful build-up of tension, as much importance is attached to the characters and their relationships with each other as to the suspense of the plot. In *The Fire-Raiser, The Champion, The Fat Man, Orchard Street* and *Hostel Girl* much of the interest lies in the psychological study of the adult characters; and there is always a sense that there is more going on than the child protagonists understand. In most cases the action revolves around the activities of the adult characters, who are presented in some depth. Several of the adult characters – Edgar Marwick, Herbert Muskie and Errol Parkinson – are psychotic; and Gee successfully 'delves into their psyches' to reveal the motives for their reprehensible behaviour, so they evoke pity as well as condemnation from the reader. The child protagonists are generally drawn into the affairs of the adult characters, and do not necessarily comprehend everything that is going on; however, they learn enough from their experiences to gain in maturity and self-knowledge, and Gee conveys this through writing vertically to reveal the changes that occur in the characters as the stories progress.

Hostel Girl is similar to *The World Around the Corner* in that they are both told from the point of view of a central female character; but where *The World Around the Corner* is a fantasy with a fairly simple good versus evil plot, *Hostel Girl* is a historical novel with a complex plot which blurs the boundaries between right and wrong. *The World Around the Corner* is a gentle story for young children; *Hostel Girl* is 'a young adult thriller' with a number of disturbing and violent elements.[20] *The World Around the Corner* shares the horizontal characteristics of Gee's other fantasies in that the narrative pace is fast, and the characterisation is fairly shallow, whereas in *Hostel Girl* the writing is much more vertical. Although it also has a fast narrative pace and its share of 'chases and dangerous situations', the focus of *Hostel Girl* is not just on these dramatic events but on the development of Ailsa's character, and the way she grows in maturity and understanding through her experiences and through her relationships with Calum, Gloria and Errol.

The protagonist of *Hostel Girl*, Ailsa, is 14 and no longer a child. She is starting to become interested in boyfriends and make-up, and is becoming aware of her own sexuality and the complex relationships between the sexes. The story revolves around a number of these relationships, from the tentative adolescent love affair of Ailsa and Calum to the obsessive and ultimately destructive feelings Errol has for Gloria. Gee described *Hostel Girl* as 'a young adult thriller', and there are plenty of thrills in the plot, which concerns a stalker who is sending anonymous and increasingly menacing letters to Ailsa's glamorous roommate Gloria.[21] Ailsa suspects that the stalker is Errol, the neighbour of her new friend Calum, and her attempts to unmask him involve her in frightening situations, such as a bicycle chase through the dark streets, pursued by the stalker she has been trying to follow. Even more chilling is Calum and Ailsa's clandestine visit to Errol's house, where they discover a room with boarded-up windows and Gloria's name embroidered on the pillow. The story culminates in Errol's knife-point kidnapping of Gloria, and a subsequent pursuit that results in Errol's death under the wheels of a train.

The characters of *Hostel Girl* are much more complex than those of *The World Around the Corner*. Ailsa and Caroline are both solitary only children who observe rather than participate in the lives of the adults around them. However, Ailsa at 14 is considerably more self-aware and introspective than eight-year-old Caroline, and is able to analyse her feelings: 'She felt her troubles like a black cloud rolling over her; but heavier than a cloud; pressing her flat like a medicine ball' (108). Ailsa is an admirable character: intelligent, honest and loyal to her friends; but although she appears confident and even brash to outsiders, she is aware of her own inadequacies when confronted with adult emotions and situations outside her experience. For example, when Gloria thinks she may be pregnant, Ailsa does not know what to say: 'She felt large and ugly, crashing around where she should be delicate ... Ailsa felt her mind shrink. Everything she might answer went away; and even in the small part that was left she could find nothing' (99). Ailsa is presented in greater depth and breadth than Caroline, and she is shown as changing as a result of her experiences. Her initial dislike of Calum turns to affection as she gets to know him better; and, as a result of her involvement in Gloria's affairs, she is much more mature at the end of the book. The character of Ailsa is sufficiently developed that Gee was able to use her as the protagonist of his adult novel *Ellie and the Shadow Man* virtually unchanged. Though Gee does not 'delve into her psyche' as deeply as he does with Ellie, the treatment of her character is considerably more vertical than that of Caroline.

The other characters in *Hostel Girl* are given a more vertical treatment than those in *The World Around the Corner*, too. Calum, Gloria and Errol all play important roles and are presented as credible and well-rounded personalities. Calum is embittered by the polio that has left him with a limp, and by his mother's refusal to accept his disability; but his relationship with Ailsa alters his perspective and allows him to come to terms with his situation. Gloria, whose brittle, sophisticated exterior masks her vulnerability, also changes as a result of the traumatic experiences she undergoes. Although she is scarred both mentally and physically, she is able to look forward to a happier future with her sister in Auckland. Gloria reappears in *Ellie and the Shadow Man*, with her name changed to Dolores, but otherwise unaltered. Psychopathic Errol Parkinson is quite unlike the villains of the horizontal fantasies, who are simply embodiments of evil. With his repertoire of accents and costumes, and his house filled with pictures of pure and dreamy girls, he is a far more complex character. He lives in a fantasy world in which he constantly changes roles – a movie star with cigarette and a panama hat, a perfect civil servant in a grey suit, a stalker in a long coat and black wig – until the death of his wife and the revelation that Gloria is not the pure young girl of his dreams shatter his delusions. Although Errol's obsession with Gloria incites him to criminal violence, Gee presents him as pitiable rather than simply depraved. Minor characters in *Hostel Girl* are also given greater depth and complexity than those in the more horizontal fantasies; for example Ron Stack, the hostel boiler man, who sits on a sack of coal daintily drinking tea from a bone-china cup but who is roused to heroism when Gloria is attacked; and Miss Cotter, who suffers from a stomach growth and believes that juvenile delinquency is caused by swimming pools. Gee suggests that these characters have much more going on in their lives (and psyches) than Ailsa realises.

Hostel Girl, like *The World Around the Corner*, is set in a real place with which Gee was very familiar, in this case the Hutt Valley, but the setting has a different role from the 'horizontal' landscapes of *The World Around the Corner*. While the Nelson landscape is convincingly portrayed and plays an important role in the story, the plot could conceivably be transplanted to another setting without substantial alterations. The plot of *Hostel Girl*, on the other hand, could not occur anywhere else, as it depends entirely on its specific physical and temporal setting – Upper Hutt in 1955. Although this period lacks the dramatic historical events (the two world wars, the Depression and the watersiders' dispute) that Gee used as the backgrounds of his previous historical novels for children, the 1950s provided an ideal setting for the type of social history he wished to write. As critic John Stephens observes:

> Since practically and traditionally the function of setting in fiction is to convey atmosphere, attitudes and values, it is inevitable that writers of historical fiction, obliged as they are to pay careful attention to setting, would also use it as part of the process of signification ... Setting is thus more than mere background, but an element that contributes to making a character act in a particular way.[22]

It is clear that the actions of many of the characters in *Hostel Girl* are strongly influenced by the 'atmosphere, attitudes and values' of the setting. Not only was the 1950s a period when gender roles and issues of morality were more clearly defined than the present, it was a time when these topics were at the forefront of public consciousness. Historian Michael King considered that:

> The only apparent interruption to the even tenor of New Zealand life in the 1950s was the atmosphere of moral outrage and panic that surrounded hearings of the 'Special Committee on Moral Delinquency in Children and Adolescents' and the release of the committee's Mazengarb Report in 1954. The inquiry was launched as a result of police and newspaper allegations of adolescent sexual activity in Wellington's Hutt Valley ... Its thrust was to confirm existing social and moral values. It laid the blame for loose sexual behaviour on the absence of working mothers from the home and on 'oversexed or morally degraded' young women, who allowed young men to have their way with them.[23]

The Mazengarb Report (which derived its name from Oswald Mazengarb, the chairman of the Special Committee) provides the circumstances for a novel in which sexual behaviour and morality are major themes, and which explores both the role of working mothers and the consequences for young women who 'allowed young men to have their way with them'.[24] The report devotes several pages to a narrative of 'The Hutt Valley Cases', including testimony from a 15-year-old girl who was a member of a 'Milk Bar Gang' which met 'mostly for sex purposes'; and a table showing numbers of boys and girls involved in occurrences of 'sexual misconduct' in 1952 and 1954.[25] There are many references in *Hostel Girl* to the Mazengarb Report and to the allegations it made about adolescent behaviour. (Ironically, it is not the teenagers in Gee's novel who are involved in inappropriate activities, but older, 'sophisticated' Gloria and her boyfriend, and the middle-aged stalker Errol.)

Gee draws on another historical happening, the polio epidemic of 1947, to give further authentic background to the story. Although the epidemic was over by 1955, the year in which *Hostel Girl* is set, its effects continued to be felt. For example Calum, a former tennis champion, has to walk with the aid of callipers; and Ailsa recalls how a polio victim was ostracised by her schoolmates because of a misguided fear that she would pass on her germs. Other historical details include a reference to the Parker–Hulme murder in Christchurch in June 1954, and Ailsa and Calum's visit to a milkbar 'full of bodgies and widgies in leather jackets and short skirts'.[26] The YWCA hostel, with its eight houses 'sardined with dental nurses and farm girls and single women, secretaries, shop workers, hoping to find husbands before long' (6) is typical of the 1950s.

Much of the language in *Hostel Girl*, too, has a deliberately outdated ring. Underwear is referred to as 'scanties', table tennis is 'ping pong', and it is not yet considered politically incorrect to describe a boy who limps as 'crippled'. Idioms such as 'someone with a screw loose', 'throw a wobbly', 'get the dirty end of the stick' and 'she thinks he's a pill' add a period flavour to the text.[27] As in his other historical novels, Gee helps establish the setting by referring to music, films and literature that were popular at that time. The girls at the hostel play 'Mairzy doats' on the piano, listen to Vic Damone singing 'Powder your face with sunshine' on the radio, and dance to the music of the Mellow Masters. They watch *Brigadoon* and *Mildred Pierce* at the Prince Edward Theatre and talk about filmstars like Errol Flynn, George Sanders, Ann Blyth and Claire Bloom. Ailsa reads books by Dennis Wheatley; her mother prefers travel books by Joy Packer. These details are all authentic, as Gee took them from the schoolgirl diaries of his wife Margareta, who lived in the Woburn Hostels for three years while her mother was matron of House 4. As Gee acknowledges, 'The whole hostel background is there … the books she was reading, the movies she was going to, her friends, the sport she played – all that sort of stuff was in these little diaries that she kept.'[28]

The physical setting is just as important as the temporal one; for example, the way the Hutt Valley is divided into two distinct parts by the railway line is instrumental to the plot. The eastern side is 'the wrong side of the tracks' (6) where the houses are smaller and scruffier and there are factories and hostels. The YWCA hostel at Woburn actually existed, and provides Gee not only with a large cast of potential characters but a credible setting for a plot involving a stalker. Ailsa lives in the hostel and feels an affinity with the working girls who live there – the more so because her mother has two jobs, at the biscuit factory and the hostel, to make ends meet. Because of the *Truth* allegations, Ailsa's mother removes her from Hutt Valley High and sends her to a girls' school run by the church, and Ailsa thus comes into contact with people who live on the other side of the tracks, where 'the houses were bigger than the ones on her side and the sections grew more trees. There were no state houses. The cars were parked in garages, not on the front lawn.' (9) On this side Ailsa meets girls who talk differently, and whose fathers are lawyers, ambassadors and MPs. She also meets the Page family and is able to compare their standard of living and way of life with her own. There is a marked contrast between the Pages' privileged lifestyle (they have a large house with a tennis court, two cars and a yacht, and Mrs Page does not go out to work), and Ailsa's life at the hostel, sharing a bedroom and eating in the dining room 'with the roar of 300 voices all around, the clatter of 300 knives and forks, and mutton, mashed potatoes, grey cabbage on the plate'. (6) Ailsa manages to fit in to both of these environments, but she is acutely aware of the difference between them. She sees the overbridge over the railway lines as the link between the two:

> She felt lonely on the overbridge. Sometimes she imagined it existed outside the world. She went down from it, one way or another, into places where her life was tangled, where too much trying was asked of her. She liked to linger on the bridge and look up and down the shining rails that cut the Hutt Valley into halves, and in a way cut her life in half. (*HG* 6)

Gee's historical novels for children have a strong sense of place and of historical authenticity, and they are vehicles for investigating a variety of social, moral and cultural issues. The themes that he revisits and explores in the five historical novels are varied, and include racism, xenophobia, class structures, family dynamics, bullying and other forms of violence. In *Hostel Girl*, because of the older intended audience, he is able to address questions of sexual morality and the relationship between the sexes: he counterpoints the tentative adolescent love affair between Ailsa and Calum with the exploitative sexual relationship of Gloria and Bevan; and he compares the obsessive and ultimately destructive feelings Errol has for Gloria with the unassuming and heroic devotion of the hostel boiler man Ron Stock, who unobtrusively keeps watch over Gloria and rescues her from Errol. The prevailing mores of the 1950s provide a context for the various relationships; for example, Gloria's affair with Bevan is a serious flouting of conventions and risks severe repercussions. She does not have access to an effective form of contraception, and if she became pregnant she would be expelled from the hostel and face either a back-street abortion or trying to raise a child on her own. Girls were supposed to be 'pure', and Errol's homicidal rage when he discovers that Gloria is not the chaste maiden of his fantasies is an extreme reflection of society's attitudes. Even Mrs Nimmo, Ailsa's liberal social studies teacher, is shocked when she thinks that Ailsa may be pregnant, and urges her not to have sex.

The moral schematism of the fantasies is less in evidence in the realistic novels, and the distinctions between black and white have blurred into shades of grey. The villains of the fantasies are creatures of unadulterated evil and they are overthrown by the efforts of the 'good' characters, but in the realistic novels characters are not as easily classified into 'good' and 'bad'. Errol Parkinson's behaviour in *Hostel Girl* is reprehensible, and the lengths he goes to in his obsession with Gloria are frightening, but he is pitiable as well. He is deluded rather than evil, and while his death under the train might be considered just punishment, the two people most closely concerned, Ailsa and Gloria, feel sorrow rather than relief. Even the 'good' characters are depicted as less than perfect. Gloria, for example, swears, smokes and is far from being the chaste young woman Errol imagines her to be. Nor do things always end happily for the 'good' characters: Gloria receives horrific injuries, and it seems likely her beautiful face will be permanently scarred. Nevertheless, Gee suggests that his protagonists are compensated for the traumas they undergo by a growth in self-knowledge and awareness, and books such as *Hostel Girl* offer readers the possibility of a similar increase in understanding.

A number of Gee's books examine class structures and challenge the concept of New Zealand as an egalitarian society. One of the underlying premises of *Hostel Girl* is that it is better to be working class than to belong to a higher socio-economic group. Ailsa is proud of her boiler-maker father and her mother who has to work at two jobs to make ends meet. She sees her parents as superior to the Pages, despite Mr Page's professional status as a lawyer and the family's comparative wealth. She criticises Mrs Page and her daughter as shallow snobs, and is scornful of Mr Page who is unhappy but lacks the courage to act. Only Calum Page is presented as a sympathetic character. Ailsa also feels that the girls at Willowbank are no better than those at Hutt Valley High: they may be the daughters of 'lawyers and ambassadors and MPs', but they swear more and are just as likely to get pregnant.

Ailsa is frowned on by Mrs Page because she is from the wrong side of the railway line, from the part of the Hutt Valley where there are state houses and hostels. Mrs Page disapproves of the fact that Ailsa's mother works for a living (though her own, non-working life is depicted as empty and meaningless). She thinks Ailsa is common, and assumes that because she is of a lower socio-economic group she must therefore have lower moral standards; she describes her as 'straight out of the Mazengarb report' (109). Her prejudice blinds her to Ailsa's good qualities, and she disapproves of Ailsa's friendship with her son, to the extent of saying she '[had] sooner he stayed in a wheelchair than run around with girls of that sort' (109). She is ashamed of Calum for getting polio because 'People like us don't get polio, it's working class' (51). Her tendency to dismiss whole sections of society as inferior means that she is isolated from other people, and it damages her relationship with her husband and son. It is ironic that Mrs Page rejects the company of 'real' people like Ailsa and her mother in favour of her neighbour Errol, whose veneer of gentility is merely an act. Ailsa realises the first time she meets Errol in his garden that he is playing a part, and that the setting (the wicker chair and table with the glass of pale drink), the costume of silk shirt, cravat and panama hat, and the rich, milky voice are all deliberately contrived.[29] Ailsa is sufficiently sensible and clear-sighted to see through Errol's various disguises, and to refuse to be cowed by Mrs Page's snobbery. She is aware of the differences between the two halves of the Hutt Valley, and the two halves of her life, but she is able to see the good and bad aspects of both and to accept them, and embrace the richness this duality brings to her life. In Ailsa's attitude and her friendship with Calum, Gee is once again providing positive examples for achieving the egalitarian society Clippy Hedges optimistically claims for New Zealand in *The Fire-Raiser*.

Another issue Gee explores in many of his novels, for both children and adults, is that of family dynamics. 'Whose hideous invention was the family?' Kingsley Pratt asks in *Games of Choice*;[30] and family tensions feature in all of Gee's historical novels for children. Errol's manipulative attitude towards his sick wife is only one of the unsatisfactory family relationships portrayed in *Hostel Girl*. Mr and Mrs Page are unhappy in their marriage, and Mrs Page treats her son Calum with callous disregard. Gloria's family, with its bullying father, is also imperfect. The warm and trusting relationship between Ailsa and her widowed mother is the only positive family experience in the novel. The fractured families in Gee's novels can be seen as a microcosm of a fractured society. Similarly, the violence of various types which is another recurrent theme in Gee's novels reflects the violent nature of society as a whole. The ending of *Hostel Girl*, when Errol kidnaps Gloria at knife-point and is subsequently run over by a train, is an example of this. The 'shadows behind the story', therefore, are considerably darker than those behind *The World Around the Corner* and Gee's other horizontal fantasies.

Conclusion

The World Around the Corner and *Hostel Girl* represent the two extremes of Gee's junior fiction. One of Gee's original objectives in writing for children was to get away from the 'delving into psyches' and 'deep-shaft mining' of his adult novels, and he achieved this aim with his first five fantasy books. With his realistic fiction, as the subjects and the age of the intended readers have moved closer to those of his adult novels, the writing has become increasingly vertical; and even when he returned to fantasy with the young adult *Salt* trilogy, Gee retained the more vertical style of the realistic novels rather than reverting to the horizontal writing of the earlier fantasies. 'Writing vertically' has allowed Gee to create more complex characters and introduce more sophisticated plots and themes; nevertheless, the horizontal style of writing, with its emphasis on action and narrative pace and 'tell[ing] a story as a story pure and simple', was the right choice for the fantasy/adventure stories with which he began his career as a children's author. *The World Around the Corner* and *Hostel Girl* exemplify Gee's skill in writing both horizontally and vertically, and his ability to adapt his style to the story he wants to tell.

6 PATTERNS OF EXCHANGE
Setting, hero, villain and child in *The Champion* and *The Fat Man*
Vivien van Rij

Maurice Gee is well known as a writer of realistic novels for adults and children; and one who draws on a childhood spent largely in Henderson, a small town situated west of Auckland, in order to create historically accurate detail. Indeed, Henderson's railway station, jam factory, Falls Hotel, Millbrook Road and Newington Road, in which the Gee family lived, and the vineyards, orchards and the creek where he once observed a swagman bathing all find their way into his novels in some shape or form. However, discussing his narrative technique in 'The way of a writer', Gee has commented that things in his books 'get charged with significance [and] there's a lot of making pregnant'.[1] By this, he seems to refer to the depth, patterning and complexity that underpin his plots, and to the fact that local settings and individual characters operate on levels that are macrocosmic and emblematic, hence reflecting socio-political situations and related value systems. This chapter examines two of Gee's novels for children – *The Champion* and *The Fat Man* – and considers themes of race, war, imperialism, depression, subjugation and power. It focuses on the significance of the settings, and characters and their roles, and ways in which these undergo patterns of reversal and exchange.

The settings of Gee's novels transcend historical reality to become microcosms of conflict that involve the particular, cultural and universal. In *The Champion* the fictional township of Kettle Creek seems to have been named to evoke, as Rex puts it, a 'tin-pot town'.[2] However, with its creeks, swamps and mud, it recalls the battlefields of Guadalcanal, which is explicitly mentioned in the novel. Indeed, Rex, the 12-year-old protagonist (who as an older man narrates the story), and Jack, the black American soldier (who shelters in Kettle Creek after fighting in Guadalcanal, and whom the younger Rex befriends) both see the landscape in terms of Guadalcanal's battles, creatures and terrain. When he is paddling up the creek with his friend Leo, Rex imagines that 'Jap subs could hide up here' (34); and Jack, venturing out at night, hears 'a strange noise [like] the croaking of frogs ... in the Solomons' (141). Gee extends the parallel between fiction and reality by depicting imagined versions of amphibious battles that recall the battles actually fought in Guadalcanal. Sitting in his grandfather's homemade amphibian, Rex sees himself 'in the amphib, speeding at a beach with machine gun rattling, then roaring up the sand with no loss of speed, and Japs in the trees falling over and lying dead' (65). Furthermore, the fictional Kettle Creek recalls the United States during the Civil War. Battles between North and South, and whites and blacks are echoed in the conflicts between the racist American soldiers Marv and Herb – termed by a local as 'the US Cavalry' (94) – and Jack, whom they call a 'nigra' (85). And Chattanooga, an important battle site in 1863, is evoked at the school gala when Jack plays the popular song 'Chattanooga Choo-choo' on his mouth organ. As Rex comments: 'It was the outside world coming to town. It was the USA in Kettle Creek' (98).

Gee extends the significance of the setting by fusing characters' views with his own. For instance, parallels exist between the fictional Kettle Creek and its nonfictional namesake – Kettle Creek in Georgia, in the United States. Where the fictional Kettle Creek is at war with imperialist forces in February 1943, the nonfictional Kettle Creek (a similarly swampy area) was the site of a major battle against imperialists in February 1779, during the American Revolution.

Aside from social and political connotations, Kettle Creek has a mythical dimension. To some it is an Eden, but to others it is a hell. Rex's mother sees it in terms of the physiological, as is made clear when she personifies it in a poem as 'Funny little town with your feet in the mud ... and your head lifted up to the hills' (13–14). To the imaginative Rex its landscape is primordial, exotic and enticing. When he explores its interior, it reflects his fascination with adventure, decay and death, but at the same time it is potentially animate:

> We glided over the water ... heading along the edge of cliffs and past the fringes of the mangrove jungle. It was half tide and the incoming water helped us along. The nearer mangrove trees had drowned trunks. A fizz and crackle sounded further in, where advancing water ran into crab holes. A smell of salt and rot and

ripeness hung in the air. It would have been easy to imagine crocodiles basking in the mud and snakes sliding in the crooked trunks. (*TC* 33)

While Rex may be engaging with the landscape in terms of a collective primordial past, his perceptions are further influenced by his reading, particularly of comics (*Champion* was his favourite boys' magazine), and by heroic characters such as Daniel Boone, Tarzan and Rockfist Rogan of the RAF. In identifying with imperialist heroes who have in effect conquered the wilderness, Rex projects onto the vegetable garden of his naturist grandmother his fantasies of the exotic. Thus Rex seems to experience a mutual correspondence with the garden during which he and it are dependent on each other for sustenance. Imagery of ingestion suggests his bliss and his fears:

> Grandma's garden affected me differently each time. I might hear growth humming and roots drinking and sap running and fat leaves creaking as they turned to follow the sun, and might start humming myself and feeling my own sap rising in my limbs. Or I might see tendrils reaching and marrows like pythons curled in the shade, and feel that I was threatened, food for them. Or I might imagine myself in Africa and put my foot on a pumpkin, a beast I'd shot. Or simply be hungry – pick a tomato, crunch a butter bean. (*TC* 61–62)

In *The Fat Man* Gee depicts a landscape that is similarly primordial and anthropomorphic – there are headlands, a tongue of bush, a throat-like gorge, and white beaches in bites of land. The landscape reflects the novel's setting during the social and economic depression of the 1930s, as is suggested by the fact that the creek is situated in an area that is geologically depressed, airless and still. Gee is careful, though, to balance death and despair as embodied by the creek with excitement and hope as embodied by the world above that is full of movement, light and life:

> The creek was in a gorge and the world of streets and houses, and paddocks and cows, was on another level, where sunshine poured down and breezes flapped clothes on the washing line. The wind never blew down here at all and the air was still. When [Colin] heard dogs bark off in the distance or heard trains whistle on the railway crossing, he sometimes felt there was no way up from the creek.[3]

Gee sets the dangerous creek in *The Fat Man* against the safety and security of the home, specifically that of the Potter family, including

Maisie and Laurie, the parents, and their son Colin (the novel's protagonist). The polarisation of the creek and home is emphasised by the depiction of these settings initially within separate chapters. However, with the arrival of Muskie (the eponymous fat man), a change is anticipated. Not only do his ablutions pollute the creek, but he stirs up its waters. Hence the melancholic creek world encroaches on the domestic world and disrupts its normal routines and, as the novel progresses, creek scenes and domestic scenes occur in the same chapters and intertwine. Similarly, the fear and gloom associated with the creek pervade characters' more rational thoughts. Thus the creek embodies the psyche's shadow side and represents not only the social and economic Depression but additionally mental depression.

The close integration in *The Fat Man* of the characters and setting is echoed in characters' relationships, and ways in which Gee's and their perceptions fuse. Patterns of projection and absorption occur here. When Jackson Coop arrives in Kettle Creek Rex expects a white hero. Instead he is shocked by Jack's colour and the fact that he is 'a Negro' or 'black' (37). Having imaginatively orientalised Kettle Creek's landscape, Rex now sees Jack in similar terms as an extension of his primitive self. Ironically, in viewing him as 'Monkeyface' (40) and as some sort of exotic gladiatorial beast – 'one of those African animals brought to ancient Rome, an ostrich, or hyena, or giraffe' (39) – Rex anticipates Jack's later public appearance in the makeshift boxing arena. During the night when he shares his bedroom with Jack, Rex perceives him as a savage killer. However, during the day, when shooting at images of Hitler and Tojo with his BB gun, Rex has, in his words, 'blasted holes in the enemy' (42). Ironically, then, it is Rex who more closely resembles the primitive and murderous savage.

The name 'Rex' has connotations of 'wrecks' and 'king' – as spelt out by Gee in *Going West*. Rex's hero worship of the comic-book character Rockfist Rogan, boxer airman of the RAF, leads him to emulate imperialist ideology. As illustrated in *The Champion Annual for Boys*, Rogan seems to be little more than a comic-book outline, and may, in his very lack of complexity and substance, provide Rex with the space in which to imagine himself. Representational of the racism of the times, Rogan, on an African adventure, refers to natives as 'coloured boys', 'pop-eyed', 'a horde of black figures' and 'the black tide' – and it is this very sort of prejudice and aggression that Rex projects onto Jack.[4]

Viewed adoringly by Rex's mother as a version of the black American singer and scholar Paul Robeson, Jack is the complete antithesis of how Rex perceives him. Indeed, he seems almost too entirely kind and good – qualities that Gee emphasises by establishing him as a sort of Christ figure (as his initials 'J.C.' might imply); and the scar on his shoulder which he has acquired, presumably from a bayonet, while fighting in Guadalcanal suggests he may indeed have suffered for mankind. Absorbing the good side of Jack, Rex overturns his initial opinion of him as evil. At the gala, when Jack woos the crowd with his mouth organ, he also wins Rex's heart. Indeed, as Jack leans forwards and back it is as though a form of courtship or 'lovemaking' occurs:

> Jack reached in the pocket of his pea jacket and brought out a mouth organ. He played very softly in time with the band ... Jack's music was soothing – and later on, throaty, wild, vibrant, wailing, sweet. It made me catch my breath. It made my heart swell until I thought it would leap out through my mouth on to the grass. We had a crowd around us before long. Jack stood up and played with his body swaying. Sometimes he bent forwards and sometimes he leaned back, and his hands, cupped over the instrument, imprisoned and let free wonderful sounds. (*TFM* 98)

Resembling a lasso-throwing cowboy hero, and centrally placed in the arena, Jack seems to loop his music out over the crowd to capture and conquer it – and Rex: 'The music went out and over the crowd, it looped out like a rope and caught them in. If you'd been high in a tree you would have seen them flowing in to a point, and Jack there like the hub of a wheel' (98). Rex's respect for Jack as a figure of power is enhanced by the adulation of the mob, and by the music itself. Not only do the throaty, wailing, soothing sounds have a sexual quality, they seem primal, organic and pre-linguistic. Rex's pleasure in the music recalls his earlier blissful integration with a primordial landscape and suggests a longing to lose his more fascist self in nature.

Colin and Muskie in *The Fat Man* similarly operate in antithesis to form patterns of exchange and reversal. However, the child and adult characters are constructed in a manner that is the reverse of *The*

Champion. Gee now suggests, in Colin, the sort of gentle, thoughtful but cowardly and conformist child that Jack might once have been; and in Muskie, the aggressive and nasty character that Rex could easily have become.

Like Rex and Jack, Colin and Muskie have dimensions that transcend everyday reality. Larger than life, Muskie is a composite of a number of roles. An archetypal 'baddie', he is established as such from the moment he first enters the story, when he seems closely entwined with the landscape. As though thrown up by the creek, he appears to have erupted from a dark hole in the earth, and to embody its waste matter: 'His eyes were angry. They were small and deep and blacker than sheep pellets. Herbert Muskie was like something that had rushed into daylight from the back of the cave' (14). He may well have emerged from the underworld of the Halfmen of O: 'The fat man had come up out of the ground, as though he had been sleeping there, buried for years, waiting for something to wake him – or come up from the deep pools of the creek, dripping slime' (26). Muskie is obsessed with cleanliness, while sensually engaging in play with water and mud. At the same time he is a freak adult who, seemingly all body, is perverted and sexual.

As 'the fat man', Muskie recalls the hydrogen bomb of the same name that was dropped on Nagasaki during World War II. Obese, but light on his feet, able to float, and with a magnetic personality, Muskie seems gaseous. Childhood repression is responsible for his explosiveness, which on a much smaller scale recalls the nuclear explosion that occurs with compression. Certainly Muskie is destructive, and he desires to bring down the structures of Loomis. Not only does he seek revenge on Colin's parents for the bullying he experienced during boyhood, he wants to avenge himself on his mother, with whom he has had a dubious relationship.

The theme of destructive adult power is emphasised by an apparent parallel between Herbert Muskie and former New Zealand prime minister Robert Muldoon (who appears in derogatory form in a number of Gee's novels). There is the obvious similarity of their names, and they have many features in common: obesity, facial disfigurement, gimlet eyes, a magnetic and manipulative personality, vice-like grip and an obsession with power. Both Muskie and Muldoon lived during periods of economic recession, were teased at school, had fathers who experienced business failure and died during the Depression, and were brought up by fawning mothers. The destructive maternal influence is further suggested by what Gee has called 'a straight steal' from a story by Frank Sargeson.[5] The fact that Gee's mother, a promising amateur writer, had a story selected by Sargeson for publication in an anthology, and that Gee along with several other New Zealand writers (known as 'Sons of Sargeson') were recipients of Sargeson's generous assistance, must have made him aware of his enormous debt to the older author.[6]

Gee draws on Sargeson's 'An affair of the heart' in constructing the fictional relationship in *The Fat Man*. In Sargeson's story, old Mrs Crawley, widowed and beaten down by the Depression years of poverty and toil, trudges nightly to the local bus shelter to await the return of Joe, her long-absent son who has possibly had a criminal career. Having indulged him as a child, she remains hopeful that she will see him again, but he never returns. Similarly, in Gee's novel, old Mrs Muskie, widowed, impoverished and unhinged by the Depression, walks daily to Loomis Railway Station to await the return of her son Herbert whom she has spoilt as a child, and who has become a gangster during his 13 years away in the United States. Each mother has sought to embellish an empty existence by projecting her physical and emotional needs onto her son. However, unlike Mrs Crawley's son, Muskie does return, first secretly to steal his mother's jewels, and second to stage for his mother a heroic arrival by train. (Interestingly, we learn of Muskie's second return through the sentimentalised account of the town watchdog and gossip, Mrs Sargent, who may be an ironic coded acknowledgement of Sargeson, the clear-sighted storyteller.)[7] Muskie goes on to murder his mother. Their unhealthy relationship, in which they have been 'more like two old sweethearts than mother and son' (112), is explicit in this line from a song which Muskie has his wife Bette sing after the funeral. More than simply a backdrop, the Depression has become integral to Mrs Muskie's social and mental condition which, projected on to Muskie, has then been turned back on her to make both mother and son victims of it and of each other.

Colin of course does not at first see Muskie as a victim. His perception of Muskie fuses with that of the third-person narrator (who is closely aligned to Gee) so that much of the time it is a projection of Colin's fear that the reader is given. In weaving various roles into Colin's thoughts, Gee draws on movies that Colin (and possibly the young Gee) may have seen in the local hall. A popular movie of the time, *Scarface*, is the story of Al Capone and the underworld of gang warfare and drink-related crime in Chicago during prohibition.[8] Both Tony Comonte (the movie's eponymous 'Scarface', alias Al Capone) and Herbert Muskie have a scarred face, wear a slouch hat, drive a Buick, flick their fingers defiantly and whistle hollowly. Both switch roles according to different contexts and change from 'tough guy' to 'lost kid', and both are frighteningly vacuous and unstable. Certainly Colin, who is threatened by Muskie, sees him as a gangster – a role that Muskie, newly arrived from America, seems to affect:

> [Muskie] took his jacket from the ferns and shook it out and put it on. It made him look even bigger. He took a tie from the pocket and knotted it round his neck. Then he put his hat on, careful not to disarrange his hair, and flicked the brim up with his fingernail and turned the front one down on an angle. Now he looked like a gangster. Maybe he wanted that. Colin wondered if he had a gun. (*TFM* 19–20)

Gee also aligns his settings and characters to those in westerns, and in so doing may be strongly influenced by Zane Grey, whose many novels Gee read avidly as a teenager. As he has acknowledged, he found in Grey's novels 'a landscape ... more than the purple sage, the dry gulch, the endless range', which served 'below the level of full consciousness' to represent 'the human condition'.[9] Grey's influence is explicit in several of Gee's children's novels, including *Orchard Street*, in which Ossie, the adolescent protagonist, notes that he has read *The Lone Star Ranger* and sees himself in terms of its cowboy hero, Buck Duane. As we shall see, Grey's landscapes are present in *The Fat Man* on an implicit level.

Initially in *The Fat Man*, however, Gee pokes fun at the western genre by creating parallels between Laurie (Colin's father) and Herbie, and Laurel and Hardy, the comic duo of American movies. In terms of their names, physiques and personalities, the similarities between the two skinny weaklings and the two fat bullies are obvious; but Gee stresses a darker side. In the movie *Laurel and Hardy Way Out West* the comic pair travel by wagon over a western landscape and Hardy tips into a creek where, in a scene very similar to Herbie's first appearance in chapter 1, he sits spouting water from his mouth.[10] Colin seems familiar with Laurel and Hardy movies in that, threatened by Muskie in his gangster role, he attempts to control his fears by recasting him in the role of Hardy: 'The most you can do is shrink them a little, perhaps by remembering things supposed to be funny: a bald head with hair pasted on it, a Laurel and Hardy jacket looking ready to burst' (40).

Like Jack and Rex, but more by force and threat than seduction, Muskie possesses the child. Obviously for Colin it is an experience that is extremely unpleasant. In chapter 1 the images of chocolate and spit are depicted as filth and have nasty implications, particularly when Muskie force-feeds them to Colin. A parallel incident occurs in *Sole Survivor* when Raymond Sole (the protagonist) visits the home of Sutton and Bluey Considine and observes Sutton dropping 'a gob of spit' into Bluey's cup of tea. Raymond realises that 'this was [Sutton's] way of having Bluey and of forcing Bluey to have him', and that 'each tea drinking is a communion'.[11] As such the feeding of spit is an expression of love. Muskie's force-feeding of Colin, on the other hand, is analogous to rape and is an expression of hate. Colin is literally the recipient of the satanic fat man's juices and symbolically is impregnated with the seed of evil. It is little wonder, then, that Colin is reduced to an infantile state resembling Muskie during his cavorting in the creek and that, shortly after this episode, he feels as though Muskie 'takes up residence in [his] mind' (40). Where Rex, pregnant with Jack's image as hero, felt as though his heart would burst, Colin, pregnant with Muskie's evil image, feels his mind to be possessed.

The domination of Rex by Jack and Colin by Muskie is temporary, however. Gee shows that in the struggle for power, roles are again overturned. In elevating Jack to hero status at the gala, Rex wants to be centrally placed himself and to enter into Jack's character as he did into Rogan's. Projecting his comic-book heroes on to Jack, Rex believes he has captured him:

> I stood by Jack, beaming with pride. He was mine, and every bit as good as Buddy Storm ... Before the crowd came swirling across, with chatter and grin, I was alone, and I realised my victory. I had my Jack. I had my Buddy Storm, my Rockfist Rogan (*TC* 98, 100).

The closer identification of Rex, the primitive and innocent child, with Jack, the urbane and experienced man, leads to a narrowing of the distance between them. After the boxing match Rex sees Jack as 'Brown Bomber' (111) – a nickname for nonfictional black American boxer Joe Louis – and starts to accept Jack's racial identity. Rather than a primitive animal or a comic-book character, Jack becomes more fully human to Rex, though in terms of racial politics Rex's patronage of Jack is disturbing and something he never properly acknowledges.

When Rex and his friends Dawn and Leo show Jack how to swim, the symmetrical arrangement – one on each side of Jack and one underneath – suggests balance. However, Rex's adoption of the role of teacher anticipates an exchange of personality traits and an end of innocence for Rex, as well as a return to innocence for Jack. In the water, then, it is the helpless Jack who resembles a child, while Rex seems to be the more reasonable and responsible adult:

> It was his helplessness in the water that calmed me down and made me start behaving in a reasonable way again. I think we all felt the same towards him – protective, and yet somehow protected by him. Equal to him, accepted, yet innocent and simple and silly alongside Jack and all the things he knew (*TC* 110).

The pattern of exchange and reversal continues, with the night preceding Jack's departure explicitly recalling his first night at Kettle Creek. In a Christ-like way Rex now takes on the suffering and pain that Jack, Christ-like, had earlier borne for mankind: 'Just as on that first night, [Jack's] face came forward from the dark and sank away. The scar turned pink and faded out in time with it. I felt a dull ache in my own shoulder' (10). The ache Rex feels reflects the ache Jack must have felt when bayoneted in his shoulder in Guadalcanal. His empathy with Jack is evidence of a growing conscience and imaginative maturity.

However, this more sympathetic view of Jack is challenged when his recuperative period in Kettle Creek ends and he sets out to return to Guadalcanal but instead goes AWOL. Having seen Jack first as savage animal, second as comic-book hero, and third as human being, Rex is forced now to see him as coward and again as animal. Returning to the creek and resembling a 'hippo wallowing' and a 'giant fish' (125) Jack descends in Rex's view to what seems to be a pre-human marine existence that is even lower and more primal than his earlier simian status as 'Monkeyface' (40). The swamplands appear to be conspiratorial and hungry for food, as though they are anticipating Jack's drowning – recalling Rex's earlier fascination with being subsumed by primordial nature: 'There we stood, triangular, waiting for Jack to show himself. Nothing moved. The tide made little whispers and sucks in the mangrove trunks' (124). However, what Rex is now projecting onto the landscape is a more pronounced fear of Jack's and his own mortality.

Rex is thus concerned with transcending his mortality, which is dependent on further reducing Jack. In the exchange of power between Rex and Jack, Jack's descent to a pre-human state is matched by Rex's increasing 'good sense' (129), responsibility, and rise to the role of saviour. The literal exchange of gifts just prior to Jack's final departure in chapter 16 is, in addition, a metaphorical exchange: when Rex hands over his *Champion* comic he relinquishes innocence and romance and faces maturity. When Jack gives Rex his Purple Heart medal he relinquishes his heart and life and faces a pre-innocent, pre-human state equivalent to death. Effectively, therefore, Rex receives a medal for his suffering much as Jack once did in Guadalcanal, but ironically, having battled for the heart of his hero, he no longer wants to possess it. Jack on the other hand receives an embodiment of Rex's heroic ideals but he is an unwilling champion. By wishing to set Jack free Rex seems to want to free himself, but by vanishing completely Jack possesses Rex for life.

In a sense Jack's death by drowning is a sort of sacrifice that saves Rex's soul and Rex becomes a much nicer human being who, although he tries to be a saviour, cannot manage to save Jack. What is interesting, though, is that Rex's premonition of Jack's absorption into the landscape comes true, and that his maturity and transcendence of Jack may have contributed to Jack's reduction and death. As the first-person narrator who writes the entire novel, the older Rex seems to relinquish earlier prejudices and dreams. As he points out at the end of *The Champion*: 'I don't need to dream [of Jack's existence]. I've never forgotten Jack and never will' (173). Certainly he is positioned on the periphery of the novel where his point of view at the beginning and end provides a frame for Jack's portrait. Unlike the earlier caricatures of Tojo, Hitler and Rockfist Rogan, it is a portrait that is rounded and substantial and that effectively saves Jack after all by eternalising him within the novel's pages. However, in writing the novel and remembering and reliving his childhood, the older Rex moves back towards innocence in a progression similar to Jack's at Kettle Creek. It seems, therefore, that where Jack existed in the novel largely as a projection of the younger Rex, the older Rex, possessing and possessed by the memory of Jack, might in the future almost become him.

An exchange of power between outsider adult figures and the children they fascinate marks the relationship of Muskie and Colin in *The Fat Man*. Just as Rex's rise to maturity and role of saviour depend on Jack's return to innocence and obliteration, so Colin's rise to maturity and a different sort of saviour role depends on Muskie's regression to infancy, the elemental and death. Colin starts to see past the movie stereotype to the infantile side of Muskie when, in chapter 7, he observes Muskie hugging his drowned mother 'on his chest, like a doll' (107) and later hugging her pillow; and Verna notes that he 'cries in it too [and sucks] his thumb' (112). In chapter 8, kidnapped by Muskie, Colin listens to Muskie's story of his childhood at Loomis School:

> 'Did I tell you, kid, what Pottsie and his mates used to do to me at Loomis school? They'd come lookin' for me at lunchtime and they'd get all around me friendly like, and Pottsie would say, "We've got a sandwich for you, Herbie." One of them would hold it out, and then they'd pull it back and say, "We'll just make it taste better, eh?" They'd take the top off, see like this.' He took the last sandwich from the bag and lifted the top off, showing the ham. 'Then they'd all spit on it, each one. Four or five of them, like this.' He did not spit on the ham but out to one side. 'Then they'd put it back together again and make me eat it. Spit sandwich was its name. I ate one of those every day.' (*TFM* 133–34)

Muskie's forced consumption of the bodily fluid of Laurie and his friends is analogous to a gang rape. Symbolically, then, Laurie has become part of Muskie's psyche in much the same way as Muskie has of Colin's. Thus the sins of the father are visited on the child, and it is Laurie's bullying behaviour that Muskie has projected back on to Colin. In chapter 1, therefore, when Muskie forced Colin to eat the chocolate on which he spat, the implication may be that, indirectly through Muskie, it is Laurie who symbolically raped Colin. As Colin now realises, Muskie's memory hastens his regression to the child he once was many years ago: 'Something in him shifted and gave way. Herbert Muskie had turned into the fat boy again, running from the playground gang at Loomis School' (138). The moment is a revelation for Colin who, psychologically impregnated by a bullying father, must now accept first, that beneath Muskie's evil exterior exists a victim and, second, take responsibility for his father's sins.

Perhaps it is this new insight that triggers Colin's empathy for Muskie. As though Zane Grey's westerns, and comic western and gangster movies have merged to take over the fictional reality – including the landscape, which is elemental but depicted in cinematic style – both characters in the final chapter are on the run from the police. Now, however, Colin moves with instead of against Muskie; and Colin, Muskie and Gee (the utterly sympathetic and integrated narrator) all operate in correspondence with each other. Implicitly recalling Grey's landscapes – their rugged cliffs, ravines, creeks and gorges – the almost symbolic landscape is now fully activated and no mere projection:[12] it dwarfs them but, in a brief synchronicity, moves with them – to run, climb, crumble, fall, and experience a hunger for life and a longing for death:

> Scrubby hills, eroded with slips, fell away to the distant coast. A cold wind was blowing and clouds were piling up on the higher hills behind them ... Yellow clay broke under the wheels and clods bounced down into the gully. Far off, the sea glittered and white beaches showed in bites of land ... Grey clouds, piling up, moved across the sun ... A little further off, towards the coast, a stretch of highway showed, running flat in the valley ... The track climbed out of the bush, crossed a shallow ford, made a right-angle turn, and ran along the side of a new hill ... They ran again and reached another spur. Another hillside, on a steeper plane, ran down to the edge of a gorge. Smooth rock walls dropped out of sight. (*TFM* 133–38)

When Muskie enters the cage of the flying fox his progression to an infantile state is complete: '[He] squatted like a child in a box too small for it, holding the couplings with two hands' (139). As he falls, the shift from 'Herbert Muskie' to 'the fat man' suggests a further loss of identity and reversion to the archetypal role in which he made his first appearance in the novel, and which now is all that is left. With his descent into the river he joins the element from which he seems originally to have come. His falling underwear inverts the traditional idea of the spirit's heavenward ascent upon death, and makes an ironic comment on his tragic soulless state:

> Herbert Muskie fell. The fat man fell. He turned over once and struck the rocks at the side of the river and slid down them into the white water and was gone. His suitcase fell too. It opened out its lid and his shirts and underpants circled down like birds. (*TFM* 140)

Colin's progression towards maturity and empathy exactly reverses Muskie's progression to infancy and the elemental. Although Colin is effectively participating in a movie, he releases Muskie from stereotyped movie roles. Hence Colin comes closer to Muskie as an individual with an identity and a real name. Running beside Muskie, Colin clearly sees the human frailty and gaseous emptiness that accompany his reduction: '[Colin] ran with the fat man along the side of the gorge, listening to him pant and wheeze, seeing him stumble' (139). Referred to by Muskie as 'Pottsie' (139), and thrust into his father's childhood role, Colin reverses his father's earlier bullying behaviour. In cutting the rope of the flying fox he effectively cuts the umbilical cord that has bound him to Muskie, but also Muskie to Laurie – and in so doing, he saves Muskie from an unbearable life and gives him the freedom to die.

Colin's action is psychologically complex. Before he cuts the rope, Colin is shown to be fully aware of the possibility of death. At the same time he recognises in the flying fox the effects of a vast elemental hunger, which now seems to be echoed by the river in the throat-like gorge below: 'Colin saw how eaten with rot the planks of the cage were. It strained to get away down the wire. The river ran below, deep in the gorge, white and green' (139). Colin seems to apply the insight to Muskie who, as consumed by rot as the cage, similarly longs for freedom and death: '"Please, Pottsie," Herbert Muskie wept ... "Pottsie, cut it, eh. Go on, do it, kid"' (140). Colin's release of Muskie is therefore a fully conscious killing, but as one critic has argued it is also 'an extraordinary act of compassion and deep understanding'.[13]

Rex and Colin: primitive savage and coward. Both triumph over innocence to become in different ways a saviour. However, their final maturity has only been possible through exchanges with characters that are larger than life, and that literally and figuratively have been integral parts of themselves. Their triumphs must therefore be qualified, as they have been dependent on Jack's and Muskie's helplessness and deaths. Operating in microcosmic worlds, the hero, the villain and the children are caught up in patterns that are larger than they. Playing an active role in these patterns, the landscape is by no means benign: not only does it embody the human condition and reflect war, depression and dream, it represents a pre-human dimension within and outside the psyche. Becoming charged, impregnated or ravenous, it is an elemental force that ejects and devours lives.

7 REPRESENTATION AND RESPONSIBILITY in *Under the Mountain* and *The Fat Man*

Elizabeth Hale

In two of his best-known works, *Under the Mountain* and *The Fat Man*, Maurice Gee pursues what he perceives as a dual responsibility to young New Zealand readers: first, to represent their country in fiction, to show exciting action happening 'at home'; and second, to confront serious moral and ethical issues within that setting. Gee's work is profoundly moral, both in its investigation of moral dilemmas through the actions of young protagonists, and in its commitment to placing the action in a local setting. In these novels, representation and responsibility intertwine, accounting for some problematic aspects of writing for young readers, including how to represent the high cost of heroic action, and how to depict evil. To do so responsibly means balancing the need to take into account the reactions of young readers and their adult guardians with the demands of the narrative and the messages it conveys. *Under the Mountain* and *The Fat Man* have both had very positive receptions in New Zealand, but they have received some criticism. That criticism centres on the darker moments in each novel – the death of a popular character in *Under the Mountain*, and the uncompromising bleakness of *The Fat Man*. In replying to that criticism, Gee has referred to the 'covenant' that exists between author and reader, which is particularly important when writing for young readers. He eschews easy answers in his books: protagonists commit heroic acts, but acts that come at a personal cost that might best be characterised as the loss of innocence. Is it right to represent bleak, dark or tragic moments for young readers and, if so, how best to do it? Given that so many of his novels require protagonists to act as responsible representatives for the good of the community, it is small wonder that Gee takes his own responsibility as a writer seriously.

Under the Mountain and the price of being a hero

Published in 1979, *Under the Mountain* was Maurice Gee's first novel for children. It is a fantasy/adventure story about 11-year-old twins who save the world from destruction by marauding aliens.

Under the Mountain was well received by children and adults alike and has remained in print since its first appearance. Almost as soon as it was published, Television New Zealand commissioned South Pacific Pictures to adapt the novel for the screen. It was New Zealand's most successful locally produced children's television series of the 1980s, popular at home and selling well overseas. A further adaptation, this time for film, was produced in 2009, funded by the New Zealand Film Commission. In 2004, the book was awarded the Gaelyn Gordon Award for a Much-loved Book by the Storylines Children's Literature Foundation. This award 'honours a book by a New Zealand author that has proved itself a long-standing favourite with New Zealand children.' On accepting the award, Gee remarked that *Under the Mountain* 'seems to get itself remembered by some bit of magic that I don't understand'.[1]

One 'bit of magic' comes from Gee's skilful exploitation of Auckland's dramatic geography. He describes how, on casting about for a setting that would give New Zealand children 'an "our story" feeling', he was inspired by the sight of Mount Eden:

> What better than Auckland's volcanic cones? It was seeing Mt Eden looming in the misty rain one morning that really got it started. Everything, monsters and all, followed from that ... I wanted settings New Zealand children would recognise, with New Zealand the most important place in the world, as it is for the children who live here.[2]

It seems to have been an inspired choice: Auckland, New Zealand's largest city, possesses a dramatic geography, with a spectacular harbour and several extinct or dormant volcanoes – a fitting backdrop for exciting fantasy/adventure action. Gee's depiction of the city is carefully – and explicitly – realistic. Early in the novel the twins marvel at a panoramic view of Auckland, the sweep of the harbour bridge, the glittering towers of downtown, and the looming volcanoes, Mount Eden and Rangitoto; and the dénouement of the novel takes place during a chase sequence around those same locations. In contrast to the spectacle offered by the city's dramatic geography, the suburban sections of the novel provide a sense of everyday New Zealand life as the twins walk down the streets of Takapuna, visit the local library, and take in the different architectural styles of the houses.

The 'our story' aspect of *Under the Mountain* is surely part of what appealed to the TVNZ producers who commissioned the six-part series in 1981. *Under the Mountain* aired on TV One on Sunday nights at 7.30, in peak family time, and was a nationwide hit. The series deliberately drew on this sense of 'our story': most scenes were shot on location in Auckland – Takapuna, Rangitoto and Mount Eden; and popular entertainers such as Ray Woolf and Billy T. James appeared in cameo comic roles. This use of familiar locations and TV personalities emphasised the representative and recognisable elements of the novel and gave viewers a sense of inclusion. Further, the show was a wholly local production: a casting search in Auckland schools found local children to play the protagonists Theo and Rachel. This sense of representation and participation is part of what makes *Under the Mountain* resonate still, especially with readers and viewers, who remember its initial screening.[3]

Representation does not mean mere celebration, however. Gee's depiction of Auckland and its inhabitants may appear neutral at first. But in a subtle critique of urban expansion and capitalism, the Auckland of *Under the Mountain* is a spreading urban space, contrasted with the peace of the country (where the twins come from); and the lifestyle choices of city dwellers are decadent or tasteless. Gee's critique plays out more starkly in the main story. The evil Wilberforces, last of the 'People of the mud, who conquer and multiply', are intent on colonising Earth and destroying its ecosystem in order to create their own ideal habitat; their totalitarian focus and greed is a clear allegory for the destructive nature of human urban expansion. Even the Wilberforces' earthly name – 'will' plus 'force' – indicates the drive towards total power, and the name of their species, 'people of the mud, who conquer and multiply', points to their drive towards a chilling ecological devastation. Gee pulls out all the stops in his depiction of these unpleasant creatures, who shapeshift into human form in order to move about the city undetected. As humans, they are a grim family of undertakers who live in a decayed and lonely house by Lake Pupuke in the centre of Takapuna; in their natural state, they are large slug-like creatures who leave a trail of dry grey slime and kill whatever they touch. Their appearance reminds Theo of German helmets (another reference to totalitarianism). Gee's critique of human (or non-human) morality ranges from the subtle to the not-so-subtle: his use of unpleasant and gothic imagery ensures that the Wilberforces are immediately recognisable as being evil.

Rachel and Theo are needed to represent humanity and conquer the evil aliens. They are chosen for the task by Mr Jones, the last representative of the 'People who understand', a 'good' race of aliens who have used telepathy and telekinetic forces to fight the Wilberforces throughout the universe and to drive the last survivors to our world and to the volcanic caverns beneath Auckland. To defeat the Wilberforces, Mr Jones needs twins with telepathic abilities to wield the two magic weapon-stones designed by his race. The two middle chapters of the book show Mr Jones explaining to the twins why they must destroy the Wilberforces, and training them to develop their telepathic powers and learn to use the stones.

It is in the twins' differing responses to their heroic obligations that the richness of *Under the Mountain* becomes apparent. Rachel, the humanist, who easily accesses her telepathic powers, questions the need to kill the Wilberforces; because they are the last of their race she fears she will be committing genocide. Mr Jones reminds her that the Wilberforces themselves will destroy everyone on Earth, and she agrees to his request. However, she continues to feel profound regret and grief for the Wilberforces, even up to the moment when she activates her weapon by hurling it into the crater of Rangitoto and uttering a ritual cry of destruction. In contrast Theo, the scientifically minded twin, initially accepts the necessity of killing the Wilberforces but has difficulty suspending disbelief long enough to use his telepathic powers properly. Theo drops his weapon at a crucial moment, critically weakening his power over it. When he hurls it into the crater of Mount Eden, it causes the Wilberforce worms to explode instead of disintegrating, destroying swathes of the city. Though the threat to Earth is averted, it has come at a heavy cost for the city – and for Rachel and Theo. The novel ends on a bleak note: their aunt and uncle may be dead or injured; their cousin Ricky is certainly dead, and the city will suffer greatly (though total annihilation has been avoided). The note of melancholy, so striking in all of Maurice Gee's books for young readers and present throughout *Under the Mountain*, sounds keenly in this conclusion.

The twins succeed in defeating evil – that is part of the contract of a fantasy/adventure novel of this type – but at a heavy cost. This cost reveals some of the ambivalences about writing for young readers that run through Gee's work. The death of the twins' older cousin Ricky is a case in point. When the twins arrive in Auckland to stay with Ricky and his parents, he meets them at the train station and drives them home through the city. Not quite an adult, not quite a child, Ricky represents city glamour, in contrast to the children from the country, and crucially he possesses his own transport. He helps the twins with their mission by driving them around the city in his buggy or across the harbour in the family speedboat to locations where key moments in the action happen. In the endgame of the novel, Ricky is killed while acting as a decoy to distract the Wilberforces' attentions from the twins. He is killed offstage in the novel, and the narrative remains with the twins, who learn of his death from Mr Jones. (In the television adaptation, Ricky is killed by the Wilberforces onscreen, just before the commercial break in the final episode: the camera lingers on his lifeless body floating in the harbour, as the words 'end of first part' roll up the screen. Ricky's death was thus positioned to have maximum impact on viewers of the television series.) Helper figures regularly die in stories requiring heroic action; their deaths indicate the seriousness and scope of the evil that the hero is fighting against. Indeed, the death of an individualised character has more effect in reinforcing the scale of a battle than does wholesale destruction. Nevertheless, Ricky's death had an impact on readers, and Gee has indicated that he regularly receives letters protesting Ricky's death.

When Gee talks about his writing for children, as he does periodically in interviews and speeches, he often justifies or critiques elements of his books. He has been haunted by a remark he made about writing for children – 'a horizontal, straight-line sort of storytelling, nice and simple' – and he seems to be similarly haunted by his decision to kill Ricky in *Under the Mountain*.[4] In a 1995 interview, he explains the decision:

> It seems to me that in so much children's literature the children go through terrifying adventures; they face great danger, they are heroic; they do all these things and come out the other end victorious. There is no price paid. No consequences. And life's not like that.[5]

Gee's intention here appears to transcend the merely practical elements identified above. For him, Ricky's death is more than a narrative trick to underscore the challenge and evil posed by the Wilberforces; it makes a strong moral point that life is hard and battles are not easily won, even for the greatest hero. Even so, some years after writing the novel, Gee indicated that he felt he had played a cheap trick on his young readers:

> It had seemed to me, on no good evidence – because I wasn't widely read in children's literature – that the children in adventure and fantasy stories win their victories too easily. They go through dreadful danger, emerge unscathed and unchanged, and presumably get on with their lives. I wanted to say that there's a price to pay – and the price in *Under the Mountain* is the death of Ricky, a likeable teenage boy. I've had many letters about the book over the years and time and again I find the children saying, Why does Ricky have to die? There's no answer except that the author decided it was lesson time. I'd overlooked completely that many children would identify with Ricky. I know now that you can't have a lesson as hard as his death suddenly appear in stories that proceed on a different set of assumptions – that's to say, the fantasy/adventure set of assumptions. It's a breaking of the covenant that exists between writer and reader. If I were writing *Under the Mountain* today I'd save Ricky.[6]

In admitting that he underestimated his readers' identification with Ricky, and the assumptions underlying the fantasy/adventure genre, Gee indicates that he now sees Ricky's death as proceeding from outside of the demands of the story, and as being an unnecessary and intrusive authorial imposition on his readers. Ricky's death, in this formulation, does not proceed organically from the action. In the novel, the brusque, almost offhand way in which the narrative treats Ricky's death (reported in a speech, and dealt with in less than a page) undermines its proper effect: his death is important only for the effect it has on Theo's later actions. This may be what Gee regrets. The television series corrects this somewhat by placing his death before a commercial break and by lingering on his final moments, paying more honour to the character.

Yet Ricky's death, and Rachel and Mr Jones' immediate grieving for him, does serve an important moral purpose (as Claudia Marquis observes in her chapter in this book). Until that point, Theo has unquestioningly accepted the need to kill the Wilberforces. Losing Ricky means that he suddenly understands the meaning of death and, therefore, the meaning of killing – which complicates his ability to do it properly. On the one hand, it makes him angry, and vengeful:

> Anger drove him on – anger with Mr Jones for getting Ricky killed and anger with the Wilberforces for killing him. There was nothing to do about Mr Jones – he was on their side. But at least he could get back at the Wilberforces. He was going to turn them into dust. (149)

On the other hand, Theo learns what death means. When he finally throws his weapon into the crater of Mount Eden, his death cry is weakened: '"We bring you the gift of …" he cried. And the final word was nearly lost. Why didn't they say death when they meant it? "oblivion."' (152)

The television series cannot make such swift changes between dialogue, narrative and internal reflection; indeed, it sacrifices the novel's contemplative aspects in favour of a fast-paced and exciting story. In the television version, as he prepares to throw his weapon, Theo says, 'This one's for Ricky,' explicitly linking his actions to vengeance. Neither he nor Rachel utters the death cry, 'We bring you the gift of oblivion,' and so the novel's attempt to understand the meaning of death – or, rather, the meaning of dealing out death to those who deserve it – is lost. But if the TV series is less profound, it is also more optimistic. Ricky's death is explicitly avenged, and the final episode closes with a view of the towers of downtown Auckland, still standing despite the cataclysmic eruption that has destroyed the Wilberforces. The blare of police and ambulance sirens, rather than indicating massive destruction, reassures viewers that systems are still in place and that the city is still intact. Interestingly, the makers of the 2009 film adaptation of *Under the Mountain* decided to keep Ricky alive. In doing so they showed that Ricky's death is a vital part of the story; and the film, without it, is somewhat muted and conventional. Not only does it lack the contemplative qualities of the novel, more seriously, it lacks the awareness of heroic sacrifice that Ricky's death provides. Though the film ends with a lavish set piece in which the various volcanoes of Auckland erupt for a period before the Wilberforces are conquered, the sense of a larger ethical framework is missing.

Theo's anger is directed not only at the Wilberforces but at Mr Jones. After all, 'The People who understand' have driven the Wilberforces to Earth, and Mr Jones has used the twins as his weapons. It may be Mr Jones who has 'got Ricky killed', as much it is the Wilberforces who have done the killing. Who is the more ruthless – the greedy Wilberforces or the implacable Mr Jones? Whose desire is more questionable? The Wilberforces are only doing what comes naturally, building their own habitat, and they are not using children to do their work for them. Ultimately, of course, we recognise (as does Theo) that the side of good requires the sacrifice of the few for the sake of the many, and that Mr Jones is 'on their side', whereas the Wilberforces, who are not on their side, will willingly destroy the many for their own sake. Ricky's death, then, not only provides a genuinely tragic note but is part of the moral debates flowing through *Under the Mountain*, through which Gee challenges some of the conventions of fantasy literature for young readers.

The Fat Man and the cost of coming of age

The Fat Man is a historical novel set in the Depression years in a fictionalised version of Henderson, a community in West Auckland where Gee spent his childhood. In his realist fiction, Gee is bound less strictly by the rules of fantasy/adventure writing and, as such, seems less concerned about the 'covenant' between reader and writer. Realist fiction gives more scope generally for engaging with hard issues front-on. However, when it is realist fiction for young readers, it runs some risks nonetheless. *The Fat Man* is a story of revenge and betrayal that culminates, like *Under the Mountain*, with the destruction of a villain by a child protagonist. In his reflections on the novel, Gee makes the point that evil is 'contained' within the pages, that the successful overthrow of an evil character enables a satisfying conclusion. However, *The Fat Man* shows that evil cannot simply be concentrated in the form of one wicked character and easily dispatched.

In this novel, Herbert Muskie, the fat man of the title, returns to Loomis after a period overseas. He is a criminal who is wanted by the police in America and in New Zealand for bootlegging – and worse. He has become very wealthy through his criminal activities, and he uses this wealth as a weapon to exact vengeance on the people of the community, teachers and pupils alike, who bullied him and made his childhood a misery. Now, with money, in a community hit hard by the Depression, he is able to exert control over them.

The action is observed by Colin Potter, the 11-year-old son of two of Muskie's former tormenters, Laurie and Maisie. Colin watches with growing fear as they are pulled into Muskie's sphere of influence. Muskie takes sadistic pleasure in tormenting his victims who, it emerges, include not just former bullies but his wife and stepdaughter too. And he continues his criminal activities. Eventually, the police find him and pursue him. Muskie snatches Colin, along with Muskie's stepdaughter Verna (in whom he takes an unhealthy interest), and flees. Hunted into the hills nearby, he tries to escape across a ravine in a flying fox – a cage on a wire. He is unable to detach the cage from its starting point and asks for Colin's help. Both Colin and Muskie know that the cage will not bear his weight. Colin cuts the rope, sending Muskie out across the ravine, where he falls to his death. The town is eventually able to recover, but through the events he has witnessed, Colin has learned unpalatable truths about his parents' weakness, which he is unable to forget.

The Fat Man received considerable critical acclaim in New Zealand and overseas. The Library and Information Association of New Zealand Aotearoa (LIANZA) awarded it the 1995 Esther Glen Medal for the 'most distinguished contribution to New Zealand literature for children and young adults'. It also received the Supreme Award in the 1995 AIM Children's Book Awards, as well as winning the Junior category, for readers aged 8–12. There is little doubt that *The Fat Man* is a good book, yet its inclusion in the AIM Children's Book Awards shortlist and its eventual winning of the awards led to controversy. In the months following the announcement of the award a serious debate took place in the Letters pages of the *New Zealand Listener* and literary magazine *Quote UnQuote*. Critics such as the reading advocate Dorothy Butler argued that the themes of the book, particularly the sexual themes, were too advanced and indeed disturbing for junior readers, and that the book should have been placed in the category above. Moreover, Butler felt that the book 'neatly equated evil with physical imperfections'.[7] Conservative writer Agnes-Mary Brooke felt that the book was part of a literary movement that would 'deprive children of their childhood'; and she criticised Gee's attraction to bleak and depressing themes.[8] Gee himself expressed his surprise that the book was entered in the junior category; he had thought of it as written for older readers (i.e. young adults).[9] It appears that decisions about categories were based on the age of the protagonist – in this case, 11-year-old Colin Potter – and not on any other factors.

Fellow novelists supported *The Fat Man*. Jack Lasenby wrote that attacks on it amounted to censorship, while Paula Boock saw in the controversy a misunderstanding of the kinds of stories children like to read:

> Children have a natural awareness of cruelty and evil in the world – they will invent bogeymen under the bed or witches in the dark with or without literature to represent such things ... One could argue that frightening characters in books acknowledge and validate the fears children already have, and bring them into the open where they are more controllable.[10]

The debate continued for some time after the correspondence closed. It was reopened in 1999 when Boock's *Dare, Truth or Promise*, a lesbian love story for young adults, won the Supreme Award – which provoked 'an even greater storm'.[11] Similar controversies have occurred in other countries: for example, in Australia in 1999, when the Children's Book Council awarded Book of the Year to Sonya Hartnett's *Sleeping Dogs*, a young adult novel with themes of incest, set in Depression-era Australia. As Tessa Duder observes, it is likely that had they not been given such attention by awarding bodies, these potentially controversial novels might have escaped such extreme reactions. Nevertheless, the controversy surrounding *The Fat Man* is worth considering because it shows, in a different way to the television adaptation of *Under the Mountain*, the strength of public response to Gee's writing: for one thing, it seems to have struck a far deeper chord of fear in adult readers.

We do not see adult readers or writers complaining that *Under the Mountain* is too frightening for children; indeed, the publicity for the 2009 film adaptation of the book delightedly announces that the television series 'terrorised and thrilled a generation of Kiwis'.[12] The Wilberforces are not so different from Herbert Muskie in terms of their appearance, destructive impulse and power to terrify, except for one important difference – their terror is allegorical rather than real: the genre of *Under the Mountain*, despite its carefully representative New Zealand setting, is science fiction or fantasy. The terror in this book is thus more benign; children can be safely afraid reading it; the moral drama is displaced into an 'other world'. In contrast, *The Fat Man*'s realistic Depression-era setting, which draws on the New Zealand of Gee's youth and the New Zealand of Frank Sargeson's stories, is not escapist. As Vivien van Rij and Diane Hebley note in their chapters, Gee's realist historical novels incorporate a sense of lived moral drama to the New Zealand reader's experience. And if that moral drama is dark, with the possible sexual abuse going on in Herbert Muskie's family and the assisted suicide of the endgame, then perhaps a realist setting makes for an overload of darkness – especially for the local reader.

Gee's realism is uncompromising, and critics of *The Fat Man*, while they acknowledge the skill of his realist setting and style, dislike what they see as the 'unpleasant' imagery of Gee's persistent depressing and dark vision. In a 1995 interview Gee responds to this criticism; he claims for his vision an observant realism that goes back to his childhood:

> A woman down south asked in a letter to the paper why everything had to be so ugly. Why, she said, is the man's hair pasted to his chest like slime? Why when he blows creek water from his mouth, why must it be like a draught horse peeing? My answer is, I lived by a creek for the whole of my boyhood and saw people swimming in it every day in summer and I know what wet black hair looks like on a white chest; and every day of my life back then I passed a paddock with two draught horses in it. The likenesses are not ones I invented at sixty, they're ones I saw for myself at six.[13]

However carefully or realistically Gee may have drawn on his childhood observations of the abject for his depiction of Herbert Muskie and other elements of *The Fat Man*, comments like this do not really refute the charge of unpleasantness, ugliness or darkness of vision. Through realistic details such as those Gee mentions, Muskie is powerfully depicted, even more powerfully than the 'bogeyman' Paula Boock identifies. Muskie has a thrilling horror to him, because he combines realism and abjection in his appearance and actions.

Critics disliked the way that horror was localised in the fat body of Herbert Muskie, arguing that it demonised the physically different. (Indeed, the many unattractive villains who appear throughout Gee's work bear out this argument, to some degree.) However, *The Fat Man* is more subtle than that. Herbert's fatness causes him to be both villain and victim. As a fat boy, he is vulnerable to bullying, which is one cause of his later desire for vengeance. To some extent, the evil Muskie was created by the town of Loomis, by the repeated and vicious bullying he suffered as a child at the hands of Colin Potter's father Laurie and his friends, and by the complicity of a community that failed to intervene. So readers are invited to view Muskie with fear, for he is a terrifying figure, but also with pity. It is a complex representation, and we (and the narrative, and the protagonist, 11-year-old Colin) are not able just to dismiss Herbert Muskie as a mere baddie.

Complexity, contained in seemingly simple stories, is a hallmark of Gee's approach, and the ability to see the victim in the villain distinguishes *The Fat Man* from many other books for young readers. In a 2000 article for *Landfall*, Margaret Mahy singles it out as an example of what serious writing for children should be. *Landfall* asked writers to discuss a major literary event or text in New Zealand publishing in the twentieth century; Mahy wrote:

> I am choosing, as a key twentieth century literary event in New Zealand, the publication of *The Fat Man*, a young adult book by Maurice Gee which is both a single event and the exemplification of a twentieth century process which allows children's books to be taken seriously as literature.[14]

Mahy identifies a combination of complexity and truth that elevate Gee's books, and particularly *The Fat Man*, from the usual fare for children:

> Gee is telling a story which, like many of his adult books, draws on complex and sometimes dark themes, but he writes with truth, including truths that children's writers are generally expected to avoid or symbolise, since appreciation of those truths calls for a perception that most children have not had a chance to develop. And I think that, with *The Fat Man*, Maurice Gee's writing for young readers becomes one with his most central adult writing. One feels the author is engaged in a primary way.[15]

As Kathryn Walls observes, a common theme in Mahy's writing about literature is her interest in its ability to tell the 'truth': she sometimes puts it as the relationship between 'story truth' and 'real truth', where story truth is transforming and visionary.[16] What Mahy sees happening in *The Fat Man*, in terms of the complex truth she argues it tells, causes her to suggest it should be seen as 'literature' rather than children's literature:

> I think the publication of *The Fat Man* was a challenging literary event because the book was written without imaginative reduction ... and I think it takes writing for young adults seriously as literature, rather than as peripheral entertainment or as a source of moral example.[17]

In truth, then, lies complexity: *The Fat Man* is truthful because it is not reduced or boiled down for children. Gee himself refers to this in 'Creeks and kitchens' when he says that the book is 'fully imagined':

> I wrote the book with full commitment. It's fully imagined. I don't think you'll find a page in it that is merely invented. I knew that it might be judged as unpleasant and disturbing, but believed that this would be a misjudgement if the book was seen as a whole.[18]

In these references – Mahy's to 'truths that children's writers are generally expected to avoid or symbolise', and Gee's to the observed truth of the novel and its being 'fully imagined' – we have the crux of the matter. Much as he did (or perhaps didn't) with the depiction and death of Ricky in *Under the Mountain*, Gee negotiates the competing requirements of literature for young readers. With *The Fat Man*, it seems clear that Gee and Mahy are actually saying these requirements do not, and should not, compete: that is to say, telling the 'truth', even if it is challenging, controversial or dark, is better for young readers than sliding over uncomfortable places in a story.

Considering some of the elements of *The Fat Man* reveals many uncomfortable places: the monstrous depiction of Herbert Muskie, the warped relationship with his mother, his sadistic treatment of his wife and the other people in his power, as well as the hints of sexual abuse in his relationship with his stepdaughter. Perhaps most uncomfortable is the pain that Muskie himself has undergone. The bullying in his childhood is a case in point – he has been singled out for his unfortunate appearance, and ganged up on by people who should know better, because they are technically 'good' people. Who made Muskie? Is he naturally evil, or was he made evil? He is so vicious that it is easier to fear him than to pity him; yet Gee asks us to, and he shows Colin Potter as able to do so. As reviewers Diane Brown and Jennifer Roback commented:

> [W]hat is most fascinating about this horrific story is the author's ability to project Colin's pity for the evildoer. In a final chase scene, Colin catches a glimpse of the tormented fat boy beneath the fat man, and understands the cruelty he himself has suffered. Gee brilliantly allows readers to see the child within each adult, and to recognize the complexity of the consequences one's actions can yield.[19]

As in *Under the Mountain*, pity for the soon-to-be-vanquished villain is most clearly seen at the end of the novel. Here Muskie, on the run from the police who have finally caught up with his criminal activities, abducts Colin and his stepdaughter Verna. They drive through the hills to a ravine, where he leaves Verna and runs with Colin towards the flying fox. He asks Colin to help him into the cage of the flying fox.

> The fat man stepped onto the platform. He put down his case and panted, hands on knees. 'WE can – cross. WE can – get away.'
>
> 'No,' Colin said. 'It'll break.'
>
> 'You tellin' me what to do, kid?' Suddenly he was Herbert Muskie again, snarling at Colin. The worm twisted, fattened in his cheek.
>
> Colin stepped back. He was safe. He could run.
>
> 'You're too heavy for it,' he said.
>
> Tears leaked from the fat man's eyes and dripped on the platform. He was changing back and forth. 'Pottsie, you're helping me now. Aren't you, Pottsie?'
>
> 'If you want.'

'Help me get in here, Pottsie. You and me are mates.'

The policemen were running down the hill, yelling at them.

The fat man put his suitcase in the cage. He lifted one leg heavily and got it over the rail. The wire sagged with his weight, but he heaved the other leg in and squatted like a child in a box too small for it, holding the couplings with two hands. 'They're coming, Pottsie. They're going to get me. Untie the rope.'

Colin saw how eaten with rot the planks of the cage were. It strained to get away down the wire. The river ran below, deep in the gorge, white and green. (139)

Note the way that Herbert Muskie shapeshifts in this passage, between being 'the fat man' and Herbert Muskie. As 'the fat man' he is an object of fear, with a wormlike scar in his cheek, who snarls at Colin and calls him 'kid'; as Herbert Muskie he is pitiable, weeping, 'like a child', and he calls Colin 'Pottsie' and considers him a 'mate'. In his final moments, when he persuades Colin to cut the rope that holds the flying-fox cage on the edge of the ravine, the distinction between these two identities dissolves:

'Please, Pottsie,' Herbert Muskie wept.

Colin saw there was no way of untying the knot. The fat man's weight had pulled it too tight. He took the razor from his pocket and unfolded it.

'Do you want to go?'

'Yeah, Pottsie, cut it eh. Go on, do it, kid.'

Colin cut the rope. (140)

In giving the gift of oblivion both to Herbert Muskie and to the fat man, the villain and the victim, Colin is committing an act of vengeance, but also an act of compassion. He kills the one (the fat man) and releases the other (Herbert Muskie). The simple act of cutting the rope contains a very complex and powerful set of intentions and meanings.

Colin has rid the town of Loomis from the terror of Herbert Muskie's reign; he also rids it of its shame for the complicity that helped create Muskie. Yet Colin himself never quite loses that shame: for him his parents are diminished by his knowledge of their past and present weakness. Gee finds this satisfying and he believes his readers will too:

There's a poem by Dan Davin that he uses as an epigraph to his short story collection, *The Gorse Blooms Pale*. Two of the lines read 'My father was a hero once, Now he is a man.' That happened to me – twice, in fact – with my jaw-punching father and my jailbird grandfather. It happens to Colin Potter in *The Fat Man*. His father stops being a hero and becomes a man. His mother too becomes more real, becomes fallible. I imagine that to ten, twelve, fifteen-year-old readers that can be very satisfying.[20]

I suspect that this point may underlie critics' unease with the book – an unease that goes beyond the more obvious points about the cruelty and horror that lie within the novel. Colin cannot go home again; he can no longer be an innocent child, unquestioningly admiring and looking up to his parents. On the one hand, this is because he takes on the hero's role – he is the one to rid Loomis of Herbert Muskie – and he therefore exceeds the abilities of his parents. Novels for young readers that have heroic action in them, be they science fiction, fantasy or historical, often sidestep this issue. Parents are often conveniently dead, missing or out of the way somehow, so the child hero does not have to reflect on their weakness or frailty. Certainly this is the case with Gee's fantasy novels, in which parents seldom appear. Nevertheless, his realistic fiction requires child protagonists to be confronted by the powerlessness of their parents. Sometimes this is powerlessness in the face of evil; sometimes it is powerlessness in the face of convention or social custom. In *The Fat Man*, it is both: Laurie and Maisie have given in to convention very early in their lives, making them weak bullies as children, and weak victims as adults.

At some point, most children will encounter and recognise adult weakness, whether in a parent or some other authority figure. To some degree it is a vital step in coming of age and separating from what could become an unhealthy dependence on one's parents. A common theme among the villains of Gee's novels for young readers is an unnaturally close relationship between parent and child, where the child has not managed to cut free from a domineering or co-dependent parent: this is certainly the case in *The Fat Man*, *The Fire-Raiser* and *The Limping Man*. If Gee has a bias, it is towards independent thought – whereby the young protagonist learns how to identify good or bad role models, and ultimately how to think for him or her self. At the conclusion of *The Fat Man*, Colin has used his own judgement to act for the good – ending up sadder but wiser. Perhaps this is one more price of heroic action: with wisdom comes knowledge; with knowledge comes pain – another aspect of the melancholy note that sounds throughout Gee's work, and indeed throughout his New Zealand landscape. Gee's young protagonists undergo a far greater, darker and more reflective coming of age than in many novels for young adult readers.

In 'Creeks and kitchens', where Gee talks in some detail about *The Fat Man*, he expresses his satisfaction with the containment that the novel represents:

> [W]e must think of that 'story' which gives control by holding everything inside a structure. The terrible event does not exist in isolation but takes its place within a sequence of events that continues to move and grow, that continues to answer the question, 'what happens next?', and that is completed in a way that satisfies. The fat man, Herbert Muskie, is frightening all right, but he's held in control, he's inside a story that carries on answering the question and reaches an end that should make the reader give a sigh of satisfaction and say, Yes, that's right.[21]

Herbert Muskie's death – like the death of the Wilberforces in *Under the Mountain* – represents the story's containment of horror. Readers of the book will be afraid while they are reading the book, while they are 'in' the story. The characters in the book are changed by the events they have been part of. Colin Potter will be (as will be Rachel and Theo) 'very deeply affected by what has happened to them'.[22] When Gee talks about his writing for children, he shows his concern to be responsible to his readers, to contain the truth within a safe structure. While he has done that in these novels, in terms of showing child protagonists confronting and conquering evil or wickedness, his work teaches hard lessons about the world, especially the frailties of adults and authority.

If Gee went in to writing literature for young readers with the assumption that it would be easy work, he must have been surprised by the challenges he faced in negotiating the demands of the genre: responsibility to young readers, to his characters, and to the ideas that pervade the novel. Judging by the remainder of his novels, he never again killed off an attractive helper figure in so cavalier a fashion as he did with Ricky. He certainly has not shied away from engaging in the moral dimension of literature for young readers, or from possible controversy resulting from that approach, as the two novels discussed here admirably show.

NOTES

Editors' note
1. Trevor James, 'Beyond realism: Maurice Gee and a critical praxis', in *Journal of New Zealand Literature* 4, 1996, 111.
2. Denis Welch, 'A creek runs through it', *New Zealand Listener*, 8 October 2005, 38.
3. Elizabeth Hale & Sarah Fiona Winter (eds), *Marvellous Codes: The fiction of Margaret Mahy* (Wellington: Victoria University Press, 2005).

Elizabeth Hale: Introduction
1. Andrew Johnston, 'Maurice Gee: Our superb storyteller', *Evening Post*, 3 July 1993.
2. Awarded by the Storylines Foundation, a major advocate for children's literature in New Zealand.
3. Ginette McDonald (director), *The Fire-Raiser* (Auckland: Television New Zealand, 1986); Maurice Gee, *The Fire-Raiser* (Auckland: Puffin Books, 1986).
4. Ginette McDonald (director), *The Champion* (Auckland: Television New Zealand, 1989); Maurice Gee, *The Champion* (Auckland: Puffin Books, 1989).
5. *The Report of the Special Committee on Moral Delinquency in Children and Adolescents* (Mazengarb Report) (Wellington: Government Printer, 1954).

1 Claudia Marquis: The early fantasy novels
1. Quoted by Cate Brett in her biographical article 'The Gee genius', *North and South*, September 1995, 101. Ireland's comment relates, of course, to Gee as author of major adult novels.
2. Brett, 'The Gee genius', 99.
3. The early fantasy novels are, in order of publication, *Under the Mountain* (Wellington: Oxford University Press, 1979) (*UM*), *The World Around the Corner* (Wellington: Oxford University Press, 1980) (*WAC*), *The Halfmen of O* (Auckland: Oxford University Press, 1982) (*HO*), *The Priests of Ferris* (Auckland: Oxford University Press, 1984) (*PF*) and *Motherstone* (Auckland: Oxford University Press, 1985) (*M*). Reference in the text is to these editions.
4. Bill Manhire, *Maurice Gee: New Zealand writers and their work* (Auckland: Oxford University Press, 1986), 9.
5. See Gee, 'Creeks and kitchens: The 2002 Margaret Mahy Award Lecture', in *The Inside Story: Year Book 2002* (Auckland: Children's Literature Foundation of NZ, 2002), 18.

6   See 'Maurice Gee/Interview by Brian Boyd', in Elizabeth Alley & Mark Williams (eds), *In the Same Room: Conversations with New Zealand writers* (Auckland: Auckland University Press, 1992), 171. It is worth noting that Gee distinguishes his own work in this genre from Margaret Mahy's, which, he feels, possesses the kind of complexity he himself reserves for his adult fiction.

7   See 'Maurice Gee/Interview by Brian Boyd', 171; Gee notes the generic factor in his writing for children at this point – 'adventure fantasy', or thriller. For a rather different observation on this fiction, see his interview with Andrew Johnston, *Evening Post*, 3 July 1993: 'Children's fiction began partly as a deliberate attempt to widen my writing base, and also because I had young children and wanted to write something for them, but certainly it was an attempt to make more money. That's why I went to TV, too.' (www:andrewjohnston.org/gee.htm).

8   *NZ Bookworld*, March 1980, 29; quoted by Manhire, *Maurice Gee*, 70, n. 15. Gee describes his first effort to publish the story, c. 1974, and its eventual publication in revised form in 1979, in 'Creeks and kitchens', 18–19.

9   The Gaelyn Gordon Award celebrates a work of children's fiction that is still in print, although it won no award at the time of publication. Gee has received many awards for these novels, including New Zealand Children's Book of the Year for *The Halfmen of O* in 1983.

10 Diane Hebley, *The Power of Place: Landscape in New Zealand children's fiction, 1970–1989* (Dunedin: University of Otago Press, 1998).

11 Anna Jackson (ed.), *A Made-up Place: New Zealand in young adult fiction* (Wellington: Victoria University Press, 2011). The most substantial discussions of the fantasies are in essays by Geoff Miles ('Utopia') and Tatjana Schaefer ('Religion'). Miles notes that the *O* trilogy as portal/ quest fantasy 'raises ... issues about the ways in which utopia may decline cyclically into dystopia' (96); while Schaefer argues that Gee's 'myth' is Christian and biblical in origin but, as taken up in his fantasy, reflects a history of religious divisions in New Zealand and comments on 'the dangers of religious authoritarianism and the distorting effect of religious belief' (147). Both concentrate on *The Priests of Ferris*.

12 Vivien van Rij, 'The pursuit of wholeness in Maurice Gee's *O* trilogy', in *International Research in Children's Literature* 3, 2010, 148–61. For the thesis, see Vivien van Rij, 'The pursuit of wholeness in Maurice Gee's fiction for children', Victoria University of Wellington, 2008, especially chapter 1, which deals with the *O* trilogy. Most of the thesis deals with with Gee's historical novels for children; neither thesis nor article discusses *Under the Mountain*, *The World Around the Corner* or the *Salt* trilogy.

13 Given its date, it is not surprising that the list of 'Critical studies and articles' in Bill Manhire's 1986 monograph on Gee's fiction includes

no reference to any study of his writing for children. Cathe Giffuni's bibliography of Gee's works and studies of his writing, four years later, notes the children's writing to date, but expressly includes no criticism; see *Australian and New Zealand Studies in Canada* 3, 1990, 36–42. Manhire himself, as already noted, does have a little to say about it, although he is clear about the limits of any such discussion: 'It would be wrong to subject Gee's work for children to the sort of close attention demanded by the adult novels' (*Maurice Gee*, 11). What is necessarily missing is 'the serious exploration of character'. It is worth noting that the writing for children that dominates in the period from 1986 until 2007 is realist in mode – and that it is this writing that has attracted most critical attention, not infrequently read in relation to Gee's adult fiction.

14 Colleen Reilly, 'An Interview with Maurice Gee', *Australian and New Zealand Studies in Canada* 3 (1990), 1–8.
15 Gee, 'Creeks and kitchens', 18.
16 Ibid., 16.
17 Colin Manlove, *The Impulse of Fantasy Literature*, 30–31, quoted in Peter Hunt (ed.), *Alternative Worlds in Fantasy Fiction* (New York: Continuum, 2001), 9.
18 Gee, 'Creeks and kitchens', 20.
19 Manhire, *Maurice Gee*, 9.
20 It seems to me important to emphasise that in each of the adventure fantasies considered here, Gee has characters make statements that have something of the force of a dictum, but are so grounded in their history, experience and situation that they demand to be read as aspects of the fiction, rather than as lessons, standpoints that might be taken as the thematic business that drives a narrative. Accordingly, while I find much of interest in Vivien van Rij's essay on the *O* trilogy, I remain fundamentally at odds with her view that 'Jungian critique' gives access to 'Gee's ideologies' and identify Gee – 'once a teacher' – as 'consciously aiming to teach the young reader about the self' ('Pursuit of wholeness', 153).
21 Brett, 'Gee genius', 99.
22 In his Margaret Mahy Award lecture, Gee admitted he wrongly resisted his wife's urging to change the conclusion in this respect, since a death like Ricky's breaks fantasy's generic 'covenant that exists between writer and reader': 'If I were writing *Under the Mountain* today I'd save Ricky'; in saying this, he reverses his earlier claim for 'consequences', referring to it as 'a bit of moralising' ('Creeks and kitchens', 19).
23 Gee does discuss this problem, to which Bridget Williams, his editor, alerted him; his answer was to set his story up by means of a prologue, introducing the old man as both a figure of otherworldly power and 'benign'. See 'Creeks and kitchens', 19.
24 See, for example, Tolkien, whose grey magician must become white in order

to compete with the Dark Lord; or Susan Cooper's *Dark Is Rising* series; or, from the other side of the Atlantic, the claim made by Ursula Le Guin's wizard, 'It is light that defeats the dark.'

25 Tzvetan Todorov, *The Fantastic* (Cornell: Cornell University Press, 1975); first published as *Introduction à la littérature fantastique* (Paris: Editions du Seuil). Todorov refers to fantasy in the common sense as the 'marvellous'. For useful accounts of Todorov's thinking, compared with conceptions developed by other modern writers on fantasy, see Rosemary Jackson's *Fantasy: The literature of subversion* (London: Methuen, 1986) and Christine Brooke-Rose, *A Rhetoric of the Unreal: Studies in narrative and structure, especially of the fantastic* (Cambridge: Cambridge University Press, 1981).

26 Todorov, *The Fantastic*, 33.

27 Gee both underplays the textual importance of this code and points it up in terms of the 'lessons in those books [the *O* trilogy], if the child readers can find them – about the pollution and degradation of the environment and of natural things, about the danger of nuclear weapons, about the abuse of political power, and so on' ('Creeks and kitchens', 20).

28 This piece of early personal history is brought up, with irony, in his interviews with Anthony Hubbard ('Obsession of a quiet man', 17) and Cate Brett ('Gee genius', 95).

29 See his Introduction to *Alternative Worlds in Fantasy Fiction*, 2.

30 See especially Tolkien's essay 'On Fairy-Stories', in *Tree and Leaf* (London: HarperCollins, 2001), 3–81.

31 Tolkien, 'On Fairy-Stories', 49.

32 Ibid., 68.

33 Ibid., 71.

34 Ibid., 48.

35 Ibid., 57.

36 Gee, 'Creeks and kitchens', 20.

37 Reilly, 'Interview', 7. Gee says something very similar in his interview with Anthony Hubbard: 'I frequently find when you talk to writers ... that what we utter is banal. The contents of a writer's mind are not particularly interesting ... The interesting thing about a writer occurs somewhere in an area of creative ability, so that you can take the most banal ideas, ordinary and trite ideas and make good fiction out of them' ('Obsession of a quiet man', 17). Nevertheless he also claims that 'in ferreting and working at the truth of certain situations he's subversive, because the truth is likely to be different from popularly accepted beliefs, and official ones too, about the way things are' (Reilly, 'Interview', 8).

38 Gee, 'Creeks and kitchens', 20. Gee instances Jimmy Jasper's proficiency with the axe, crucial to the advance of the adventure in O, but validated by the A&P shows, back in New Zealand, that he shares with the (New Zealand) reader.

39 Gee, 'Creeks and kitchens', 24.
40 See Tzvetan Todorov, 'The grammar of narrative', in *The Poetics of Prose* (Oxford: Basil Blackwell, 1977), 111. For a reading of children's fiction from this point of view, similar to mine, see J.G. Appleyard, *Becoming a Reader: The experience of fiction from childhood to adulthood*. Appleyard turns to Todorov and Northrop Frye to provide theoretical support for his observation of 'a large affective dimension in the adventure story's balance of diversity and sameness' (63). In this 'affective dimension', I suggest, we register ideology at work, whether it is acknowledged or not.
41 Quoted in Hunt, *Alternative Worlds*, 91. But note also Gee's response to Reilly's question, 'Is the only reason we must acknowledge evil to be able to withstand it, as Bill Manhire suggests?' [Gee:] 'The act of standing against it is worth something, even if you're defeated in the end' (7).
42 In her interview with Gee, Colleen Reilly cited Brian Boyd's claim that, for Gee, the 'root of all evil' is 'the will'. Gee's response is interesting, although he (typically) downplays its value: 'One of my obsessions, rather than with the will, is with evil. I'm very simple in my obsession – I can't understand how human beings can be evil and some of them quite plainly are. I don't think it's got much to do with will – it's something that exists in a pure state' (8).
43 In *Areopagitica*; see *Milton's Prose Writings* (London: Dent, 1958), 163.
44 The reach of the cult's control of human society on O suggests, in fact, that Gee intends his fiction to have the aggressively cautionary thrust of great liberal statements like E.M. Forster's essay, 'What I believe'.
45 See van Rij, 'Pursuit of Wholeness', 154.
46 Gee's trilogy seems to me to show little interest in Jungian psychological theory, in fact; although the vaguer stuff of Jungianism – Jung in popular discourse – may have some importance for a reading of Gee's fantasies. Comparison with Ursula Le Guin is useful in this regard; see her collection, *Language of the Night: Essays on fantasy and science fiction* (New York: Putnam, 1979) and especially her essay 'The child and the shadow', in *Quarterly Journal of the Library of Congress* 32, 1975, 139–48.
47 From this point of view, it is worth considering again the significance of placenames. Farah Mendlesohn notes that, following Tolkien, maps and histories have become something of a 'trend' – for signalling entry into the genre – in the case of portal/quest narratives; see Mendlesohn, *Rhetorics of Fantasy* (Middletown, Conn.: Wesleyan University Press, 2008), chapter 1, pp. 14 and especially 30–38. She notes that maps no more correlate with geography than chronologies do with history in such fiction. Nevertheless, Gee (perhaps more in the fashion of Arthur Ransome's *Swallows and Amazons* etc) provides a map of Auckland, Takapuna and the Waitemata harbour in the endpapers to *Under the Mountain*, a real aid to any outside reader who wishes to trace the directions taken by Rachel and Theo in their adventurous trips around the region. He also provides a map of O in

The Priests of Ferris, which likewise seems useful, since the high-energy adventuring of the fantastic narrative tends to make distance and direction indistinct. Nevertheless, Gee also plays games: the compass image that orients the map cries out to be read left to right, so that it keys the reader to the narrative in terms of ethical, rather than spatial directions, in reading W-O-E. We might then say the kind of playfulness this suggests (and Gee has confessed his pleasure in textual play) probably makes the fantasy a most remarkable, but entirely Kiwi, O-E-xperience!

48 'Gee's young heroes tend to be granted character traits (one character is dreamy, another practical) rather than characters' (Manhire, *Maurice Gee*, 11).
49 Gee, 'Creeks and kitchens', 18.
50 Reilly, 'Interview', 7.
51 Gee reports that he killed Jimmy Jaspers off in the first version of *The Halfmen of O* but, faced with his family's objections, revised Jimmy's fate – to his authorial profit, since Jimmy expands the range of characters in succeeding stories but also anchors different plotlines.
52 See Shelley, 'A defence of poetry', in *Essays, Letters from Abroad, Translations and Fragments*, 2 vols (London: Edward Moxon, 1840).
53 See Derek Brewer, *Symbolic Stories: Traditional narratives of the family drama in literature* (Woodbridge: Boydell & Brewer, 1970).
54 See Williams, 'Maurice Gee/Interview by Brian Boyd', 171. Gee also notes critical comment on his pessimism in his interview with Anthony Hubbard, but emphasises not a movement towards self-knowledge, but a common focus in his novels on solitary characters: 'It's not a fixed belief of mine that we are all inevitably solitary, but that seems to be the way that most of the characters move' (Obsession of a quiet man', 17). In fantasy/adventure, of course, you get to be solitary because you – first – get to be chosen.
55 Gee, 'Creeks and kitchens', 17.

2 Diane Hebley: The good, the bad – and ironic reversals

1 Maurice Gee, 'Beginnings', *Islands* 5, March 1976, 284–92; and 'Creeks and kitchens: The 2002 Margaret Mahy Award Lecture', *The Inside Story: Year Book 2002* (Auckland: Children's Literature Foundation of New Zealand, 2002), 11–25.
2 Cate Brett, 'The Gee genius: Stalking the middle classes', *North and South*, September 1995, 91–101.
3 Brian Boyd, 'Maurice Gee: Ironies of growth and judgement, Part 1: The early fiction', *Islands* 8, October 1980, 268–81.
4 Bärbel Czennia, 'Cross-cultural encounters and xenophobia in contemporary New Zealand children's literature: Maurice Gee's historical novels *The Fire-Raiser* and *The Champion*', in *The Inside Story: Year Book 2002* (Auckland, Storylines: Children's Literature Foundation, 2003), 71–92.

5 Gee, 'Creeks and kitchens', 21.
6 Steve Braunias, 'Our man in Loomis', *New Zealand Listener*, 24 July 2004, 54.
7 Iain Sharp, 'Dial Gee for Gruesome', *Sunday Star-Times*, 29 August 2004, C7.
8 Boyd, 'Maurice Gee: Ironies, Part 1', 269.
9 Brett, 'The Gee genius', 99.
10 Sharp, 'Dial Gee for Gruesome', C7.
11 As do many of his adults. See Lawrence Jones, 'Three views of a changing scene: The *Plumb* trilogy', *Barbed Wire & Mirrors: Essays on New Zealand prose*, 2nd edn (Dunedin: University of Otago Press, 1990), 182.
12 Mark Williams, *Leaving the Highway: Six contemporary New Zealand novelists* (Auckland: Auckland University Press, 1990), 174.
13 Williams, *Leaving the Highway*, 188.
14 Tom Fitzgibbon & Barbara Spiers (eds), *Tea-tree and Iron Sands: A guide to present-day New Zealand children's writers* (Auckland: Auckland College of Education, 1986); revised as *Beneath Southern Skies: New Zealand children's book authors and illustrators* (Auckland: Ashton Scholastic, 1993), 36.

3 Elizabeth Hale: Mining Gee

1 There are exceptions: *The World Around the Corner* has only one child protagonist, nine-year-old Caroline; the heroes of *The Fire-Raiser* are a group of four children; and the protagonist of *The Champion*, Rex, joins forces with Dawn and Leo, forming a trio.
2 Maurice Gee, *Gool*, (Auckland: Puffin Books, 2008) 202.
3 Perry Nodelman, *The Hidden Adult: Defining children's literature* (Baltimore: Johns Hopkins Press, 2008), 65.
4 Dorothy Butler, 'Children's fiction – what message?', in *New Zealand Listener*, 13 May 1995, 12; Maurice Gee, 'Creeks and kitchens: The 2002 Margaret Mahy Award Lecture', in *The Inside Story: Year Book 2002* (Auckland: Children's Literature Foundation of New Zealand, 2002), 24.
5 See chapters in this book.
6 Maurice Gee, *The Limping Man*, 64–65.
7 John Milton, *Paradise Lost*, Book XII, lines 648–49.
8 Judith Holloway, 'A fat boy, a creek and a personal responsibility', *New Zealand Books* 3, 5, August 1995, 22–24.
9 Roberta Seelinger Trites, *Disturbing the Universe: Power and repression in adolescent literature* (Iowa City, IA: University of Iowa Press, 2000).
10 Maurice Gee, *Salt*, 84.
11 Mikhail Bakhtin, 'Form of time and chronotope in the novel', in Michael Holquist (ed.), *The Dialogic Imagination: Four essays* (Austin: UTP, 1981), 84–258.
12 Maurice Gee, 'Creeks and kitchens,' 18.

4 Kathryn Walls: 'What I must steer clear of'

1. Prefatory notes: (i) Lydia Wevers, Director of the Stout Centre, Victoria University, provided me with the opportunity to develop my ideas about the maternal influence on Gee in a Stout Centre Seminar in 2005. (ii) A condensed version of the first section of this chapter (on *Mihi and the Last of the Moas*) appeared in *New Zealand Books* 76, December 2006, 12. (iii) The title quotation comes from *Meg* (London: Faber & Faber, 1981), 9. Meg, writing her autobiography, resolves to rid her writing of the 'fancies' so disliked by her son Raymond.
2. Marion McLeod (in a valuable *New Zealand Listener* piece coinciding with the publication of *The Champion*) writes: 'The parents and grandparents [in *The Champion*] are quite unlike his own, except that Gee's mother, like Rex's, wrote poetry' ('A champion tale', *New Zealand Listener*, 7 May 1988, 29). Maurice Gee told Steve Braunias: 'There was a lot of writing going on in my family. My mother wrote. An aunt was a poet' (*New Zealand Listener*, 24 July 2004, 52). Nelson Wattie, writing in Roger Robinson & Nelson Wattie (eds), *Oxford Companion to New Zealand Literature* (Auckland: Oxford University Press, 1998), is an exception to the rule in that he does not mention Gee's mother's published work at all, while at the same time he attaches serious influence to her (oral) 'tales of family history' – judging them 'important to Gee's developing sense of storytelling, providing a sense of social history and its implications for families, couples and individuals' (197). Wattie appears to have gathered this view from Maurice Gee himself. Interviewed by Thomas E. Tausky in 1991, Gee described his mother as 'a story-teller of some talent and skill'. See '"I let the story make its own demands": An interview with Maurice Gee' (*Australian and New Zealand Studies in Canada* 12, 1994, 156). Most recently, speaking to Kathryn Ryan on National Radio's *Nine to Noon* on 25 July 2007 after winning the 2007 Montana Book Award, he identified his mother's stories about her family as an important influence, adding that she 'mythologised' her father.
3. Lyndahl Chapple Gee is Harriet Gee's penname; it incorporates the name she was evidently known by and her maiden name.
4. In his autobiographical essay 'Beginnings,' published in *Islands* 17, 5:3, 1977 [not 1976 as on the cover], 284–92, Gee alludes to a story involving a swagman and a foreman, but he does not identify its title (289).
5. No date of publication appears in the book; 1943 is the date given in the National Library Catalogue entry.
6. Lyndahl Gee, '*Mihi and the Last of the Moas: The adventures of Mihi, a little Maori boy, with the very last of the moas*' (Oswald-Sealy, 1943), 14.
7. Maurice Gee, *The Priests of Ferris* (Auckland: Puffin Books, 1987), 66; *PF* was first published in 1984.
8. Maurice Gee, *The Halfmen of O* (Auckland: Oxford University Press, 1982), 38 (emphasis in the original).

9 Gee, *Halfmen of O*, 104–11. Although Gee's Birdfolk, unlike his mother's birds, are not native New Zealand species – which makes sense, given that O is another planet – Gee does recall her Morepork character when Nick uses a morepork's cry to alert Susan to the fact that he is coming to her rescue (*HO* 53).
10 Underground locations feature not only in the *O* trilogy, but in almost all Gee's fantasies for children. In *Under the Mountain* the evil Wilberforces, inhabiting the bodies of giant slug-like creatures, worm their way beneath Auckland via a network of tunnels and caves – part of which is entered by the child protagonists Rachel and Theo. The more recent *Salt* trilogy (2007–10) features burrows (as the dwelling-places of the oppressed masses) and the deathly mine known as Deep Salt (as a kind of gulag). But it is in the *O* trilogy that Gee's indebtedness to *Mihi* is most extensive and obvious.
11 Gee complements the underground journey, as his mother did not, by having Nick and Susan journey over land and sea, and by including episodes of flight. These journeys work together to create a metaphor of the wholeness that planet O has lost. On wholeness in Gee, see Vivien van Rij's chapter.
12 Maurice Gee, *The Champion* (Auckand: Puffin Books, 1989), 173.
13 Latterly, while implicitly excluding *Mihi*, Maurice Gee has mentioned how well he knew his mother's 'poetry'. According to Polly Greek of the *Dominion Post*, '[Maurice Gee] says there are no children's stories that he remembers growing up with. His mother was a poet, however, and used to recite her poetry to him so often that he came to know large chunks of it' (13 May 2006, 4). Speaking to Louise Guerin in 1984, however, he had given an almost contrary impression – recalling *Mihi*, but implicitly denying that he had come to remember any of his mother's verses: 'My mother *must have read to us, I suppose*. She wrote short stories herself and had a little children's book in verse published called *Mihi and the Last of the Moas*' (*New Zealand Listener*, 13 October 1984, 20) (emphasis added).
14 Frank Sargeson (ed.), *Speaking for Ourselves* (Christchurch: Caxton Press, 1947), 23–30.
15 Lyndahl Gee, 'Double Unit', 25–26.
16 'Bully' and 'Sissy' are what each boy considers the other (25). For the aggressive father on the Italians, see 27.
17 Vivien van Rij elaborates on this point in chapter 6.
18 The antithetical characteristics emerge 142–50. Susan distinguishes them quite quickly: 'He [Seeker] became her favourite. Finder was more bossy' (142–43).
19 In a lecture given in 1930, after interpreting a subject's dream of a spiral as 'the attempt of the unconscious to penetrate the consciousness' (an attempt that, if successful, would result in a loss of distinction between the two), Jung went on to comment: 'Also, by intuition, you have something here that suggests the Taoist symbol. In the black you have the white spot, and in the white the black spot, indicating that when Yang has reached its culmination,

Yin is born again': see William McGuire (ed.), *Dream Analysis: Notes of the seminar given in 1928–1930 by C.J. Jung* (London: Routledge & Kegan Paul, 1984), 524–25. (The Taoist symbol is reproduced as an illustration in this volume, 524). Gee's halves clearly refer to this symbol. See *The Halfmen*, 15, 195 and (for a description incorporating the contrasting spot) 120. My emphasis on Jung is obviously *pace* – Claudia Marquis (c.f. chapter chapter 1, n. 20, 183–84).

20 Marion McLeod, 'A champion tale' (*New Zealand Listener*, 7 October 1989), 29.
21 This sympathy is more clearly evident in a remark Gee made to Steve Braunias in reference to *Mihi:* '[Gee] "I've never forgiven the bloody *Listener* for their review." [Braunias] "It reads, in its insufferable entirety: 'The printers have done their work well.'" [Gee] "That really is the most dismissive comment to make. She was mortified by it. Yeah."' (*New Zealand Listener*, 24 July 2004, 52). (Lyndahl might, however, have been almost equally 'mortified' by her son's assessment of her work in 'Beginnings'!)
22 Thomas E. Tausky, '"I let the story make its own demands": An interview with Maurice Gee', *Australian and New Zealand Studies in Canada* 12, December 1944, 156.
23 Harold Bloom, *The Anxiety of Influence: A theory of poetry* (New York: Oxford University Press, 1973).
24 Maurice Gee reaffirmed his commitment to 'character' above all in his National Radio interview with Kathryn Ryan, 25 July 2007. My discussion of 'character' resonates with those of Elizabeth Hale (Introduction, 21–27; chapter 3, 97), Claudia Marquis (chapter 1, 46–47) and Louise Clark (chapter 5).
25 The implication that writing for children is easier than writing for adults is somewhat countered by Gee's (perhaps equally dismissive) suggestion that it pays the bills. When discussing his children's writing with Kathryn Ryan (in the interview noted immediately above), Gee spoke of his children's fiction in the context of his need to 'make a living'. In the same interview, however, he also spoke of his children's writing as 'broaden[ing his] range', thus recognising in a perhaps more positive sense the exceptional character of his children's fiction within his work as a whole. Gee called children's writing 'far less satisfying' in conversation with Louise Guerin (*New Zealand Listener*, 13 October 1984, 21).
26 In conversation with Louise Guerin (*New Zealand Listener*, 13 October 1984, 21).
27 Tausky, '"I let the story make its own demands"', 160 (emphasis added).
28 In conversation with Louise Guerin (*New Zealand Listener*, 13 October 1984, 21) (emphasis added), c.f. Louise Clark, chapter 5, 123.
29 'It would be wrong to subject Gee's work for children to the sort of close attention demanded by the adult novels. The element that is conspicuously missing from the children's writing is the serious exploration of character.' See Bill Manhire, *Maurice Gee* (Auckland: Oxford University Press), 11.

30 Maurice Gee, *Sole Survivor* (London: Faber & Faber, 1983), 212 (emphasis added).
31 Maurice Gee, *Meg* (London: Faber & Faber, 1981).
32 Gee in conversation with Tausky, in "'I let the story make its own demands'", 154: 'But I *know* – I knew my mother so well, and I was so close to her. I know the accuracy of my portrait of that type of woman. I referred constantly to my mother when I wrote the novel. I don't mean that I asked her about it, but I checked it against my memories of her and my knowledge of her all the way through.'
33 See *Meg*, 27.
34 As Gee has said, in the course of a brilliant analysis of his procedure throughout the *Plumb* trilogy, each of his three protagonists (Plumb and Raymond, that is, as well as Meg) 'tells his or her life story' ('The way of a writer', *New Zealand Listener*, 17 January 1987, 42). But while it is, of course, true that *Plumb* and *Sole Survivor* are written 'in the first person', they are not written *by* the first person.
35 Gee's names are frequently puns (cf. 'R. Sole').
36 Gee has frequently recalled how his mother 'mythologised' her father, e.g. in the interview with Kathryn Ryan, National Radio, 25 July 2007. In *Plumb* Gee takes on the counter-task of demythologising him.
37 For Meg's 'Bab' phase, see 76–77. For Meg's revised attitude, cf. 190, where Meg laughs at Alfred's account of his (male) lover's first 'romantic' approach to him – 'He sounds as if he'd been reading *Bab of the Blackwoods*.' It must be acknowledged, though, that genuine 'true love' existed between Alfred and John. The point seems to be that a cliché may on occasion be apt.
38 Without identifying the mature Meg with himself, as I do here, Gee himself has drawn a clear association between Meg's limitations (specifically, her 'sentimentality') and those of his mother as a writer: see Tausky, "'I let the story make its own demands'", 156. But where, according to Gee, his mother never managed 'to write herself past that [sentimentality]', the mature Meg has (at least to a very large extent) done exactly that.
39 Meg notes her tendency to return to 'Capitals' when depressed, revealing that they are inherently mythologising: 'I had thought I was moving nicely to my conclusion but suddenly I was trapped in uncertainties. Capitals reared up and hung like clouds over me. I thought of my brothers and sisters in the Dark Wood' (*Meg* 15).
40 It was while he was writing *Meg* that Lyndahl died. This may be why Gee has Meg 'remember' Raymond's criticism, keeping him at two removes from the immediate action of the novel at that point. His voice is thus a ghostly one, just as Lyndahl's had become for Maurice Gee. Once again the parallel is between Gee and Meg, not Gee and Raymond.

5 Louise Clark: Writing horizontally and vertically

1. Maurice Gee, 'Creeks and kitchens', *The Inside Story: Year Book 2002* (Auckland: Storylines Children's Literature Foundation of New Zealand, 2002), 18.
2. Miles McDowell, 'Fiction for children and adults: Some essential differences', *Children's Literature in Education* 10 (1973), 51.
3. Virginia Haviland, *Children and Literature* (London: Bodley Head, 1974), 203.
4. Brian Boyd, 'Maurice Gee/Interview by Brian Boyd', in Elizabeth Alley & Mark Williams (eds), *In the Same Room* (Auckland: Auckland University Press, 1992), 171.
5. Gee, 'Creeks and kitchens', 21.
6. Ibid., 20.
7. Maurice Gee, *The World Around the Corner* (Auckland: Oxford University Press, 1980), 38.
8. Gee, 'Creeks and kitchens', 18.
9. 'Simply because life is like that, there are no satisfactory conclusions. Life goes on. ... It seemed to me that in so many children's books children are put though terrible adventures and put into great danger and come out the other end unscathed and with no price paid, and no change made in them, no difference made.' *The Authors,* vol. 3, Videotape (Christchurch: Christchurch College of Education Video Production Unit, 1995).
10. Gee, 'Creeks and kitchens', 18.
11. Gee, *The Authors,* vol. 3.
12. Maurice Gee, *Prowlers* (London: Faber & Faber, 1989), 4.
13. Russell Haley, 'Games of choice', *Spleen* 6, December 1976, 8.
14. Bill Manhire, *Maurice Gee* (*New Zealand Writers and Their Work*) (Auckland: Oxford University Press, 1986), 67.
15. Ibid., 68.
16. Ibid., 10.
17. Gee, 'Creeks and kitchens', 20.
18. Ibid., 22.
19. Ibid., 21.
20. Ibid., 23.
21. Ibid., 23.
22. John Stephens, *Language and Ideology in Children's Fiction* (London: Longmans, 1992), 209.
23. Michael King, *Penguin History of New Zealand* (Auckland: Penguin, 2003), 430.
24. *The Report of the Special Committee on Moral Delinquency in Children and Adolescents* (Mazengarb Report) (Wellington, Government Printer, 1954).
25. Ibid., 8–9.
26. Julie Glamuzina & Alison J. Laurie, *Parker & Hulme: A lesbian view* (Auckland: New Women's Press, 1991) sets the murder in its social and

political context. The chapter devoted to the social and cultural situation in New Zealand in 1954 portrays its 'dreary and dull conformity' and 'the conservative and judgemental atmosphere of the times towards anyone who defied the status quo' (48); Maurice Gee, *Hostel Girl* (Auckland: Puffin Books, 1999), 111.
27 *Hostel Girl*, 'Scanties' (12), 'ping pong' (12), 'crippled' (13), 'someone with a screw loose' (59), 'throw a wobbly' (80), 'get the dirty end of the stick' (73), 'she thinks he's a pill' (86).
28 Denis Welch, 'Gee Gee', *New Zealand Listener*, 12 May 2001, 59.
29 Errol seems to be trying to recreate a scene like that of the 1930s tennis party Gee describes in *The Scornful Moon*, and in fact many of the elements are identical – the Hutt Valley setting, the wicker furniture, and the refreshments served out in the garden after a game of tennis (*HG* 13–20).
30 Maurice Gee, *Games of Choice* (Auckland: Oxford University Press, 1976; reprinted 1985), 90.

6 Vivien van Rij: Patterns of exchange

1 Maurice Gee, 'The way of the writer', *New Zealand Listener*, 17 January 1987, 42.
2 Maurice Gee, *The Champion* (Auckland: Puffin Books, 1989), 37.
3 Maurice Gee, *The Fat Man* (Auckland: Viking Press, 1994), 11.
4 Hal Wilton, 'Rockfist Rogan the boxing airman', *The Champion Annual for Boys* (publishing details omitted, 1950), 141–51.
5 Maurice Gee in interview with Vivien van Rij, Wellington, December 2003.
6 See Kathryn Walls' chapter for details on Gee's mother's publication. For more on 'Sons of Sargeson', see Martin Jones, 'Frank Sargeson House', Heritage New Zealand Pouhere Taonga (2004): www.historic.org.nz/TheRegister/RegisterSearch/RegisterResults.aspx?RID=7540
7 For a detailed comparison of Sargeson's and Gee's stories see Vivien van Rij, 'A straight steal: "An affair of the heart" and Maurice Gee's *The Fat Man*', *Kotare* 6, 2006, 31–34.
8 Brian de Palma (director), *Scarface* (Los Angeles: Universal Pictures, 1983).
9 Maurice Gee, 'Early reading', *Education* vol. 24, no. 8, 1975, 25.
10 *Laurel and Hardy Way Out West*, directed by James W. Horne (Universal Pictures, 1937) [on DVD].
11 Maurice Gee, *Sole Survivor* (Auckland: Penguin Books, 1984), 89.
12 For examples of Grey's emblematic landscape, see Zane Grey, *The Spirit of the Border* (Wisconsin: Whitman Publishing Company, n.d.).
13 Agnes Nieuwenhuizen, 'Know the author: Maurice Gee – Creek, kitchen & the art of language', in *Magpies: Talking about books for children* 12, 1, 1997, 4.

7 Elizabeth Hale: Representation and responsibility

1. Maurice Gee, '*Under the Mountain* by Maurice Gee: the 2004 Gaelyn Gordon Award recipient', *The Inside Story*, Yearbook 2004 (Auckland: Storylines: Children's Literature Foundation of New Zealand, 2004), 31.
2. Ibid., 30.
3. Chris Bailey (director), *Under the Mountain* (Auckland: TVNZ, 1981); Jonathan King (director), *Under the Mountain* (Auckland: Index Films, Liberty Films, 2009).
4. 'Maurice Gee/Interview by Brian Boyd', in Elizabeth Alley & Mark Williams (eds), *In the Same Room: Conversations with New Zealand Writers* (Auckland: Auckland University Press, 1992).
5. Judith Holloway, 'A fat boy, a creek and a personal responsibility', *New Zealand Books* 3, 5, August 1995, 22–24.
6. Maurice Gee, 'Creeks and kitchens: Margaret Mahy Lecture, 23 March 2002', *The Inside Story*, Yearbook 2002 (Auckland: Storylines: Children's Literature Foundation of New Zealand, 2003), 19.
7. Dorothy Butler, 'Children's fiction – what message?' in 'Letters', *New Zealand Listener*, 13 May 1995, 12.
8. Agnes-Mary Brooke, 'Children's fiction – what message?' in 'Letters', *New Zealand Listener*, 10 June 1995, 14.
9. Gee, 'Creeks and kitchens', 24.
10. Paula Boock, 'Children's books – what message?' in 'Letters', *New Zealand Listener*, 1 July 1995, 13.
11. Tessa Duder, 'Much ado about The Fat Man', www.tessaduder.co.nz/res_fatman.html. I am grateful to Tessa Duder for alerting me to this controversy.
12. 'Under the Mountain (2009)', *Weta NZ* promotional website: www.wetanz.com/under-the-mountain
13. Holloway: 'A fat boy, a creek and a personal responsibility', 22.
14. Margaret Mahy, in 'Bookmarking the century (Literature)', *Landfall* 199, 2000, 38–39.
15. Ibid.
16. Kathryn Walls discusses Mahy's allegiance to truth in '"True-seeming lyes" in Margaret Mahy's fiction', in Elizabeth Hale & Sarah Fiona Winters (eds), *Marvellous Codes: The fiction of Margaret Mahy* (Wellington: Victoria University Press, 2005), 148–67.
17. Mahy, 'Bookmarking the century', 38.
18. Gee, 'Creeks and kitchens', 24.
19. Diane Brown & Jennifer Roback, 'The Fat Man (1994)', *Publishers Weekly*, vol. 244, no. 44, 27 October 1997, 77.
20. Gee, 'Creeks and kitchens', 25.
21. Ibid.
22. Holloway, 'A fat boy, a creek and a personal responsibility', 24

CONTRIBUTORS

Louise Clark graduated MA (Hons) in English from Canterbury University, and worked as a research assistant and librarian before returning to academic life as a tutor in English at the University of Waikato. She subsequently convened a paper in children's literature for a number of years. In 2005 she completed an MPhil thesis on the relationship between Maurice Gee's fiction for children and for adults, followed in 2010 by a PhD thesis on New Zealand historical fiction for children and young people.

Elizabeth Hale grew up in New Zealand and studied English literature and Latin at the University of Otago before gaining her MA and PhD in English Literature at Brandeis University in the United States. She now lives in Australia, where she is senior lecturer in English and Writing at the University of New England. She teaches children's literature, media and creative writing, and she has published widely on topics in children's literature, nineteenth-century literature, and classical reception studies. With Sarah Winters, she was co-editor of *Marvellous Codes: The fiction of Margaret Mahy* (Victoria University Press, 2005).

Diane Hebley was writer and course director for The New Zealand Experience in the Christchurch College of Education's National Diploma in Children's Literature. She completed her PhD on children's literature at the University of Waikato, and from this published *The Power of Place: Landscape in New Zealand children's fiction, 1970–1989* (University of Otago Press, 1998). Her poetry, essays and short stories have been published widely in magazines such as *Landfall* and the *New Zealand Listener*, and in books such as *The Oxford Companion to NZ Literature* (Oxford University Press, 1998) and in *Marvellous Codes: The fiction of Margaret Mahy* (Victoria University Press, 2005). In collaboration with her husband Gary she has published five picture books for children; together, they were joint recipients of the New Zealand Children's Literature Association's 1997 Award for Service.

Claudia Marquis is senior lecturer in the Department of English at the University of Auckland, teaching courses in Renaissance and Victorian literature, African and Caribbean literature, and adolescent fiction. Her research concentrates on Caribbean literature as well as children's fiction, especially the work of New Zealand writers. Her most recent publication is the editing of a 'symposium' in *Children's Literature Association Quarterly* on the writing of Margaret Mahy. Her current projects include a book-length study of nineteenth-century fantastic works written for children.

Vivien van Rij has a background in performing arts and primary school teaching. These days she lectures in literature and literacy in the Faculty of Education, Victoria University of Wellington, and enjoys introducing teacher trainees to some of the wonderful books that can be used with children. Vivien has a special interest in primary school-level readers, particularly New Zealand's *School Journal*, and ways in which changing perceptions of childhood and learning influence its form and content. Vivien is also interested in Maurice Gee's books for children, on which she completed her doctoral thesis. She is currently working on a comparative study of children's novels by Gee and Jack Lasenby.

Kathryn Walls is a professor in the School of English, Film and Theatre at Victoria University of Wellington. She is the author of *God's Only Daughter: Spenser's Una as the Invisible Church* (Manchester University Press, 2013), and editor (for the Renaissance English Texts Society of America) of *The Pilgrime* (the seventeenth-century adaptation by William Baspoole of a seminal fourteenth-century allegory of life). Her interest in writing for children has borne fruit in book chapters and journal articles on C.S. Lewis and on Margaret Mahy.

BIBLIOGRAPHY

Appleyard, J.G., *Becoming a Reader: The experience of fiction from childhood to adulthood* (Cambridge: Cambridge University Press, 1991)

The Authors, vol. 3 (Martin Baynton, Sherryl Jordan, Maurice Gee), Videotape (Christchurch: Christchurch College of Education Video Production Unit, 1995)

Bailey, Chris (director), *Under the Mountain* (Auckland: TVNZ, 1981)

Bakhtin, Mikhail, 'Form of time and chronotope in the novel', in Michael Holquist (ed.), *The Dialogic Imagination: Four essays* (Austin: University of Texas Press, 1981), 84–258

Bloom, Harold, *The Anxiety of Influence: A theory of poetry* (New York: Oxford University Press, 1973)

Boock, Paula, 'Children's fiction – what message?' in 'Letters', *New Zealand Listener*, 1 July 1995, 3

Boyd, Brian, 'Maurice Gee: Ironies of growth and judgement, Part 1: The early fiction', *Islands* vol. 8, no. 3, October 1980, 268–81

—, 'Maurice Gee: Ironies of growth and judgement, Part 2: Structure and irony in Plumb', *Islands* vol. 8, no. 4/vol. 9, no. 1, June 1981, 136–60

Braunias, Steve, 'Our Man in Loomis', *New Zealand Listener*, 24 July 2004, 50–54

Brett, Cate, 'The Gee genius', *North and South*, September 1995, 91–101

Brooke, Agnes-Mary, 'Children's fiction – what message?' in 'Letters', *New Zealand Listener*, 10 June 1995, 14

Brooke-Rose, Christine, *A Rhetoric of the Unreal: Studies in narrative and structure, especially of the fantastic* (Cambridge: Cambridge University Press, 1981)

Brown, Diane & Jennifer Roback, 'The Fat Man (1994)', *Publishers Weekly*, vol. 244, no. 44, 27 October 1997, 77

Butler, Dorothy, 'Children's fiction – what message?' in 'Letters', *New Zealand Listener*, 13 May 1995, 12

Campbell, Joseph, 'The hero with a thousand faces', in E. Hale and S.F. Winters (eds), *Marvellous Codes: The fiction of Margaret Mahy* (Wellington: Victoria Unvirsity Press, 2005)

Czennia, Bärbel, 'Cross-cultural encounters and xenophobia in contemporary New Zealand children's literature: Maurice Gee's historical novels *The Fire-Raiser* and *The Champion*', in *The Inside Story: Year Book 2002* (Auckland: Storylines: Children's Literature Foundation of New Zealand, 2003) 71–92

de Palma, Brian (director), *Scarface* (Los Angeles: Universal Pictures, 1983)

Duder, Tessa, 'Much ado about The Fat Man', www.tessaduder.co.nz/res_fatman.html, accessed 28 February 2014

Fitzgibbon, Tom & Barbara Spiers (eds), *Tea-tree and Iron Sands: A guide to present-day New Zealand children's writers* (Auckland: Auckland College of Education, 1986); revised as *Beneath Southern Skies: New Zealand children's book authors and illustrators* (Auckland: Ashton Scholastic, 1993), 36

Gee, Lyndahl, 'Double Unit', in *Speaking for Ourselves: Fifteen stories edited by Frank Sargeson* (Christchurch: Caxton Press, 1947), 23–30

—, *Mihi and the Last of the Moas: The adventures of Mihi, a little Maori boy, with the very last of the moas* (Auckland: Oswald-Sealy, 1943)

Gee, Maurice, 'Beginnings', *Islands* vol. 5, no. 3, March 1977, 284–92

—, *The Champion* (Auckland, Puffin Books, 1989)

—, 'Creek and kitchen', *Through the Looking Glass: Recollections of childhood from 20 prominent New Zealanders, selected and introduced by Michael Gifkins* (Auckland: Century Hutchinson, 1988), 83–92

—, 'Creeks and kitchens: Margaret Mahy Lecture, 23 March 2002', *The Inside Story: Year Book 2002* (Auckland: Storylines Children's Literature Foundation of New Zealand, 2002), 11–25

—, 'Early reading', *Education* vol. 24, no. 8, 1975, 25

—, *The Fat Man* (Auckland: Viking, 1994)

—, *The Fire-Raiser* (Auckland: Puffin, 1986)

—, *Games of Choice* (Auckland: Oxford University Press, 1976; repr. 1985)

—, *Going West* (London: Viking, 1992)

—, *Gool* (Auckland: Puffin, 2008)

—, *The Halfmen of O* (Auckland: Oxford University Press, 1982)

—, *Hostel Girl* (Auckland, Viking, 1999)

—, *The Limping Man* (Auckland: Puffin, 2010)

—, *Motherstone* (Auckland: Oxford University Press, 1985)

—, *Orchard Street* (Auckland: Viking, 1998)

—, *The Priests of Ferris* (Auckland: Puffin Books, 1987)

—, *Prowlers* (London: Faber and Faber, 1989)

—, *Salt* (Auckland: Puffin Books, 2007)

—, *Sole Survivor* (London: Faber and Faber, 1983)

—, *Under the Mountain* (Wellington: Oxford University Press, 1979)

—, Author interview with Vivien van Rij, Wellington, December 2003

—, 'The way of the writer', *New Zealand Listener*, 17 January 1987, 42

—, *The World Around the Corner* (Wellington: Oxford University Press, 1980)

—, 'Maurice Gee/Interviewed by Brian Boyd', in Elizabeth Alley & Mark Williams (eds), *In the Same Room: Conversations with New Zealand Writers* (Auckland: Auckland University Press, 1992), 159–73

—, Colleen Reilly, 'An interview with Maurice Gee', *Australian and New Zealand Studies in Canada* 3, 1990, 1–8

—, Interview with Kathryn Ryan, National Radio, 25 July 2007

Giffuni, Cathe, 'Maurice Gee: A bibliography', *Australian and New Zealand Studies in Canada* 3, 1990, 36–42

Glamuzina, Julie & Alison J. Laurie, *Parker & Hulme: A lesbian view* (Auckland: New Women's Press, 1991)

Grey, Zane, *The Spirit of the Border* (Wisconsin: Whitman Publishing Company, n.d.)

Guerin, Louise, 'A balance of good and bad', *New Zealand Listener*, 13 October 1984, 21

Haley, Russell, 'Games of choice', *Spleen* 6, December 1976, 8

Haviland, Virginia, *Children and Literature* (London: Bodley Head, 1974)

Hebley, Diane, *The Power of Place: Landscape in New Zealand children's fiction, 1970–1989* (Dunedin: University of Otago Press, 1998)

Holloway, Judith, 'A fat boy, a creek and a personal responsibility', *New Zealand Books* vol. 3, no. 5, August 1995, 22–24

Horne, James W. (director), *Laurel and Hardy Way out West* (Los Angeles: Universal Pictures, 1937)

Hubbard, Anthony, 'Obsession of a quiet man', *Dominion Sunday Times*, 25 October 1987, section 2, 17

Hunt, Peter (ed.), *Alternative Worlds in Fantasy Fiction* (New York: Continuum, 2001)

Jackson, Anna et al., *A Made-up Place: New Zealand in young adult fiction* (Wellington: Victoria University Press, 2011)

Jackson, Rosemary, *Fantasy: The literature of subversion* (London: Methuen, 1986)

Jones, Lawrence, 'The novel', in Terry Sturm (ed.), *Oxford History of New Zealand Literature in English*, 2nd edn (Oxford: Oxford University Press, 1998), 119–245

—, 'Three views of a changing scene – The *Plumb* trilogy', in *Barbed Wire & Mirrors: Essays on New Zealand Prose*, 2nd edn (Dunedin: University of Otago Press, 1990), 177–203

Jones, Martin, 'Frank Sargeson House', Heritage New Zealand Pouhere Taonga (2004): www.historic.org.nz/TheRegister/RegisterSearch/RegisterResults.aspx?RID=7540

Johnston, Andrew, 'Maurice Gee: Our superb storyteller', *The Evening Post*, 3 July 1993

Jung, Carl, *Man and His Symbols* (New York: Dell, 1968)

King, Jonathan (director), *Under the Mountain* (Auckland: Index Films, Liberty Films, 2009)

King, Michael, *Penguin History of New Zealand* (Auckland: Penguin, 2003)

Le Guin, Ursula, 'The child and the shadow', *Quarterly Journal of the Library of Congress* 32, 1975, 139–48

—, *Language of the Night: Essays on fantasy and science fiction* (New York: Putnam, 1979)

Mahy, Margaret, 'The Fat Man', *Landfall* vol. 199, no. 8, 2000, 38

Manhire, Bill, *Maurice Gee (New Zealand Writers and Their Work)* (Auckland: Oxford University Press, 1986)

McDonald, Ginette (director), *The Champion* (1989; Auckland: Television New Zealand)

—, *The Fire-Raiser* (1986; Auckland: Television New Zealand)
McDowell, Miles, 'Fiction for children and adults; some essential differences', *Children's Literature in Education* 10 (1973), 50–56
McGuire, William (ed.), *Dream Analysis: Notes of the seminar given in 1928–1930 by C.J. Jung* (London: Routledge & Kegan Paul, 1984)
McLeod, Marion, 'A champion tale', *New Zealand Listener*, 7 October 1989, 29
Milton, John, *Areopagitica*, in *Milton's Prose Writings* (London: Dent, 1958)
Nieuwenhuizen, Agnes, 'Know the author: Maurice Gee – Creek, kitchen and the art of language', in *Magpies: Talking about books for children*, vol. 12, no. 1, 1997, 4–6
Nodelman, Perry, *The Hidden Adult: Defining children's literature* (Baltimore: Johns Hopkins Press, 2008), 65
Report of the Special Committee on Moral Delinquency in Children and Adolescents (Mazengarb Report) (Wellington, Government Printer, 1954)
Seelinger Trites, Roberta, *Disturbing the Universe: Power and repression in adolescent literature* (Iowa City, IA: University of Iowa Press, 2000)
Sharp, Iain, 'Dial Gee for Gruesome', *Sunday Star-Times*, 29 August 2004, C7
Stephens, John, *Language and Ideology in Children's Fiction* (London: Longmans, 1992)
Tausky, Thomas E., '"I let the story make its own demands": An interview with Maurice Gee', *Australian and New Zealand Studies in Canada* 12, 1994, 155–63
Todorov, Tzvetan, *The Fantastic* (Cornell: Cornell University Press 1975); first published as *Introduction à la littérature fantastique* (Paris: Éditions du Seuil)
—, 'The grammar of narrative', in *The Poetics of Prose* (Oxford: Basil Blackwell, 1977)
Tolkien, J.R.R., 'On Fairy-Stories', in *Tree and Leaf* (London: HarperCollins, 2001)
van Rij, Vivien, 'The pursuit of wholeness in Maurice Gee's fiction for children', PhD thesis, Victoria University of Wellington, 2008
—, 'The pursuit of wholeness in Maurice Gee's O trilogy', in *International Research in Children's Literature* 3.2 (2010), 148–61
—, 'A straight steal: "An affair of the heart" and Maurice Gee's *The Fat Man*', *Kotare* 6, 2006, 31–34
Walls, Kathryn, '"True-seeming lyes" in Margaret Mahy's fiction', in Elizabeth Hale & Sarah Fiona Winters (eds), *Marvellous Codes: The fiction of Margaret Mahy* (Wellington: Victoria University Press, 2005), 148–67
Wattie, Nelson, in Roger Robinson & Nelson Wattie (eds), *Oxford Companion to New Zealand Literature* (Auckland: Oxford University Press, 1998), 197–99
Welch, Denis, 'Gee Gee', *New Zealand Listener*, 12 May 2001, 58–59
Weta NZ, 'Under the Mountain (2009)' (Weta NZ promotional website), accessed 28 February 2014, www.wetanz.com/under-the-mountain

Williams, Mark, *Leaving the Highway: Six contemporary New Zealand novelists* (Auckland: Auckland University Press, 1990)

Wilton, Hal, 'Rockfist Rogan the boxing airman', *The Champion Annual for Boys* (publishing details omitted, 1950), 141–51

INDEX

action/excitement 28, 43, 82, 98, 124, 136, 137, 146, 163, 164
AIM Children's Books Awards 1995: Supreme Award 172; Junior category 171
adolescence 50, 54, 73, 78, 82, 86, 93, 138, 143; *see also* coming of age, Mazengarb, Oswald
aliens 31–32, 37, 47, 49, 84, 87, 89, 90, 91, 96, 97, 164, 166
allegory 45–46, 117, 165, 173
A Made-Up Place (Anna Jackson) 27
ambiguity 31–38, 96
'A Mother's Love' (Lyndahl Chapple Gee) 119
Auckland 32, 33, 38, 41, 49, 50, 54, 62, 81, 98, 101, 139, 147, 164–67, 169, 170
Avondale College 38

Bakhtin, Mikhail 96
'Beginnings' (MG) 114
Blindsight (MG) 132
Bloom, Harold, *The Anxiety of Influence* 115, 117, 118
Boock, Paula 172; *Dare, Truth or Promise* 172, 174
Botanical Hill (Nelson) 130
Boyd, Brian 53, 59, 124
Brett, Cate, 'The Gee genius' 58
Brooke, Agnes-Mary 172
Brown, Diane 176
bullying 55, 58, 61, 62, 68–78, 79, 81, 82, 90, 110, 143, 145, 152, 158–59, 160, 174, 176
Butler, Dorothy 172

Campbell, Joseph, *The Hero with a Thousand Faces* 103
capitalism 165

Champion (boys' magazine) 113, 149, 157; *Champion Annual for Boys* 150
characterisation, character types 29, 30, 32, 35, 37, 46–53, 59, 61, 63, 65, 66, 68, 70, 72, 73, 77, 78, 82, 88, 90, 95, 96, 97, 111, 112, 115, 116, 117, 124, 125, 126, 129, 130, 134, 136–40, 144, 146, 147, 148, 150, 151–52, 154, 156, 160–61, 171, 172, 179
Chattanooga 148
Children's Book Council (Australia) 172
classism, class struggle, class structure 55, 56–58, 60, 62, 73–74, 78–82, 112, 143, 144–45
comedy *see* humour
coming of age 69, 72, 83, 86, 93–95; *see also* adolescence
compassion 37, 42, 50–51, 72, 160, 177
Cowley, Joy 26
'Creeks and kitchens' (MG) (Margaret Mahy Award lecture 2002) 28–29, 55, 97, 123, 175, 179
critics, criticism 26, 27, 30, 45, 101, 115, 140, 160, 163, 166, 171, 172, 173, 174, 178
cruelty 38, 43, 58, 61, 65, 68–72, 97, 111, 172, 176, 178
cults *see* religion

dark themes/vision 25, 93, 94, 146, 154, 163, 173, 174, 175, 179; *see also* depressing themes
darkly comic 67, 81; see also humour
darkness (light and dark) 32, 36, 37, 38, 43, 47, 48, 58, 60, 67, 70, 80, 81, 84, 90, 93, 95, 98, 102, 105, 120, 126, 130

202

INDEX

Davin, Dan, *The Gorse Blooms Pale* 177–78
deformity 89–91
depressing themes/vision 94, 123, 172, 173; *see also* dark themes
depression (economic) 69, 78, 82, 140, 147, 149, 150, 153, 161, 170, 171, 172, 173
depression (mental) 76, 150, 172
Dickens, Charles 46, 54
disability 112, 128, 139
'Double Unit' (Lyndahl Chapple Gee) 109–13, 114, 116, 121
Duder, Tessa 172
duty, sense of 29
dystopian 83, 95

ecology *see* environmentalism
egalitarianism 144, 145
Elidor (Alan Garner) 127–28
Ellie and the Shadow Man (MG) 139
endings 28, 31, 41–47, 53, 54, 89, 93, 95–99, 102, 110, 112, 115, 145, 167, 171, 178
enlightenment 61, 62, 66–68, 82, 86, 89, 93–95, 98
entertainment/storytelling 25–26, 29, 30, 33, 53, 82, 97, 123, 124–25, 134, 135, 167
environmentalism, pollution 30, 36, 38, 103, 45, 132, 135, 136, 165
Esther Glen Medal 171
ethical code(s)/issues 27, 28, 29, 36, 39, 41–47, 54, 83, 86, 99, 163, 170; *see also* morality, moral codes(s),
eucatastrophe *see* happy endings
evil *see* good and evil
excitement *see* action/excitement

fable 109, 115
family: dynamics 50, 82, 88–89, 93, 97, 104, 114, 143, 145, 178; familial love 51; continuity 55; Gee's own 101–21, 147; history 119; types/structure 55, 56–58, 62–64, 70, 71, 73, 76, 78, 82, 88–89, 91, 94, 142, 144, 145; *see also* parents, mothers, fathers
fantasy/adventure genre 25–54, 83, 93, 94, 95, 96, 97, 103, 117, 123–24, 125, 127–30, 133, 135, 136, 137, 146, 164, 167, 168, 170, 173, 178
fathers 35, 47, 56, 57, 58, 62, 63, 64, 66, 67, 69, 70, 73, 74, 76, 77, 78, 79, 81, 83, 85, 87, 88, 89, 91, 103–04, 110, 113, 115, 118, 119, 126, 131, 135, 142, 144, 145, 153, 154, 158, 159, 160, 174, 177–78; *see also* parents
frailty/fallibility 88, 93, 160, 178, 179
freedom of choice 44

Gaelyn Gordon Award for a Much-loved Book 2004 26, 164
Garner, Alan, 124; *Elidor* 127–28; *The Weirdstone of Brisingamen* 28–29, 127
Gee, Lyndahl Chapple 101–21, 153; A Mother's Love' 119; 'Double Unit' 109–13, 114, 116, 121; *Mihi and the Last of the Moas* 101–09
Gee, Maurice, childhood 101–21, 147, 170, 177–78; childhood observations 174; on writing for young readers 27–28, 116, 123–25; on writing landscape 130–32; relationship with his mother 101–21, 153
Gee, Maurice, publications: 'Beginnings' 114; *Blindsight* 132; 'Creeks and kitchens' 28–29, 55, 97, 123, 175, 179; *Ellie and the Shadow Man* 139; *Going West* 150; *Gool* 83–99, 125; *Hostel Girl* 78–82, 87, 88, 112, 123–46; *Meg* 101, 114, 117–21, 132;

Motherstone 40, 41–42, 43, 44, 45, 51, 53, 54, 103, 123, 128, 129; *Orchard Street* 55, 72–78, 80, 87, 88, 125, 137, 154; *O* trilogy, the 28, 30, 31, 35, 36, 38–41, 47–53, 54, 87, 94, 98, 101, 103–07, 110–12, 123, 124–25, 128, 135; *Plumb* 26, 47–48, 55, 101, 118; *Prowlers* 26, 132, 133; *Salt* 83–99, 125; *Salt* trilogy, the 83–99, 125, 146; *Sole Survivor* 118–19, 155; *The Champion* 55, 62–68, 69, 70, 74, 76, 94, 101, 107–09, 112–13, 115, 123, 137, 147–61; *The Fat Man* 40, 55, 68–72, 73, 74, 80, 87, 88, 90, 98, 125, 135, 137, 147–61, 163–79; *The Fire-Raiser* 55, 56–62, 63, 66, 70, 75, 80, 88, 125, 130, 131, 133, 137, 145; *The Halfmen of O* 30, 40, 42, 43, 47, 48, 49, 87, 88, 90, 103–05, 110–12, 116–17, 120, 125, 129; *The Limping Man* 51, 53, 83–99, 125; *The Priests of Ferris* 44–45, 47, 49, 50, 51, 103, 106–07, 120; 'The way of a writer' 147; *The World Around the Corner* 28, 31–38, 53, 90, 97, 98, 103, 123–46; *Under the Mountain* 26, 28, 31–38, 41, 50, 53, 87, 88, 90, 93, 97, 98, 103, 123, 124–26, 127, 129, 134, 163–79; film 164, 169–70, 173; TV series 164, 165, 167, 169, 173, 176, 179
'Geeland' 97
gender 51, 87–88, 140
generic hybridity 31–38
Gisborne 56
Going West (MG) 150
good and evil 29–31, 32, 34, 36, 37, 42–48, 50, 83–99, 111, 116, 117, 124, 125, 128–29, 133, 136, 137, 139, 143–44, 151, 163, 166, 167, 168, 171, 172, 176, 178, 179
Gool (MG) 83–99, 125

gothic 35, 166
grandfathers 73, 148
grandmothers 62, 67, 136, 149
grandparents 62, 70, 117
Gray, Zane 29
greed 72, 89, 90, 165, 170
Gregory, Jackson, *Bab of the Blackwoods* 120
Grey, Zane 154, 159; *The Lone Star Ranger* 154
Guadalcanal 147–48, 151, 156, 157

Haley, Russell 133
happy endings *see* endings
Harry Potter (J.K. Rowling) 33
Hartnett, Sonya, *Sleeping Dogs* 172
Haviland, Virginia 124
Hebley, Diane, *The Power of Place: Landscape in NZ children's fiction* 27
Hebley, Gary 130, 132
Henderson (Auckland) 62, 68, 72, 147, 170
heroes/heroines 29, 30, 41, 49, 50, 51, 54, 67, 77, 81, 86–87, 88, 91, 93, 103, 104, 110, 126, 128, 129, 136, 147, 149, 150, 155, 156, 157, 161, 164–70, 177–78; heroes mostly girls 51
heroism, heroic qualities 29, 30, 52, 54, 62, 66, 67, 69, 73, 77, 87–88, 91, 93, 95, 99, 126, 128, 139, 143, 147, 149, 153, 157, 163, 164–70, 177–78; heroic action/s 88, 95, 99, 163, 167, 178
historical/realist novels 25, 32, 33, 35, 38, 40, 53, 55–82, 83, 88, 94, 95, 96, 97, 107, 124, 125, 136–37, 140, 141, 143, 144, 145, 146, 147, 164, 170, 173, 174, 178
Hostel Girl (MG) 78–82, 87, 88, 112, 123–46
humour, comedy 54, 62, 63, 65, 66, 82, 154, 159, 165

INDEX

Hunt, Peter 38
Hutt Valley High School 78, 142, 144

idealism 54, 89, 131
imperialism 147
individuality 89, 93–95, 97, 160, 167
individuation 117
Ireland, Kevin 25
Islands 114

Jackson, Anna, *A Made-Up Place* 27
James, Billy T. 165
Jung, Carl 27, 46, 112

King, Michael 140

Landfall 174
landscape/natural world 27, 36, 38, 42, 55, 92, 95–97, 108, 124–25, 127, 130, 135, 140, 147, 148, 149, 150, 151, 152, 154, 157, 159, 161, 179
language (Gee's use of) 40, 44, 47, 95–96, 123, 125, 132, 141
Laurel and Hardy 154–55
Le Guin, Ursula 51
Lewis, C.S., *Narnia* stories 28, 41, 128
liberalism 44
Library and Information Association of NZ Aotearoa 171
Lord of the Rings (J.R.R. Tolkien) 41, 128
Lucas, George 49

MacDonald, George, *The Princess and Curdie* 49
magic 30, 31, 33, 36, 91, 108, 113, 123, 126–35, 164, 166
Mahy, Margaret 174–75
Maitai River 130, 131
Manhire, Bill 26, 30, 46, 48, 116, 134, 135
Manlove, Colin 29

Margaret Mahy Award lecture 2002 *see* 'Creeks and kitchens'
materialism 36
Mazengarb, Oswald, *The Report of the Special Committee on Moral Delinquency in Children and Adolescents* (1954) 78–79, 82, 140–41, 144
McDowell, Myles 123–24
McLeod, Marion 113
Meg (MG) 101, 114, 117–21, 132
Milton, John 43–44, 93; *Paradise Lost* 43–44, 93
mining (as image, metaphor) 97–99, 123, 129, 136, 146
morality, moral codes(s), moral universe 25, 29, 32, 36, 37, 38, 54, 55–82, 89, 93, 95, 96, 107, 123, 136, 140, 141, 143, 144, 163, 166, 168, 169, 170, 173, 175, 179; 'moralscape' 55–82'; *see also* ethical code(s)/issues
mothers 47, 58, 60, 61, 63, 64, 70, 73, 74, 75, 76, 78, 79, 81, 84, 85, 87, 88, 91, 103, 104, 112, 113, 117–18, 134, 139, 140, 141, 142, 144, 145, 148, 151, 152, 153, 158, 176, 178; Gee's mother 101–21, 153; *see also* parents
Motherstone (MG) 40, 41–42, 43, 44, 45, 51, 53, 54, 103, 123, 128, 129
Mount Eden 164, 165
Muldoon, Robert 69, 90, 152
myth 30, 99, 107, 115, 119, 120, 148

Narnia stories (C.S. Lewis) 28, 41, 128
narrative: pace/tension 27, 29, 77, 97, 116, 123, 124, 130, 136–37, 146; clarity 27; complexity 28; conflict 46; convention 28; energy 29; expression 46; first-person 73; force 34; gothic 35; of perception 33; one-dimensional 116; portal/

205

quest 38–41; power 58; structure 89; technique 147; third-person 60, 68;
natural world *see* landscape
negotiation 50–51, 66, 93, 94, 175, 179
Nelson 59, 140
New Zealand Film Commission 164
New Zealand Listener 172
Nodelman, Perry 88
nuclear weapons 30, 45, 128, 152

Orchard Street (MG) 55, 72–78, 80, 87, 88, 125, 137, 154
O trilogy, the (MG) 28, 30, 31, 35, 36, 38–41, 47–53, 54, 87, 94, 98, 101, 103–07, 110–12, 123, 124–25, 128, 135
Oswald-Sealy New Zealand 101

pacifism, anti-militarism, 38, 39, 41, 59, 45, 67, 74, 110, 111, 113, 116, 119, 147; *see also* nuclear weapons
Paradise Lost (John Milton) 43–44, 93
parents 29, 31, 42, 55, 56, 57, 58, 61, 62, 63, 67, 68–69, 70, 72, 73, 74, 77, 78, 79, 84, 88, 91, 94, 115, 144, 150, 152, 167, 171, 177, 178; absence of in fantasy books 178; *see also* fathers, mothers
Parker–Hulme murder 141
pessimism 53, 109
plot *see* story/plot
Plumb (MG) 26, 47–48, 55, 101, 118
politics, politicians 39, 43, 45, 45, 60, 69, 72–78, 79, 82, 89, 90, 93, 111, 141, 147, 148, 156; capitalism 165
pollution *see* environmentalism
power (pursuit of, lust for, abuse of) 30, 36, 41, 43, 45, 60, 69, 70, 85, 86, 89, 90, 91, 92, 132, 135, 147, 152, 155, 165
Pratchett, Terry 41
predation 55, 73, 78–82
Prowlers (MG) 26, 132, 133

Queens Gardens (Nelson) 130
Quote Unquote 172

racism 55, 56–68, 82, 94, 108, 143, 148, 150
Rangitoto 164, 165
reading (as motif) 134, 142, 149
Reilly, Colleen 27, 47
religion/faith 44–45, 54, 72–78, 83, 85, 86, 89, 93
Revelations (Bible) 41
revenge 55, 56–72, 73, 81, 82, 152, 170
Roback, Jennifer 176
Robin Hood 29
Ruskin, John, *The King of the Golden River* 33

Salt (MG) 83–99, 125
Salt (MG) trilogy, the 83–99, 125, 146
Sargeson, Frank, 114, 153, 173; 'An affair of the heart' 153; *Speaking for Ourselves* 109, 114
scandal 82
Scarface 154
self-sacrifice 29–30
settings: 32, 33, 34, 38, 40, 47, 49, 51, 52, 54, 56, 62, 68, 78, 95–96, 105, 112, 124, 125, 126, 127, 130, 132, 136, 140, 141, 142, 143, 145, 147–61, 163, 164, 173; description of interiors 131–32; Auckland 32, 33, 34, 54, 164; Collingwood 40, 49, 51, 52; Henderson 62, 68, 72, 170; Hutt Valley 78, 112, 140–45; Lake Pupuke 34; Mount Eden 32, 34, 164; Mount Victoria 34; Mount Wellington 34; Nelson 38, 40, 52, 56, 126, 130, 132, 140; New Zealand 47, 95, 96, 124, 127, 173; North Head 34; North Shore 38; One Tree Hill 34; Rangitoto

INDEX

32, 34, 164; Takapuna 32, 165–66; Upper Hutt 140; Waitakere 62
sex/sexuality, sexual desire 51–52, 54, 71, 73, 77, 78–82, 85, 94, 97, 109, 138, 140–41, 143, 151, 152, 172
sexual abuse 173, 176
sight/seeing 132–34
Sole Survivor (MG) 118–19, 155
South Pacific Pictures 164
Star Trek 32
Star Wars 49
Stephens, John 140
story/plot, storytelling 26, 27, 28, 29, 31, 32, 33–36, 40, 43, 46, 47, 48, 50, 82, 97, 109, 110, 114, 115, 116, 123–25, 127, 130, 133, 134, 135, 136–38, 140, 142, 146, 147, 153, 164, 167, 169, 175, 179
Storylines Children's Literature Foundation 164
strikes *see* unionism
symbolism 32, 37, 42, 46, 52, 53, 54, 59, 68, 70, 71, 72, 90, 91, 98, 112, 119, 130, 155, 158, 159, 175

Takapuna 32, 165–66
Tausky, Thomas E. 114, 117
Television New Zealand 164, 165
Tennyson, Alfred Lord 92
The Champion (MG) 55, 62–68, 69, 70, 74, 76, 94, 101, 107–09, 112–13, 115, 123, 137, 147–61
The Fat Man (MG) 40, 55, 68–72, 73, 74, 80, 87, 88, 90, 98, 125, 135, 137, 147–61, 163–79
The Fire-Raiser (MG) 55, 56–62, 63, 66, 70, 75, 80, 88, 125, 130, 131, 133, 137, 145
'The Gee genius' (Cate Brett) 58
The Halfmen of O (MG) 30, 40, 42, 43, 47, 48, 49, 87, 88, 90, 103–05, 110–12, 116–17, 120, 125, 129

The Hero with a Thousand Faces (Joseph Campbell) 103
The Hobbit (J.R.R. Tolkien) 128
The King of the Golden River (John Ruskin) 33
The Limping Man (MG) 51, 53, 83–99, 125
The Power of Place: Landscape in NZ children's fiction (Diane Hebley) 27
The Priests of Ferris (MG) 44–45, 47, 49, 50, 51, 103, 106–07, 120
The Princess and Curdie (George MacDonald) 49
'The pursuit of wholeness in Maurice Gee's O trilogy' (Vivien van Rij) 27
'The way of a writer' (MG) 147
The Weirdstone of Brisingamen (Alan Garner) 28–29, 127
The Wizard of Oz 128
The World Around the Corner (MG) 28, 31–38, 53, 90, 97, 98, 103, 123–46
Todorov, Tzvetan 33–34, 35, 40
Tolkien, J.R.R. 26, 28, 38–39, 53, 128; *Lord of the Rings* 41, 128; *The Hobbit* 128
totalitarianism 165–66
Trites, Roberta Seelinger, *Disturbing the Universe* 93

Under the Mountain (MG) 26, 28, 31–38, 41, 50, 53, 87, 88, 90, 93, 97, 98, 103, 123, 124–26, 127, 129, 134, 163–79; film 164, 169–70, 173; TV series 164, 165, 167, 169, 173, 176, 179
underground journey (as motif) 102–03, 105, 107
understanding 33, 37, 42, 46, 54, 62, 70, 82, 88, 93, 98, 113, 138, 144, 160

unionism, industrial action, strikes 74, 82
universality 46, 52, 95–96, 99, 147

van Rij, Vivien, 'The pursuit of wholeness in Maurice Gee's *O* trilogy' 27, 46
violence 25, 38, 41–42, 43, 46, 49, 50, 52, 54, 71, 84, 87, 94, 97, 113, 127, 137, 139, 143, 145

war (and peace) *see* pacifism, nuclear weapons
wartime setting 55, 56, 67, 74, 76, 77, 109, 112, 119, 148, 152, 161
Williams, Mark 80–82
Woolf, Ray 165
Wyndham, John 32

xenophobia 57, 59, 143